Film at the Intersection of High and Mass Culture analyzes the contradictions and interaction between high and low art, with particular reference to Hollywood and European cinema. Written in the essayistic,
speculative tradition of Walter Benjamin and Theodor Adorno, this
study also includes analyses of several key films of the 1980s. Tracing
the boundaries of such genres as film noir, science fiction and melodrama, it demonstrates how these genres were radically expanded by
such filmmakers as Neil Jordan, Chris Marker and Georges Franju.
This work also reflects on kitsch, the star system, racial and gender
stereotypes and the nature of audience participation. While defining
the conditions under which the symbiotic relationship between high
and mass culture can be cross-fertilizing, the study stresses their inevitably contradictory characteristics.

FILM AT THE INTERSECTION OF
HIGH AND MASS CULTURE

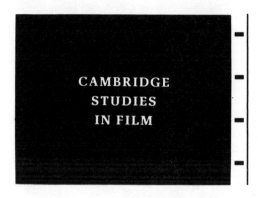

CAMBRIDGE STUDIES IN FILM

FILM AT THE INTERSECTION OF HIGH AND MASS CULTURE

PAUL COATES
McGill University

CAMBRIDGE
UNIVERSITY PRESS

#28709305

Published by the Press Syndicate of the University of Cambridge
The Pitt Building, Trumpington Street, Cambridge CB2 1RP
40 West 20th Street, New York, NY 10011-4211, USA
10 Stamford Road, Oakleigh, Melbourne 3166, Australia

First published 1994

Printed in the United States of America

Library of Congress Cataloging-in-Publication Data

Coates, Paul, 1953–

Film at the intersection of high and mass culture / Paul Coates.

p.   cm. – (Cambridge studies in film)

Includes bibliographical references and index.

ISBN 0-521-44472-1

1. Motion pictures – Philosophy.   2. Film genres.   3. Popular
culture.   I. Title.   II. Series.
PN1995.C5439   1994
791.43'01 – dc20   93-1991
                                                        CIP

A catalog record for this book is available from the British Library.

ISBN 0-521-44472-1 hardback

In dreams begins responsibility.
W. B. Yeats

We had fed the heart on fantasies,
The heart's grown brutal from the fare.
W. B. Yeats

Genuine responsibility only occurs where there is real responding.
Martin Buber

Trash has given us an appetite for art.
Pauline Kael

Contents

Preface

Two quotations from Yeats provide epigraphs for this book. One defines dream as the source of responsibility; the other evokes the brutalizing effects of fantasies. They may be aligned with two common modes of discourse concerning cinema. On the one hand, the metaphor of dream has been a constant of writing on film, from its earliest impressionism to the psychoanalytically influenced scientism of Christian Metz or Alexander Kluge's proposal (itself the echo of a thesis of Bazin or Adorno) that cinema has been with us for thousands of years as mental association and only now has assumed the concrete form of a mechanism. But there is also the tradition that sees celluloid as a factory product, unrolling unilaterally over an exploited audience. Genre, an assembly-line article, overrides individual makers and receivers (and then, when genre falters, individual films become genres in themselves, or the constant factor is the recurrent descent to earth of a 'star' who transcends any narrative he or she may traverse). If the work that brutalizes does so through lack of individuality – nobody's child, it could so easily have been aborted – then the recipe for dreams that yield responsibilities is individualization, poetic mediation. At the same time, however, generic formulae fulfil the useful function of counteracting the intensifying hermeticism attendant upon the individualism of modern art. Thus, this book argues a case for works that tune in to the wavelength of an existing genre and then overlay it with different signals: the adoption of genre is an implicit critique of individualism, while the very strength of the individuality of the artist irrigates the desert of the merely generic. (Following the logic whereby all cultures spin their opposites from within themselves, in order to achieve the status of a self-enclosed world, American individualism automatically generates machine-tooled collectivism as its own antidote.) Generic wavelengths deliver a public; reprogramming practises enlightening metacritique of the genre. Form needs matter, and high culture ascends by standing on the shoulders of the low. Where genre is sick, one can be sure that high art is also.

The essays collected here pair examples of a genre or topos of popular culture with works that dislocate them into dream. If the upshot is in the main a juxtaposition of American genres and European directors, the fault is less in American directors than in the working conditions that devastate their dreams. After all, the films of Welles, Altman and Scorsese are often as liberating as the science fiction (SF) of Marker or Tarkovsky, the *roman policier* of Truffaut or Franju's melodrama. The careers of these three Americans indicate how the deck is stacked against the American director who seeks to enrich fantasy. The extent of the lodes still untapped in apparently defunct, abandoned genres is apparent, for instance, in Truffaut's *Shoot the Pianist*, which exhilarates in its swooping descent into the imaginary of mass culture. Its scarred protagonist Charlie (Charles Aznavour) is a concert pianist who retreats to bistro playing after his wife's suicide. He is, however, no mise-en-abîme image of Truffaut himself. Charlie cannot combine high and low: he is either a bistro player or a concert hall lion. Truffaut, on the other hand, can slide playfully in and out of B-movie clichés; to be exclusively one thing or the other would be a nightmare for him.

It may be that in Truffaut's case distance from Hollywood is magical protection against it. The American who assays reworking of Hollywood's schemata may think he is bending it to his will and himself be doing all the bending. Such is the case in Scorsese's *Cape Fear*, a remake of a 1962 thriller, in which an ex-con terrorizes the lawyer who failed to defend him 'zealously', as his oath had required. Scorsese talks of having made a two-tier work, potentially receptive to a double audience, whose thriller surface harbours depths at which Max Cady (Robert De Niro), the ex-con, is a dark angel dispatched to induce his victim's repentance. Cady himself voices this view when he tells the lawyer (Nick Nolte) to look up the biblical book sandwiched between Esther and Psalms. But the narrative as surely invalidates Scorsese's subtheme as it destroys Cady. Placed in Cady's mouth, the theme becomes a mere strand in his characterization as crazy cracker zealot. Since no supernatural curtain is raised, as it is in the first chapter of Job, to reveal the hidden engines of events, we can only assume there is no other dimension. The film may deliver thriller shocks, but the technique is crude, with door slams synchronized to cuts, lighting overblown and a conventionally tingling score that has none of the contrapuntal inventiveness with which rock is used in Scorsese's *Mean Streets*. (Why not employ, say, the Stones' 'Sympathy for the Devil', as the early De Palma might have done?) There is even product placement: Pepto Bismol prominently mixed with whiskey by the private investigator the lawyer hires. The rancid, leering quality of De Niro's ex-con can indeed give one goose bumps, but the plot is concerned more with his elimination than with his comprehension. The stray hints of his otherworldliness (a bus passes his car and the car vanishes, enigmas surround his mode of access to the lawyer's house) are coy and opportunistic, degrading the supernatural into a source of momentary frisson. As often, there is no criminal more dangerous than a lower-class autodidact. The irony is that our mechanisms for pushing him down may make him bob back up: his eerie knowledge does not stem from any status as exterminating angel but from the lengthy prison spell during which he learned to read. The threat is that the outsider might discover the things whose knowledge enables us to keep him down – with the lawyer the scapegoat suffering on our behalf. The uncanny unknown is really the working class. But – as in *The Silence of the Lambs* – the real horror is to watch a gifted director immolate himself on the altar of sensational demand and self-delusion.

To pair a genre with its dreamlike dislocation is to create a double exposure. Doubly exposed images are rich in the mysterious rightness and inevitability of an *arbitrary* interpenetration of two worlds. They fuse like Siamese twins – the feelings of the one seeping into the other. The essential rightness of the two worlds' mysterious encounter lies in its revelation of the unity of the two worlds we all inhabit (male and female, rich and poor, dark and light, individual and collective and so on). The double exposure, however, prefigures reconciliation as obscurely as all prophetic speech. The reconciliation this book seeks, meanwhile, is one between the academic and the reviewer, theorist and critic: figures so often polarized so combatively in recent years. A double exposure itself, it brings together two worlds (the two sides of my own personality): with something for everyone, it may well fully please no one. For its gesture is arguably useless without a larger forum; its use may be in pointing to the utopian common space between theorist and critic. Yet such a space is more necessary than utopian: necessary to overcome film culture's division between brutal stampedes for deadlines and hermetic irrelevance on sidelines. All too often the rhythms of industry self-promotion render the critic the film's conduit, as is most signally the case at those events where film culture reveals its identity with barbarism – the festivals. Conspicuous consumption unseats aesthetic response, and lemming-like rushes to judgement generate hysterical phrase making. The theorist, meanwhile, frustratedly espousing marginalized works, seeks consolation in litanies of fetish words and retreats to an academy in which publishing matters more than gaining and persuading readers. Hence, although this book situates itself between the rival claims of theory and criticism, its author does not imagine he has resolved the dilemma. His primary hope is that readers lured by the bait of familiar fantasies may discover that they're not in Kansas anymore, as the colour control knob – the power of great directors' refigurations of often-hackneyed forms – floods the grey road with yellow (or green ...), introducing them to a magical place. It is Pauline Kael's hope, expressed in another of my epigraphs, that trash can give us an appetite for art.[1]

To argue the value of refigured genre, however, is not to advocate the postmodern pastiche that reproduces genre in the form of plastic death-mask, using knowing inverted commas to broadcast superiority to its prototype. It is not to advocate the value of a *Miller's Crossing*. Close consideration of the works that most interest me (*Solaris, La Jetée, A Short Film about Love*) should indicate that the fruitful use of convention is one that destroys it from within, living on its meat before emerging, transfigured, from the hollowed-out shell. It is not the knowing and external fossilization performed by pastiche, with its ignorance of the emotional resources secreted within genre. These transformations of genre may be likened to the lucid dreams psychologists elicit to dispel traumas. Nightmare victims can be taught to plan before sleep to break the dream's stranglehold by acting differently in the dream or telling themselves as it unfolds that they are only dreaming. Genres, like nightmares, are structures of repetition. The film-makers who interest me dream the dream and yet change it, stripping it of the predictability that is the hallmark of the syndrome.

Since each genre is part of a system whose division of the world loses that world through its apparent conquest (reality's ichor bleeding away in the gaps between its disjecta membra), the project of deepening genre involves reinserting the whole – the world – into the part. It entails a realization that each part is a world. Since this is a paradoxical undertaking, it is hardly surprising that the films that do so often teem with conundrum. Inserting the whole into the part may also be described as an effort to bring back home to the United States the Europe it thinks it has left behind. Were this to be achieved, responsibility would cease to connote the banal and boring, TV movie mediocrity. The sheer pervasiveness of the ideology of irresponsibility can be seen in the way it has seeped into the recent work of Scorsese, causing the complex dialectic of religion and escapism that made *Mean Streets* so compelling to collapse (and so one has the dream that self-deludedly masks its status as dream – the exhilaration of pure stoned fantasy in the bravura of the amazing, dubious *Goodfellas*). But if American film's industrial conditions represent the future towards which inevitable forces impel us, as so many commentators contend, injection of an element known as 'the European' is no more an instant panacea now than it was for Henry James. The difference is simply that the relative independence from conglomerate influence enjoyed by the cultural sphere in Europe permits airholes of freedom that directors utilize with various degrees of success. Just how much can be achieved, however, is apparent from such series as Reitz's *Heimat* or Kieślowski's *Decalogue.*

In the context of consideration of part–whole relations, it may be worth dwelling for a moment on the word 'culture' – a term whose slipperiness bestows on it the status of what Freud would have termed a 'primal word', a keyword that conducts social contradictions, a locus of apparent consensus covering confusion. In this case the ambiguity concerns hierarchical, part–whole relations, rather than any binary opposition. For the two senses of the word 'culture' designate, on the one hand, a whole (the anthropological view from without discerns 'a culture') and, on the other, a part ('culture', the part that justifies the whole or persists in antagonism with it, a redeeming antibody the whole treats as a virus and banishes to the museum). It is the word's ability to define a totality that causes the advocates of 'culture' – be they the more traditionalist appointed guardians of canons and the unashamedly 'high' or those who find culture's vitality in popular artefacts and responses – to promote their favoured part as worth more than the whole or as the utopian image of an unrealized or impossible totality (the poet's legislation of the world passes unacknowledged).

The preceding two paragraphs should have indicated the extent to which this book is a multilevelled meditation on part–whole relations. Its method is essayistic. This may appear both paradoxical and provocative. After all, is not the essay the fruit of an exploded, primitively premethodological impressionism? One may wonder, however, to what degree an object – in this case, the work of art – may be comprehended by an observer who lacks the sort of sympathy for it the essay displays. The effort to pluck out the heart of the mystery piquantly pursues a scientism long abandoned by science itself. Among other things, this book argues that it is far more scientific to present one's individual perceptions as such than to elevate them into systems. This is not to advocate individualism and connoisseurship, but to seek to allow the object to speak ventriloquially through one's own words: to enable it, as it were, to speak a foreign language. 'In actuality, the thinker does not think but makes himself the arena of intellectual experience', as Adorno notes in his apologia for the essay.[2] If totalities – glimpses of a system – are present in this book, they are mise-en-abîme images secreted in the corners of its parts. The whole is present only in the miniature image of the DNA spiral: it is a whole that has not been unfolded wholly. It is not obscurantism but tact, respect for the reader, that weaves a figure into the carpet. The vision of totality is momentary and unbidden; the methodical trudge up the mountainside in no way guarantees exhilaration, or even visibility, on reaching the summit.

The essayistic method of this book focuses on details, hopefully significant ones, which can be read as allegories of the whole. The speculations and apparent farfetchedness of the essay recognize the degree to which significant details become so through the ghostly presence within them of that which seems to have been voided from them, the rest of the work, the oeuvre, the career. Such moments totalize the apparent whole of which they are part. They are its negative imprints: even as they reflect it they reshape it, like the glass that both distils and curves the surrounding room in Kieślowski's *Short Film about Love*. To locate significant detail is the critical task. Hence, the difference between works of 'popular' and ones of 'high' culture may well be one between varieties of part–whole relations. In the work of high culture, the part crystallizes themes and stylistic features that radiate from it across the entire work. In the work of popular culture, the part represents a lost possibility, an open door the rest of the work, or the star's career, failed to pass through, for a multiplicity of reasons. These moments do not so much redeem a work as offer the possibility of its redemption. They will be happy accidents that are not then – as in surrealism – employed as the basis for new aesthetic laws, but pass ignored or suffer diffusion in the form of degradation. One may think of Karloff's Frankenstein (who comes into his own belatedly in *The Spirit of the Beehive*), Monroe's persona or that marvellous figure trapped not so much in a computer as in the banal schemata of an investigative reporting thriller – Max Headroom, the appalling legless Beckettian comedian turned into a parrot, a mere Coke front man.

The combinatory calculation of mass culture blinds it to the nonarbitrary nature of the few successful images its turning kaleidoscope yields. Each one of these images is what Benjamin termed a 'revolutionary chance in the fight for the oppressed past'.[3] But the critic's role is less violent and desperate than Benjamin contends: he or she does not so much blast something clear of the past as calmly remove it, a stone that has already worked itself loose; the critic underscores its nonidentity with its context. To practise such a form of criticism is to demand, like Pauline Kael, that a movie 'be totally informed by the kind of pleasure we have been taking from bits and pieces of movies'.[4] Her conclusion is that 'if we've grown up at the movies we know that good work is continuous not with the academic, respectable tradition but with the glimpses of something good in trash'.[5] The slivers embedded in trash reflect the light of the suns of the great works. And praise of those works should not be stinted, meanwhile, for fear of elitism: the ideal community the great work posits has never existed. The great works are not yet a secure canon; they have not yet come into their own. To use appreciation of 'high' culture as a badge of social belonging is to traduce their truly humanitarian promise. To accuse great works of elitism is to swallow the lies of the elite, for when the lights go down they promise a dream that will both unify crowds and whisper secrets to each and every one of their members. Only a profound sense of responsibility could realize so overwhelming a dream.

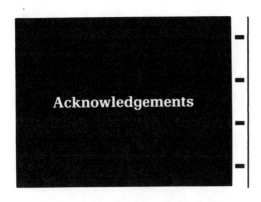

Acknowledgements

The third section of Chapter II, 'The Kindness of Strangers: *A Short Film about Love*', first appeared in a different version in the *Polish Review*, 37, no. 3 (1992). The portion of the second section of Chapter III, 'Beyond the Outer Limits of SF', dealing with Chris Marker first appeared in *Science-Fiction Studies,* 14 (1987). Earlier versions of brief sections of Chapters IV through VIII first appeared in the June 1989, June 1988, February 1990, November 1989 and February 1988 issues of *The World and I,* a publication of the Washington Times Corporation. The final section of Chapter IX, 'Revolutionary Spirits: The Wedding of Wajda and Wyspiański', first appeared in *Literature/Film Quarterly,* 20, no. 2 (1992).

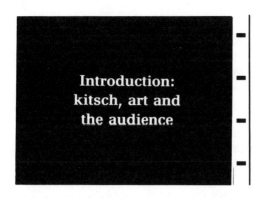

Introduction:
kitsch, art and
the audience

Kitsch, camp and mass culture

The emergence of kitsch parallels that of mass education from the mid-nineteenth century onwards. It can be argued that kitsch is generated in one of two ways: through a failure of the aspiration to art or through consigning art to the back-seat of a vehicle driven by moralism. The former is a pallid simulacrum of art; the latter, art's bowdlerization. I will deal with them in turn.

Kitsch of the former kind is ersatz art for a culture whose value system ascribes supreme importance to art, the last metaphysical activity, even as subconsciously it is sceptical of art's unverifiable claims. Its inhabitants satisfy their culturally inculcated superego by purchasing something that resembles art, while their unacknowledged disbelief is satisfied by the object's actual disparity from art. This form of kitsch is wed to the nineteenth-century cult of the Beautiful. According to Hermann Broch, kitsch arises from a concern to work 'beautifully' rather than 'well': for Broch, this preponderance of the aesthetic over the ethical fosters evil.[1] The Kierkegaardian derivation of Broch's theory is patent; for although it can account for one variety of kitsch, its definition of the ethical as the middle term in a three-stage progression from the aesthetic to the religious renders it unable to account for the specific forms of kitsch generated by art's subordination to ethics or religion. The Beauty Broch describes is skin-deep, without the polysemous layered complexity art possesses in the hermeneutics of Dante, for instance. Such kitsch may be seen as a post-Romantic phenomenon: as Romanticism came to insist upon originality as the yardstick of art and as the notion of copyright began to be codified, artists who might once have been content with the role of copyist felt compelled to attempt more. Their transformation of Romanticism into cliché gave the lie to their individualistic Romantic message. Their kitsch was the blighted fruit of a minor artist's failure of self-recognition. Where the modernists, unable to escape quotation, flaunted it, the producers of

1

this kitsch shamefully hid indebtedness. Their quotations absurdly strive to deny the yawning gulf between past and present (neo-Gothic architecture, for instance, wishes away the crisis of the nineteenth-century church) by presenting a minor derivative talent with all the afflatus of a major one.[2]

To speak of the neo-Gothic is to arrive at the variety of kitsch fostered by art's subordination to religious or moralistic ends. Here art is conceived as an illustration of what we already know, as *doxa* or tautology. The conception seeks to undo Romanticism's redefinition of art as exploration, the Baudelairean plunge into 'le nouveau', the emergence of 'the novel' as the name of the nineteenth century's major art form. Whatever its pre-nineteenth-century validity, the conception had been shattered by Romanticism's Promethean transvaluation of values. Its last-ditch battle unfolds in slow motion in Richardson's *Clarissa*,[3] where educative intent is pitched against amoral psychological investigation – or, in Bakhtinian terms, monologue enters into agonizing deadlock with the dialogue that will succeed it historically. The kitsch that follows radiates bad conscience: it is surely correct to ascribe greater importance to moral rectitude than to art, but on coming to this belief the logical conclusion is to abandon art, not to mingle inferior and superior syncretistically. It is perhaps this form of kitsch that is invoked in Syberberg's notion of kitsch as a fragment of myth.[4] It is the kitsch of the Wagnerian operas Nietzsche lambasted for the composer's insistence that they were 'more than just music' – more recently, of the quasi-Jungian films of George Lucas or so much moralizing SF; of Victorian anecdotal painting; of melodrama; and arguably, of the fictionalized, pseudonymous religious tracts of Kierkegaard himself.

There is, of course, a third term of relevance to the kitsch–art equation: entertainment. Kitsch may be bad art, but entertainment is something else entirely. Entertainment is the antiart of a world with no time for art. That has been the world, of course, as most generations have experienced it. For the reception of art requires a viewer strong – and usually leisured – enough to participate in the world's unmaking and remaking, in an activity that absorbs and changes one's life to the very depths. Entertainment is the diversion the world offers those it has rendered incapable both of the aspiration to art displayed by one variety of kitsch and of the subordination of art to ethics another kitsch displays. For Adorno that failure of aspiration is characteristic of what he terms the 'culture industry'. In his meditation upon this industry's systematic exploitation of the gulf between human beings and their culture, entitled 'Janus Palace,'[5] he speaks of a process that is turning culture into kitsch and uses the terms 'kitsch' and 'entertainment' interchangeably. Here, I feel, he is mistaken. Kitsch is a specifically modern – in particular, a nineteenth-century – phenomenon. Entertainment, however, is perennial. A Bakhtin would trace its transhistorical presence in carnivals and other mutations of popular culture. But the moment of carnival is fleeting,[6] the brief sabbath an authorized transgression that restores one for labour. If intermissions can be incorporated into regimes of exploitation, in the case of the twentieth century industrialized diversion gives off-the-job training for industrialized work: as Benjamin noted, the shocks of the cuts in a film match those of the 'apperceptive apparatus' in modern life.[7] For Goebbels, meanwhile, Zarah Leander was the best propaganda. Entertainment lacks the divided consciousness of kitsch, that crack through which nineteenth-century discontents filtered to the surface in mystified form. Its mode of address to the most superficial levels of the personality pretends that no depths exist: it would be too painful to recall the starved prisoner down below. Where art shows us human beings, presenting an often fearsome mirror to our selves and social orders, entertainment disperses humanity between the sub- and the superhuman, its dreams of redemption cynically aware of their own unreality.

By the end of the fifties in the West, enhanced purchasing power and a massive extension of the educational system – among other factors – had rendered the products of mass culture so pervasive as to secrete the dubious antidote of a new sensibility: that of camp. Where kitsch is failed art with a bad conscience and entertainment is content to be disposable, camp feeds both on the failure of low culture to become high culture (on kitsch) and on the failures of high culture itself. If high culture is shot through with failure – the most notorious instance being the compatability of reading Rilke with the operation of a concentration camp – it is partly because the Romantic, and then modernist, requirement that the artist create a world ex nihilo raised the stakes of the aesthetic endeavour to a level at which few could play, and even the remaining players often found themselves bankrupt in midcareer[8] – and partly because art could never become the religion it was widely called on to replace. Camp culture thrives on the failure of art; resigned to the production of kitsch and entertainment in our society, it tries to dispel their oppression by modifying the ways in which they are perceived. If it paradoxically transforms failure and dissonance into a sign of success, it is nevertheless dependent upon them for its shadowy substance and sustenance. Insofar as the camp sensibility is homosexual in origin, it delights in the failure of the culture that has placed gays beyond the pale. Camp is a culture of consumption rather than production – whence its rapid propagation in a consumerist society. Where kitsch producers feel the anxiety of the petit bourgeois educated beyond their tastes, and fearful of falling back into the abyss of the unlettered masses they know to be present still within

themselves, the camp consumer practises the gay science of a deconstruction incapable of construction, the academic graffiti it doodles on
culture's failed products legible in another light as a *mene tekel:* an
air of *fin de siècle,* of the end of time hastened by the biological steril-
ity of homosexual relations, hangs over it. Both belong to a culture of
the after-image: kitsch helplessly quotes the art it cannot rival and the
religion of which it falls short, while camp wastes on the dismantling
of culture the wit and energy it could have reserved for the construction of art. In terms of Jameson's description of postmodernism, camp
practises pastiche rather than parody. Its shallow euphoria of negativity frantically represses the knowledge of negativity's pain; it grins and
bears it. For the camp sensibility, the exemplary figure should surely
be Proust, whose pastiche deconstructions of other writers concluded
in the construction of *À la Recherche.*

But since, as Raymond Williams has shown, cultures comprise re-
sidual phases alongside emergent ones, there were still some prepared
to receive mass culture without mockery, to take kitsch or entertainment (Vincente Minelli ...) for art. The revaluation of mass culture in
the sixties, when pop art and structuralism unified the field of culture
by connecting its poles – Superman and the *Übermensch* – employed
the notion of intertextuality to demonstrate that even the most rarefied
works of high culture needed roots, to say nothing of casting shadows.
This revaluation of mass culture resulted among other things in the
current near hegemony of the alternative term, 'popular culture', and
involved acknowledgement of the value of one's unschooled – childhood or adolescent – apprehension of its products. This was in part a
replay of the Romantic idealization of the unstructured perceptions of
the child and of 'folk culture', whose spectre returned as youth culture.
The child experiences the hackneyed work with the freshness he himself brings to it ('he' because the films that underwent revaluation
were often such male fantasies as the Western – so that in some quarters among auteurists, the privileging of adolescent experience became
an excuse for permanent residence in that stage of life). Similarly, to
concede value to these works was to recognize or seek to recover the
social or familial roots education so often severs. Thus, the idolization
of Hollywood product by intellectuals raised on 'the great tradition'
breathed both Young Turkishness and utopian nostalgia for an inte-
gral selfhood or culture. The assumption that these could persist so
easily in conditions of modern capitalism and consumerism, however,
was mere wish-fulfilment, yielding such schizophrenic mystifications
as analyses of B movies with methodologies honed on *The Waste Land*
or the dubious assertion that a still-polarized society was now entirely
middle class. Effacing the high culture–low culture distinction could
be an ideological, as well as a utopian, undertaking.

In between the camp aesthetic, with its mockery of kitsch, and the enthusiasts' acceptance of its pretensions lay the more common reaction of those who accepted a popular culture they then rejected as corny under pressure from that culture's next wave. Adorno defines the mechanism of 'the corny effect' as follows:

Likes that have been enforced upon listeners provoke revenge the moment the pressure is relaxed. They compensate for their 'guilt' in having condoned the worthless by making fun of it. But the pressure is relaxed only as often as attempts are made to foist something 'new' upon the public. Thus the psychology of the corny effect is produced again and again and is likely to continue indefinitely.[9]

The receiver's denigration of the 'corniness' of the past obeys a Mephistophelean law of mass production, whereby everything that comes into being has built-in obsolescence: 'alles was entsteht / Ist wert, dass es zugrunde geht'. Adorno's impersonal 'attempts are made' suspends the question of agency, which it ascribes instead to the zeitgeist. The inverted commas around 'guilt' and 'new' imply that to take old for new is merely the inevitable concomitant of inhabiting what Adorno elsewhere terms 'the administered world'. He is perhaps too understanding of the all too human mechanisms involved. The passage itself is almost Mephistophelean in character, as if penned by a being whose longevity yields the melancholy conviction that there is nothing new under the sun. The zeitgeist is an illusion born of the changing of masks; in essence it is eternal. Hence, the antihistoricism of Adorno's Marxism, which sees all human societies as still steeped in myth, may render it unable to discern the emergence of true novelty. The psychology of the corny effect may or may not continue indefinitely, but it has not always been with us. Nor is the denigration of the past ever total: awareness of one's past love colours mockery with narcissistic affection. One is grateful for the existence of a work whose naïveté permits one to define oneself as sufficiently sophisticated to see through it. For to see through a thing is not necessarily to reject it, as the Reagan phenomenon's invulnerability to critique inter alia has revealed; it is rather to accept its existence as an occasion to congratulate oneself on one's experience or worldly wisdom. Adorno describes the recognition of corniness as the surfacing of fury at the compulsion to conform. He fails to grasp, however, that the fury repressed in obedience to peer pressure is vented simultaneously against the older generation. Adorno does not perceive the degree to which conformist teenage consumption of popular music, for instance, also formalizes revolt against norms established by one's elders. The analysis is surprisingly undialectical. It overlooks the dialectics of utopia and ideology in mass culture.

Utopia and ideology in mass culture

Fredric Jameson, echoing Ernst Bloch, has proposed in *The Political Unconscious* the possibility of discerning utopian elements in every work of mass culture.[10] Ideology and utopia are of course virtually inextricable: the utopia of full meaning prefigured by the great artwork becomes ideological when access to it is restricted – as it always has been – while the shallow fantasies of mass culture can justly claim to provide their audiences with approximate conceptualizations of hopes of escape.

The argument may be tested against a much-loved Hollywood film, *Meet Me in St. Louis.* The choice of example is prompted in part by the film's use by David Bordwell and Kristin Thompson, in the most influential film course book of recent years, as a typical instance of ideology.[11] The notion of ideology Bordwell and Thompson advance may be accused, however, of failing to grasp both the contradictoriness of ideology and its possible use of contradiction to generate the confusion on which false consciousness feeds. *Meet Me in St. Louis* dreams of a reconciliation of the provincial and the central, St. Louis and New York. After all, why should a land's centre be deemed provincial? And why go to New York when the spectacle of the World's Fair Exposition lies on one's doorstep? (And if home is more mute and inglorious than St. Louis, glory can still enter through the awesome moveable feast on offer at the local movie theatre.) The film turns on a transformation so improbable in its context that it has to be read as utopian: the family's father revokes his acceptance of the promotion that would take him, and them, to New York. The patriarchal law of political economy succumbs to matriarchal values of rootedness and fantasy. (Father is heavily outnumbered by wife and daughters.) The volte-face becomes necessary following the youngest daughter's decision to destroy her snow people rather than leave them in St. Louis for anyone else. The scene glosses leaving a place in infantile fashion, as the equivalent of killing its inhabitants. The daughter's murderous rage has to be halted at all costs; hence, the film presents the fantasy of changelessness as utopian, rather than as a response to the pathology of the family's youngest member. It revokes the occasion of pathology in order to deny the possibility of pathology within the family and is blind to the ideological nature of the belief that family moves should depend on the will of their youngest members. The father's improbable U-turn has been foreshadowed by a series of unexpected transformations during the Christmas ball – ranging from the surprising graciousness of the feared and hated girl from the East, who can thus be absorbed into the family, to the moment at which Esther (the Judy Garland part) dances behind a Christmas tree with her grandfather and emerges on the other side with her sweetheart. (The moment embodies a profoundly cinematic dream of time's reversibility, the metamorphosis of age into youth.)

Is this fantasy purely ideological, however? If ideology is the glue of social order, then it can be seen to deny it on one level at least: individualism, patriarchy and the economic imperative give way to the imago of an inviolate matriarchal community. And yet the idealization of the family is also deeply ideological. Another turn of the screw, meanwhile, shows that family to be utopian in its willingness to accommodate otherness: the extended family extends to the horizon, encompassing even New York, in a kind of conurbation of the soul. Nevertheless, the work's utopian features may be not so much antidotes to ideology as features of its structure. A belief that utopia is possible here and now may prevent defeatist acceptance of the way of the world (and the hardships of 1944, the film's year of release – hardships including the lack of males strangely mirrored in the film's preponderance of females), but it is blind to the barriers that separate current life from the ideal world of which the Louisiana Purchase Exhibition can only be a figure. The possibility that the dream factory itself is implicated in subjugation is never even aired, while the assertion of feminine power rings hollow in the midst of a war begun by men. And here the dangers of the Bloch–Jameson position become apparent: the argument that every form of ideology secretes a silver lining of utopia can obscure the deep disparity between our ideological life and one that would be worth living. The theoretical recognition that both components are present in all works can be a paralysing mystification, frustrating the application of criticism to determine which predominates in any particular case.

Even criticism, however, may be unable to make the necessary distinctions so long as it remains at the level of content: after all, narratives depend on oppositions (ideology *and* utopia), and most seek to affirm both. (If tragedy shows the opposites' mutual destruction, the lesson is that in this case the characters who embodied them sinned through excess: the chorus recommends the golden mean.) The danger of indiscriminate acceptance already mentioned may be averted nevertheless by seeking the criterion of the utopian on another level, that of form. From this perspective, the truly utopian work would not be the utopia whose formal resemblance to past works indicates enthrallment to old ways (More, Morris, Bellamy), but the one whose determination to make it new bespeaks true commitment to Otherness. Accordingly, the most formally achieved artworks – not necessarily the most accessible – would be the least tainted by ideology. Such works, however, are probably not the most formally innovative: as Adorno noted when discussing Stravinsky's *Histoire du soldat*, a thing's violent negation can conceal identification with it.[12] The truly utopian, able to draw on a past that includes the most recent avant-garde, is fettered neither to it nor to its programmatic negation. The avant-garde's rejection of existing formal languages at the turn of the century becomes the midwife of the great modernist works of Kafka, Musil or Proust. Expressionism's scissors cut the modernist birth cord; Picasso's cubism prepares the way for *Guernica,* which orders disjunctions into a significant syntax of rage. As they dissolve the realism–fantasy distinction on which so much popular culture rests, allowing the dreams popular culture sees as exiled irrevocably to enter reality, the great works do not just dream of reconciliation but practise it. Only utopias prepared to carry some things over from the past are ever likely to be real. They alone find bridges from the future to now.

PART ONE
Getting in on the act

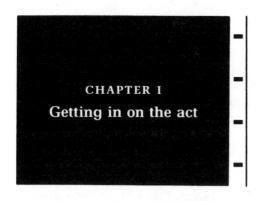

CHAPTER I

Getting in on the act

The term 'mass culture' (and still more the term 'popular culture') may prompt one to ask where the masses are in relation to an industry that in claiming to speak for them so often takes in vain the name of the seemingly deified populace. And where does the individual who views him- or herself as a carrier of 'culture' stand in relation to a culture said to be for the mass? Is the term an oxymoron papering over the cracks of a social contradiction? This essay considers several possible positions on this issue, situated on a sliding scale from total exclusion to complete absorption. In *The Day of the Locust* the frustrating illusoriness of the dream factory's product generates fury in both individual and crowd; in *The Purple Rose of Cairo,* the individual steps out of the crowd and so individualizes – and alters – the work, while in my final examples, singing along with the song may radically revise it ('Into the Groovey') or simply reinforce it (*The Player*).

The shame and the fury

At one point in Nathanael West's *Day of the Locust,* Faye Greener – the aspiring Hollywood starlet living with Homer Simpson, a smaller-scale buyer of the body she wishes to sell big-time – begins bitterly to patronize her patron:

Faye called to the waiter again.
  'He doesn't like the champagne cocktails', she said. 'Bring him brandy'.
  Homer shook his head.
  'Please, Faye', he whimpered.
  She held the brandy to his lips, moving the glass when he turned away.
  'Let him alone', Tod finally said.
  She ignored him as though she hadn't even heard his protest. She was both furious and ashamed of herself. Her shame strengthened her fury and gave it a target.[1]

The shame and fury Faye feels are virtually omnipresent in West's novel, forming part of the self-hatred dramatized in West's contempt

11

for the part of the United States that bears his own name, which it
takes in vain. Tod Hackett, who is obsessed with Faye and plans to
position her prominently in his painting *The Burning of Los Angeles,*
experiences the same shame and fury as Faye, and probably West
himself: shame at his habit of caricaturing people and his inability to
leave the Hollywood he despises. He is surely a split-off, drifting fragment of the crowd that assembles at the novel's close, lost and mystified in his incapacity to admit belonging to it. Like Faye he has
internalized the crowd that seeks relief in baiting scapegoats. Shame
goads them into furious attempts to vent self-hatred on a world that
intolerably reminds them of their incompatibility with it. Their discontent is a microcosm of the crowd's resentment of the dream factory's
conjuration of the appearance of realities that can never become real.
Both Tod and the crowd are held in Hollywood by the same thing: the
glamorous dream of the ideal. Since the essence of a dream is separation from reality, its human embodiment must be unattainable so as to
retain her dream aura. This unattainability renders Faye hateful. Unable to express directly their hatred of Faye, however – after all, she
incarnates the ideal, to reject which would be to reject the system –
West's protagonists displace it onto other things. Homer tells his story
of the repulsive naked black hen; and long before Tod informs Faye
that he and Homer have been talking about 'you, darling', we know
that the anecdote expresses frustrated hatred. Appropriately enough,
the reversal that describes the essence of white beauty as black is very
dreamlike; in a similar reversal, while hens lay eggs, the glamour Faye
personifies is irrevocably sterile. Tod's denunciation of the dangerous,
smouldering dissatisfaction of the stars' groupies is blind to his own
participation in their loss of individuality: he loses his own image in
the crowd and does not even know it is there. And when the novel concludes that 'these people had it in them to destroy civilization', it
echoes Tod's own use of the lower middle class as scapegoats for
a malaise whose source is far harder to localize, being dispersed
throughout the system. West pins the blame for Tinseltown's corrup-
tion on the audience, ignoring the guilt of moguls, corrupt artists and
others. Like Tod and Faye, he seems to be too attached to glamour –
perhaps too much himself the corrupt artist – to achieve the self-
awareness that requires a selfhood he lacks. Ever aware that West
Coast reality is a series of rackets, a dizzying variety of fronts, he is
fascinated nevertheless. It is the people with no fronts, the unappeal-
ing lower middle classes, who appal him: they are living dead, displaced reflections of the death that inhabits Tod's own name. They have
no *style.* West projects his own apocalyptic rage onto the people –
partly to mock it, but also as part of a secret effort to magnify it by

granting it the strength in numbers that allows him vicarious pleasure in its destructiveness.

The emotional displacement underlying Tod's painting is manifest in the other characters too. Everyone in the book is a displaced person, the final scene their rally. The displacement of emotions is a misplacement that fosters shame. Faye's shame over her failure to become a star and her status as a kept woman seeks relief in attacks on Homer, but the intended catharsis merely compounds the problem, prompting further shame over her unwarranted aggression. One feels shame at striking out at the wrong person, fury at one's inability to locate the proper object of one's animus, perhaps because that object is oneself, one's own blind spot: the individualistic culture says that you alone are responsible for your shortcomings. Here Tod proves cannier than Faye. In directing his anger against the crowd, which is animated by his own uglier impulses, he chooses a multiplicity of targets, thereby raising the odds of hitting the right one. Moreover, he has an alibi in the transformation people suffer upon entering a crowd: they become different, strangely bestial and aggressive. And so he can justify his apocalypticism as an assault upon a crowd that differs fundamentally from the people who comprise it: misanthropy (the burning of Los Angeles) burns the body to save the soul.

As West's characters externalize their own ugliness out of the imperative to appear nice or glamorous (the men, nice – the girls, glamorous), the figure who is unable to view himself as appealing becomes of great interest. Only Honest Abe Kusich, the book's dwarf parody of Lincoln, is capable of expressing violence directly, without displacements, a one-man apocalypse. In standing out, albeit through his freakishness, he is related to the attractive Faye – upon whose doormat Tod discovers him. Indeed, as a real object of people's stares, he is the nearest thing to a real Hollywood star in the book. (The real stars are eliminated by West's *ressentiment* and determination to show us a Hollywood that is nothing but sham. Stars being absent, it is hardly surprising that Napoleon should fail to appear at the absurd cinematic restaging of the Battle of Waterloo, where Tod's encounter with the Great Man is even more tangential than that of Stendhal's Fabrizio, which it echoes and revises: he doesn't even see the imitation Bonaparte in the distance.)

Because Tod is looking for 'a clue to the people who stared', he is fascinated by both Abe and Faye, remarking of the latter that 'she enjoyed being stared at'. That is why each is placed so prominently in his painting. Painting (the still image) becomes that which film excludes; and so all those who are unable to appear on the silver screen manifest themselves on canvas instead. Painting is, for West, the apocalypse of film: a frame that freezes to burn out, the projector breaking down and arresting life into the death-mask at which one stares. The person doing the staring is, of course, the intellectual in Hollywood. A bystander in a world that disdains art – as it simply exploits art's look as decorative camouflage for its rackets – and furious and appalled at his inability to preserve beauty (Faye) from it, he constructs his canvas as itself an act of camouflage, a displaced expression of fantasized revenge. The fact that Tod is never shown at work on it surely gives the measure of his demoralization. One may wonder if it exists, if it is only in his mind's eye that Los Angeles burns. The most prominent hands in the book belong not to the artist but to a Homer alienated from their neurotic rituals. It is as if West is hinting at his own frustration with the work of his hands, his writing. Conjured flames can hardly satisfy a burning desire for the elusive, illusive siren of the billboards.

Emma Bovary, c'est Mia

Although it is quite clear that *The Purple Rose of Cairo* is descended from *Six Characters in Search of an Author,* its meaning can best be grasped through comparison with the two other Allen pieces usefully mentioned in Pauline Kael's review of the film:[2] *The Kugelmass Episode* and his witty statement of a wish to become Gigi. As a variant of *Six Characters,* Woody Allen's film benefits from, and participates in, the popularization of modernism that was a midwife at postmodernism's birth. Perhaps inevitably, the process involves a dissipation of Pirandello's fearsome paralysis between reality and illusion and is achieved primarily through shifting the focus from the impossibility of incarnation and expressivity to the audience's role in a work's making and unmaking. The vertigo Pirandello's work evokes is due in part to its redefinition of the actor as superfluous audience and partly to the scandal of the characters' unembodied drama: the lack of a natural audience makes one wonder if one ought to be watching. The characters' insistence on playing themselves anticipates one of the key novelties of cinematic acting, thus justifying Allen's reverie on Pirandello's themes. *The Purple Rose of Cairo,* however, presents characters whose drama is already embodied fully on the screen, which only a minor character inhabited by an ambitious actor would be sufficiently frustrated to seek to escape. But certain conditions must be met for him to do so: he needs the rooting of the star-struck fan who has watched him five times on a single day. She is Cecelia (Mia Farrow), and it is 1935, in the midst of the Depression, as she sits down to watch the film within the film. Cecelia has just lost a waitressing job by bungling orders while dreaming of the screen. Unable to face her surly, thickset, abusive husband, she ducks into the local movie theatre for whatever's on – in this case, *The Purple Rose of Cairo,* a tale of Egyptian explorers and Manhattan high-life she has already seen twice (once by herself, once with her sister). As she gazes at the screen for the umpteenth time, a minor character – an idealistic pith-hatted explorer called Tom Baxter (Jeff Daniels) – casts a glance in her direction, comments that she must really love this film and steps out into the auditorium. The two slip away through a side-entrance, and the film's remainder plays witty variations on the consequent paradoxes and consternation. One subliminally expects Tom's step down from the screen – the scene in which it occurs having been shown several times beforehand, allowing one to feel the boredom that might prompt Tom's existential leap, as well as his possible desire to translate into actuality the startling Manhattan adventure of which they speak; after all, it is only just across the river from Cecelia's New Jersey. Tom is drawn out by Cecelia's love for the screen, which is translated first into love for him and then for the actor who plays him – the metonymy of Hollywood itself – when he turns up in an effort to restore his aberrant image to the screen.

Cecelia's ability to bring the star down to earth, where he glows like E.T., is the link to *The Kugelmass Episode,* in which a middle-aged Jewish professor removed Emma Bovary from Flaubert's novel, had an affair with her and then had problems slipping her back between the pages' legitimate sheets. Kael links the film to the fantasy of becoming Gigi, though she does not spell out the basis for the connection. It is, of course, the phrase 'Emma Bovary, c'est moi': in what is in effect a postscript to *Zelig* – the story of the human chameleon that is surely Allen's masterpiece – Allen himself becomes Cecelia, who in her turn lives out a feminized version of *The Kugelmass Episode.* The miracle of Tom's departure from the screen is predicated on another one, Allen's own transformation into Mia Farrow. There is perhaps another quasi-miraculous metamorphosis at work here too: the step back into the mid-thirties. Depression-era New Jersey may seem hardly an ideal fantasy destination, but Allen clearly views the thirties as a privileged period of a more popular, more utopian, mass culture than that of the present: a Hollywood character's leap into a sparsely attended matinee was still possible. Both *Hannah and Her Sisters* and *Radio Days* argue that postwar popular culture is a degraded form of the truly popular one of the age of swing. If *The Purple Rose of Cairo* and *Zelig* are Allen's richest works, it is because they exude a glow whereby the interwar years become a lost paradise. The argument is clinched in the ending of *The Purple Rose.* Cecelia finally chooses the actor, Gil, over Tom, for Gil has the advantage of being real (albeit less than perfect), while she can rest assured about Tom's fate: in his world things have a habit of working themselves out (the law of the happy ending). But Gil absconds the moment his double is safely locked up in the screen; and Cecelia's place of refuge will not be the real Hollywood to which Gil had promised to take her but its silver lining, the screen. As she enters the cinema, where *Top Hat* is now playing, and gazes at the screen, the contrast between Astaire's 'I'm in Heaven' and her desolate state may seem cruel and ironic, but as the camera continues to hold on Cecelia we become as absorbed by her as she is by the screen and notice that her face is beginning to glow. Its irradiation really is that of the light of heaven, perhaps the only heaven on this present earth: that of the star-gazer in the gutter. And we are positioned similarly, gazing rapt at Mia Farrow. Dialectically, the antidote to desolation arises out of desolation itself: the experience of art. Allen escapes Kracauerian condescension to the little shop-girls by identifying with them, by becoming one with the Emma Bovary whose literary tastes were no more exalted than Cecelia's cinematic ones. And yet there is an element of sleight of hand here too; for if *The Purple Rose of Cairo* has given way to *Top Hat,* there is progress rather than succession, the Astaire–Rogers film being far superior to the explorer picture Allen has parodied. It is the real thing – beyond parody. By ending with *Top Hat,* Allen implies that Hollywood heaven is Cecelia's final destination – the last scene becomes her Assumption – conveniently forgetting that *Top Hat* itself will be followed by inferior films, one of which (horribile dictu) may well be Gil's forthcoming Lindbergh biopic. Later in life, Cecelia may find that mass culture is a second home no longer; like Woody himself, she may seek a new one through yearning masochistic identification with an Other one can never become – such as Ingmar Bergman – with the Other of Europe. If *The Purple Rose of Cairo* is utopian, it is because in it Allen reconciles himself to a mass culture whose modern incarnations he disdains.

Brilliant parasites

Rock music lifts the dialectic of audience frustration and enfranchisement to a level far beyond Cecelia's experience. When a washboard can be a legitimate instrument and stars cannot read a note, there is little to distinguish the fan from the object of adoration. But for every group whose rise to fame through technical incompetence is democratic and liberating – as with the Sex Pistols, since desperation and guts were all one needed to look and sound as they did – there is a Duran Duran proclaiming that vacancy must be pretty to succeed; and biology has hardly been even-handed in its distribution of good looks. So what the rock machine gives with one hand it takes away with the other. Thus, although 'Saturday Night Live' traces the impulse behind

Albert Goldman's books to his apocryphal dismissal from the Beatles in their Cavern days (Elvis told them Goldman's trumpet solos were deeply uncool, and the hapless John delivered the message), the imaginary Goldman's resentment could well be fuelled by a suspicion that he was axed because his looks were no match for those of the moptops. Meanwhile, tribute groups ensure themselves audiences by mimicking the rock saviours of the day, playing only at weekends. Aware of the risks and impediments to stardom, they hold down their nine-to-five jobs, sometimes in the hope of singing their own songs further down the line. But if tribute groups can be read as parodies of the rock dream, Ciccone Youth restore reality to the parody. Usually known as Sonic Youth, an industrial music band, they renamed themselves for this project, a version of Madonna's 'Into the Groove'. The drilling sounds with which they surround the melody suggest a road-repair crew laying down tar on the image of a flattened Madonna. The strategy is driven equally by the fan's desire to sing along with the hit and by an outsider group's fantasy of revenge, remotely inflected perhaps by rock's sexist resentment of self-assertive females. The fantasy's spectacular failure is at the same time the source of its success: this brilliant record is Sonic Youth's best-known release (it made it onto the 1986 *Village Voice* 'Pazz and Jop' poll), but was not produced under their name. The ambiguity corrugates the song's texture, as – from the midst of the shuffling, drilling swathes of sound – fragments of Madonna's voice drift into audibility, with a strange poignancy far more powerful than the original version. The fragments recall the thin voice of a ghost haunting the site of its murder: an echo from the past, from the woman immured behind the wall of sound Ciccone Youth so impassively erects. Revenge and mimicry become one as the revenger is haunted by the spectre of his victim – as the listener is by this song. The song's power derives from its dramatization of the ambivalence of mimicry, which seeks to destroy the original so as to assume its place and then can never forget it wasn't there first. 'Into the Groovey' – its title restoring hipness to the suggestion in 'Into the Groove' of being in a rut – is one of the most resonant (not to say one of the loudest) songs of the eighties.

In *The Player*, meanwhile, Robert Altman shows he can make a Hollywood movie as well as the next man – indeed, better, for his preoccupied drifting camera imparts layers of richness and mystery to the scenario, as well as implying a critical refusal to pay too much attention to the cardboard characters who inhabit it. For much of the time – until the self-reflexive denouement – *The Player* simulates an attack on Tinseltown: Griffin Mill (Tim Robbins), the flakey producer whose pudgy, boyishly guilty face suggests Warren Beatty and the young Orson Welles rolled into one (the birth of films from the conjunction of two previous films is a leifmotif of the pitching patter of *The Player* – so why should not its critic use the same device?), kills a would-be screen-writer he thinks has been sending him poisoned postcards – and gets away with it. He has a recipe for movie success we are sure Altman disdains, with nudity, violence and a happy ending among its key constants. Only when the new gun in town, who began as Griffin's rival, rings Griffin, now become his boss, to float a story-line identical with the one we've just been watching, complete with the same title, do we start to add things up and grasp that in a sense we've been had. All the ingredients in Griffin's recipe are ticked off in a mental retro-spect. Is this self-reflexive wrap-up a nod in the direction of the art movie or cynical self-congratulation? The latter is very much on the cards. Altman may be accused of aiming throughout for the best of both worlds, of being himself Griffin Mill – with his box-office-oriented insistence on star presence – and Levinson, the old studio head, with his fabled youthful 'no stars' trademark, rolled into one. All the real Hollywood stars who participated almost gratis – Cher, Bruce Willis, Angelica Huston, Julia Roberts et al. – may have known what they were doing: subconscious star instinct telling them that all pub-licity is good publicity. We all sell out, the movie seems to say. The pitchers of the prison drama that had to be starless and tragic to be real gladly watch their script's reworking with Julia Roberts, multiple stars and her last-minute rescue by gun-toting Bruce Willis. What wonder if Altman himself sells out too? Whereas his early films would have extended sympathy to Bonnie, Griffin's discarded girl-friend who protests the imposed happy ending, here she is merely a loser who limps away jobless, broken-heeled. For all its seductive virtuosity, *The Player* has an ugly underside. Its 'Hooray for Hollywood' is far less clearly ironic than the end of *The Long Goodbye*. It may seem as if one of the best directors in the United States has defected to 'Enter-tainment Tonight', desperate for a hit.

The self-reflexive ending is more than just cynical, however. It ties a ribbon on a box that then starts to tick, as Altman activates the timer on his own work. The implication is that it was not worth making. You thought this five-finger exercise was a real Altman film? How could you be so blind? But if Altman chuckles over how easily we are trapped, he is entrapped also: locked in orbit round the very thing he holds at a distance. His own stylistic blood seeps into the trashy sce-nario, a transfusion that bestows on it an undeserved life. The self-absorbed, unpredictable camera movements, the signs of reverie, lami-nate the narrative sand with the pearl that obscures its true nature. So if Altman sells out, it is not consciously. Anyone curious about why the perennial outsider should cast himself as knowing Hollywood insi-der will find it hard not to conclude that on this occasion the director

Pauline Kael says works closer to his unconscious than other Americans was unconscious of what he was doing. He did not defect, he was kidnapped: as accidentally, and yet fatally, as Joe Gillis by Norma Desmond.

Unconscious of what he is doing, Altman fails to grasp that the richness of his own mining of Hollywood culture has already undercut Hollywood movie-making practice, even before the ending's imposition of art-cinema norms. His pat ending reclassifies the preceding film as merely a tour de force, mistaking it for – and welding it to – the Hollywood film he despises: it is as if his revenge fantasy required him to destroy the celluloid reflection of the object of theoretical hatred. For the perniciousness of the institution of Hollywood makes it more than just another subculture: it is the oppressive master text of the American imagination, the web that entraps it. That is why it has to be blown away. But in doing so Altman has sold his own film short. He forgets that Hollywood is not just an institution – a set of rules for the euthanasia of good films – but also the network of teeming idiosyncrasies he himself has just mapped out.

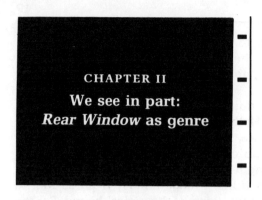

CHAPTER II

We see in part:
Rear Window as genre

One basis for distinguishing between works of art and works of mass culture is the relationship between the latent and the manifest content of the work in question. Broadly speaking, one can say that a work is to be defined as art when the manifest and latent content mesh with each other (such meshing need not necessarily occur throughout the work, thus allowing for the possibility of texts that are only intermittently works of art), whereas in the work of mass culture the two levels will diverge, the manifest content being foregrounded at points in an effort to conceal the implications of a latent content that surfaces only fleetingly, at the margins of a work that would rather repress it than negotiate its complexities. Whether or not a work of mass culture becomes 'art' depends on its ability to thematize the hints of revelation of the latent content. One work that clearly does so is *Vertigo*;[1] one that seems as if it might be about to do so, but then reinstates repression, is *The Bedroom Window*. The title inevitably cross-refers one to the problematics of looking found in Hitchcock's *Rear Window*. Hitchcock's film is often mentioned in one breath with *Vertigo* as a study of questions of voyeurism and the imagination, a pairing I find doubly dubious: partly because the theme of *Vertigo* is in fact a different one, partly because *Rear Window* is by far the lesser work.

Almost excruciatingly coy in its juxtaposition of the window-shows available simultaneously to the James Stewart character – the multiplicity of screens before him rendering him the Man Who Fell to Earth even before his own fall, or Nicolas Roeg's film of that title – *Rear Window* justifies voyeurism by endorsing the chair-bound photographer's suspicions. It thereby revokes its own earlier intimations of a critique of the idle busybody. *Rear Window*'s enormous influence may be less the result of its merits – which I would maintain are doubtful – than of the way Hitchcock's prestige emphasized the timeliness of the theme of surveillance, a crucial topos of post-sixties film-making (*The Conversation, The American Friend, Sisters, Body Double*, inter alia). One may be tempted to see the auteurs' echoes of *Rear Window* as devices for limning their works with self-reference, while accusing lesser directors of pursuing voyeurism under the cryptic coloration of sociology, but feminists would argue that the auteurs themselves are not free of voyeurism. The conclusion might then be either that the minigenre is compromised irredeemably or that it is only in Kieślowski's *A Short Film about Love*, in which the woman mimics the male and takes up the telescope herself, that its inherent pathology is exorcized. One could maintain furthermore that the pathology is reversed most completely in the short version of *A Short Film about Love, Decalogue 6*, which begins and ends with the woman as viewer: with Magda before the post office counter window usually occupied by Tomek. If the short film about love is equally effective in both its 'long' and its 'short' version, it may be because its distant prototype, *Rear Window*, itself felt like a stretched edition of a 'Hitchcock Half-Hour'. The theme is, as it were, elastic. Some of the directions in which it can be stretched are apparent in *The Bedroom Window, Body Double* and Kieślowski's film.

A foreign body: class and identification in *The Bedroom Window*

The hero of *The Bedroom Window* is Terry Lambert (Steve Guttenberg), a young executive who seduces his boss's wife (Isabelle Huppert). After the two have made love she looks at her watch and is alarmed to note how late it is (about 2 a.m.). Rising, she hears a scream outside. As she looks down through the bedroom window, she sees a young girl (Elizabeth McGovern) being assaulted in the opposite park. She fumbles to open the window, succeeds in doing so, and the would-be assailant looks up and makes off. When Terry goes to work the next day, he sees his boss holding a newspaper with a report of the assault and murder of a girl in the same neighbourhood, shortly after 2 a.m. Eager to alert the police to what his mistress had seen, but equally anxious not to compromise her, he phones them, pretending to have been the one who went to the window and saw what she did. Summoned to an identification parade, however, he is unable to pick out the man, even though the mistress has described him quite precisely, and despite the fact that – as a police officer remarks afterwards – the line-up contains one known rapist. After talking on the way out to Denise, the victim of the assault, who is also unable to identify the assailant, he follows a man from the line-up who seems to match the description. The man visits a bar, where his attention is drawn to a sorority girl who dances on a table. On later learning of this girl's death, Terry tells the police he is willing to testify in court against the man. The apparently cast-iron case collapses, however, when the hearing reveals that Terry wears contact lenses, removing them to sleep, and so when woken suddenly by the scream in the park could not possibly have seen the assailant well enough to identify him. The defence lawyer holds up a red book at the back of the courtroom, and Terry cannot see what it is. Meanwhile both the defendant and Denise have noticed Terry's mistress signalling to him across the courtroom. Since the police are now aware of inconsistencies in Terry's story, they begin to suspect him; worse still, his mistress – Sylvia – refuses to furnish him with an alibi. He follows her to the ballet and is himself followed by the defendant (whose name is Henderson), who kills Sylvia in the darkened aisle and pushes her body into Terry's arms. Fleeing the theatre, his shirt blood-stained, he runs into Denise. She has long suspected his duplicity; it had been quite clear to her at the line-up that he'd never seen her before – and she's prepared to work with him to ensnare Henderson. Herself followed by Terry, she tracks Henderson to a bar, where she behaves in the provocative manner that seems to trigger Henderson's attacks. The plan succeeds almost too well, for several mishaps excruciatingly delay Terry's efforts to warn the police of a possible imminent attack, and he is barely able to save Denise. Henderson is trapped, Terry cleared, and he and the girl are together. The illegal, adulterous couple of the film's beginning gives way to the legal pairing of the previously unattached. The jaws of an ideological trap snap shut.

Before examining some of the features that render this film profoundly ideological, I would like to pin-point the moments at which it begins to veer towards a revelation of the latent content – and towards the discourse, and self-awareness, of modern art. At the deepest level of the text, Terry and the murderer are one. What renders the text ideological is the transformation of the double into the monster (and the suppression of the intermediate term, the monstrous double).[2] In one scene the narrative flirts with the possibility of revealing the actual identity of the two: when Terry tells Sylvia how Henderson tampered with a front-door keyhole in order to lure a girl to the shadowy side of the building – there to be raped and killed – he is in fact imagining it all. He tells it graphically, in the present tense, with the camera hand-held, a cliché that indicates that 'a perverted mind' is either (a) nearby or (b) doing the looking. It is between (a) and (b) that the film equivocates; for whose mind is one entering here – Terry's or Henderson's? Sylvia interjects sceptically, 'The police told you all that – about the girl?' 'Most of it', he replies evasively; 'the rest was in the paper'. In retrospect the film will claim that Terry is able (almost magically – and here he is like a film-maker, with the final ensnarement scenario his diploma film) to translate words into images. At this level the film may in fact be dealing with a contradiction between the logocentric

bias of the novel (the film derives from a novel) and the 'seeing is believing' ideology of film in general, and this film in particular. Terry
himself stands on both sides of the opposition, for he both sees and
does not see, depending on whether or not he wears his contact lenses. We ourselves, piquantly enough, cannot see whether he has his
lenses in. In granting Terry a quasi-magical capacity to translate
words into images, the film represses the possibility that Terry himself
is the murderer and is trying to frame Henderson. (This scenario
would help explain one of the narrative's enigmas: how it is that he,
who has not seen the assailant, can be sure of his identity merely on
the basis of Sylvia's description, when Sylvia herself, as Terry points
out Henderson to her at his shipyard work place, professes to be un-
sure. It may be that she simply does not want to get involved, but the
moment may also be read as a symptom of the film's work of repression.) Having granted us a brief glimpse of this possibility, the film
retrospectively represses it by redefining it as 'really' a red herring introduced, like the Hitchcock McGuffin, to enhance the suspense and
keep us guessing a little longer. If Terry himself repeats the murderer's
trick with the locks – putting a paper-clip in his pick-up truck's igni-
tion to stall his get-away attempt – there is no implication that he has
any of the sexual hang-ups of which this specific ruse is a symptom; it
is 'merely' an ironic reversal and appropriation, the 'poetic justice' that
is deeply unjust. The detective story underlines its own intellectuality
and control; these are the defining traits of its hero, who reconciles
opposites: he both is and is not the man of action, does and does not
wear glasses. Control may be threatened, but it finally asserts itself by
creating the reality that proves its point. The blocked keyhole is like
the work itself, which refuses to allow us to insert the key to the protagonist's personality. It disavows the truth it suggests about itself.
Like so many thrillers, it relocates to plot to escape awkward questions of character.

The mechanism of disavowal in *The Bedroom Window* runs on
class feeling. In asserting the possibility of identification – of becoming another person, standing in for Sylvia – Terry is, as Denise puts it,
either 'a romantic fool or an idiot'. The process of identification that
allows him to think he can assume Sylvia's experience has to be
stopped, and it is clear why: if all the characters folded into one another, the deepest level of the text (the one at which Terry is a murderer) would become apparent. Such absurd sympathy has to be
dispensed with. It is destroyed by the reestablishment of the class barriers Terry sought at first to dissolve. (He evidently does not know
what is good for him.) Initially the removal of class barriers seems to
be in his interest: if they fall, the boss's wife will drop in his lap. But
in the end their undermining threatens identity itself. The film does

not show Terry as the first to draw this conclusion, however. It is Sylvia who first retreats to the safety of life on a higher class level. The use of a French actress, Isabelle Huppert, in the role of Sylvia subliminally reinforces her incompatibility with Terry – at the same time camouflaging the fact that the difference is founded on class. 'There's nothing wrong with *my* eyes', she remarks, distancing herself from him. Terry's failing here suggests a more generalized problem of virility that echoes Henderson's more explicitly pathological problems. When Terry tracks her down to the ballet, she says that although she's told her husband of her affair with him, she's only confessed to having slept with him once. Since neither she nor her husband wants to be mixed up in murder, she will not confess her presence in his room on the night of the assault and killing. One is reminded of her earlier words, which had prompted Terry to speak quixotically on her behalf, deluded that one can have the best of both worlds: 'Why should my life be turned upside down just because I happened to look out of the window?'

Whereas *The Bedroom Window* defines the upper class as all hardnosed calculation and control, it presents the working class as dangerously out of control. In ensnaring Henderson, Terry and Denise reassert the control the middle class has lost through its outflanking by the pincer movement of upper and lower classes. Social mobility is a false solution to the impoverishment of the middle classes in eighties America – and is rejected along with Sylvia. The true (unreal, utopian) remedy is the intraclass solidarity of Terry's pairing with Denise. Meanwhile, the redefinition of the working class as 'out of control' represses the text's awareness of just how much control Henderson has been able to achieve: he is in fact almost as 'fiendishly' cunning as Sylvia. (Id and superego are linked in their conspiracy against the beleaguered ego, the middle class.) In killing Sylvia, Henderson eliminates the only person who can provide Terry with an alibi. (After hearing a neighbour confess to Terry that she heard him coming in late on the night in question, the viewer's suspicions of Terry can only be reinforced.) Using Henderson to kill Sylvia, the film employs the double to have the best of both worlds: the revenge upon her required by the viewer identified with Terry is duly exacted, but the crime is attributed to someone else in line with a 'wrong man' syndrome that is profoundly characteristic of the thriller. Terry is defined as the wrong man in order to hide the possibility that the wrong man may be Henderson. Nevertheless, since upper and lower classes are secretly allied against Terry, the moment at which the working-class man kills Sylvia marks the alliance's demise. It is only apparently the nadir of Terry's fortunes, since although Henderson's pushing of Sylvia's body into Terry's arms when the latter is known to have cause for anger with her creates the illusion that Terry murdered her, shortly thereafter he reencounters Denise, a helpful rather than a hostile double: a 'donor' within the narrative, in fact.

The largely middle-class audience has itself surrendered control by entering the movie theatre and consenting to have the unforeseen come at it out of the dark. If it did not recover control, it might in theory never be able to leave the theatre (the nightmare ending of Buñuel's *Exterminating Angel*). It does so by translating the film to the level of metafilm, upon which it becomes merely a constructed object – not really life, only an imitation that can be comfortably abandoned as an imposture. This occurs when Terry and Denise set a trap for Henderson that is really an unacknowledged film-within-the-film. She dons a wig before following Henderson into the bar; she becomes an actress. It is so sleazy she hesitates to pass through the door; all heads swivel instantaneously when she does so. The condition of her entry is the same as that of the audience's entry into the theatre: the mechanism of disavowal, for which suspension of disbelief is really suspension of belief. 'She' isn't really there; 'we' aren't really here; 'it's only a film' (as one tells oneself frantically whenever suspense threatens to become too excruciating).

If the girl were really the sexpot she pretends to be – the film argues – then she would deserve all she has coming to her. Sylvia is seen half-naked by Henderson – and is later killed. The sorority girl makes a spectacle of herself – and she too dies. As Sylvia stands by the window, Terry tells her that people can see her standing there. Henderson's depravity is visible, for even though he inhabits a ground-floor room (in the basement, where the id and the working class belong), he doesn't draw the curtains on his nakedness before going to bed. In *The Bedroom Window* nakedness is always unattainable, always on the other side of windows or shower drapes (it is thus that we see Denise after she has made love to Terry), or else walking away from you (Terry going to the bathroom, Sylvia to the window, each shot from behind): it is the perspective of the film-goer fixated on untouchable flesh. Henderson's tendency to self-exposure links him to Sylvia. And yet he flees at the sight of the upper-class girl at the window. Although he does so for the mundane reason of not wishing to be seen, other motives permit one to classify the scene as overdetermined, the film's primal – as well as originary – scene. No wonder the film poster alludes to it. Henderson runs away: because her nakedness is unattainable, as far above him physically as Sylvia is socially above Terry (a moment of doubling between Henderson and Terry); because its appearance at the window renders pointless his assault. (Why strip one girl when another flaunts her nakedness? Anticipation of the end of one's action paradoxically prevents the action's completion; and given the problems with sexuality signalled by the blocked keyhole, it may be that Henderson is unable to consummate relations and so might assault girls primarily so as to look on their nakedness, embodying the scopophilia of the film-viewer himself, *another* theme the film broaches and represses.) It is as if his alter ego's possession of a naked girl removes the need for *him* to strip one. In this film, to stand out is to be hurt: whether one be Terry, remembered at the bar because a waitress spilled a drink on him; the sorority girl, whose table-top dance attracted the murderer's attention; or Denise, the waitress who gave barman Peter a public birthday kiss. And so we are reconciled to our position as invisible nonstars: the dark auditorium is the only safe place.

Because the film is about the pointlessness of identification (sympathy), the villain's background is never shown. This refusal of understanding is fundamental to melodrama, with its demonization of the Other. Why should we wish to discover why he acts as he does or learn the identity of the woman who bawls him out for coming home late (landlady, mother, shades of *Psycho* too?)? The film tells one to take out the contact lenses that enable one to see the distant (the unreachable upper-class girl, the film's French window-dressing) and look instead to what lies near to hand: the girl from one's own class, from the neighbouring block, who *could* be sexy if she wanted (and who will act sexy if necessary), but usually is not, for she knows it's neither quite safe nor quite right. And when the girl is close enough to touch (when she's the girl in the seat next to you, not the one on the screen), one's myopia does not matter.

The echo chamber: *Body Double*

By the time of *Body Double,* De Palma had been wearing the mask of Hitchcock's manic, mod double for a long time. The repetition, parody and reworking of images and themes from *Vertigo, Psycho* and *Rear Window* had become his characteristic forged signature, reaching a baroque peak of attenuation in *Body Double.* Over and above the obvious dense network of reference to voyeurism in Hitchcock, the film is shot through with doublings and repetitions and can even be read as the optimistic (and somewhat shallower) rewrite of his own *Blow Out,* his most powerfully felt film. Thus, the name Holly is doubled (belonging both to the fictional Holly Body and the real Holly Johnson, of the Frankies). The short-haired blonde doubles the long-haired brunette. And most pregnantly of all, as Jake (Craig Wasson) clutches Holly (Melanie Griffith) in the 'Relax' sequence, to intercut images of himself holding Gloria, accompanied by the trashily swirling romantic music that has dominated the film's first part, the spinning camera echoes the 360-degree pan around Scottie and Judy in *Vertigo,* reprises De Palma's own *Obsession* and, for good measure, indicates the presence of a dual text: on the one hand, the inner text of Jake's romanticism and the camera's identification with his point of view hitherto and, on the other, the hard reality of the text of the outer world – for the return of 'Relax' ironically puts romanticism in its place. In this remarkably convoluted sequence, the real possibility of holding Holly (a sign of her sluttishness) simultaneously signifies the impossibility of securing the rich, idealized Madonna-figure, Gloria. As a way of making vicarious love to Gloria, while at the same time denying that her image could ever be thus tainted, it becomes a form of the necrophilia that recurs at the film's end, when Holly (rescued by Jake from 'the Indian', Gloria's disguised murderer-husband) accuses Jake of morbidity. Jake as ironic vampire is the work's final image: as he stands holding a blonde in a shower (*Psycho – again*) on the set of a hard-core movie, the body double for the lead actress displays her breasts as a fine frame for the trickling blood. If the body is double, it is a construction that is always false (whence the air of falsity hanging over the film itself?), built up by the editor of events – be it 'the Indian', the director's unconvincing evil twin, or Jake, the director surrogate who finally wins. To complicate matters still further, *Body Double* itself can be split into two halves (like the image of woman, divided so as to be ruled? or divided to be perennially beyond grasp?), a break noted intuitively by Pauline Kael when she remarked that only with Holly's appearance does it become interesting.[3] This is because Holly's emergence takes the theme of deceptive appearance, previously marginal to the film (the acting milieu setting; the shot of the landscape whose shifting shows it to be painted), to its centre – and so gives it a centre. The sudden addition of a possible extra layer of events – of the plot (conspiracy) that pulls them together – shows one had been right to deem the first part, culminating in Gloria's death, superficial and repetitive. The insistent early echoes of Hitchcock become readable retrospectively as clues to the superficiality of Jake's point of view, pointers to a hollowness to be penetrated to disclose the hidden connections. (A penetration involving a downward spiral that is also the movement of the drill that screw-kills Gloria – a spiral pervasive – need one add? – in *Vertigo.*)

During the 'Relax' sequence, the film's built-in Frankie Goes to Hollywood video, Jake remarks to Holly, 'I like to watch'. Voyeurism seduces him into dutiful participation in the plot laid by Gloria's husband. With Gloria's death, however, seen from an impotent distance, he perceives the potential for pain in just watching, the voyeur's frustrated exile from action. 'I like to watch' crumbles as he realizes he has been set up to validate false appearances through his witness. As pain deepens Jake's point of view, he understands that the murder had been planned to seem the side-effect of a burglary, with Jake himself at fault for the warning phone call to Gloria that enticed her into the murderer's vicinity. The robbery had been simply a side-show: as so often in this film, the marginal becomes central. As Jake's perspective shifts, the film ceases to identify with his etiolated fascination with rich women clicking high-heeled through shopping malls (here De Palma implicitly critiques his own *Dressed to Kill*), transcending the superficiality of *mere* image. Jake's discovery that surface and depth are disjunctive permits him to act, as actor, again − playing the bewildered straight Holly initiates during 'Relax', impersonating a porn director to pique her interest, incarnating a vampire at the close. As he lies in the grave, facing live burial by the killer, he taps the actor's power of resurrective self-transformation and escapes the claustrophobia that stands for his earlier enclosure by his own point of view. Jake's limitations are almost fatal, as he lies immobile in the grave prepared for him and Holly. But if *Body Double* repeats *Blow Out* (each ends with the shooting of scenes in exploitation flicks), it does so in an altered key, as the satyr play to a tragedy. Illusion is benevolent, it seems to argue, so long as it is wrought so amateurishly as to deceive no one. (The film thus advances an apologia for its own tiredness.) Camp becomes a strangely Brechtian source of pleasure, alienation effects becoming in-jokes, for our shared knowledge of cheap conventions (Hitchcock's, the exploitation movie's, De Palma's own) means we are all alienated together. If, in *Body Double*, De Palma is simply revisiting his own old (read: *dead*) themes, as Kael complains, he does so as fearless vampire killer, digging up motifs to lay them to rest once and for all. The death of the auteur then becomes in De Palma's case the birth of *his* body double − the metteur-en-scène, the director of *The Untouchables*.

The kindness of strangers: *A Short Film about Love*

Words are our way of making sense of things, and tears are forced from us at those moment when we can no longer make sense of the world, they are the acknowledgement that, however powerful we may be, however intelligent, power and intelligence have to give way before life itself.[4]

The characters in Krzysztof Kieślowski's films move at enormous distances from one another − one reason, perhaps, why such long stretches of his short films about killing and love (and his best other works, such as *Decalogue 4*) unfold so effectively within clamps of silence. The separateness of lives is imaged in the impersonal Warsaw apartment block in which the entirety of the *Decalogue* series is set. Even people in close physical proximity have souls on remote planets.

Their faces are masks – so much so indeed that in *Decalogue 4* passion becomes indistinguishable from acting, with language existing only to conceal thought. (The daughter who claims to have opened her mother's dying letter to her, to have learned that her father is not her father really, may simply be trying to legalize her incestuous feelings and pave the way to their translation into physical possession – or she may not; she is, after all, a student of acting.) Other people exude the mystery that is a recurrent subtext of the *Decalogue*. One could of course defend oneself by assimilating others to the Other, be it political or supernatural, but this is not Kieślowski's tactic. If tears of frustration or incomprehension well up when the other is both intimate and opaque, a better defence is the irony that accepts contradiction because it feeds on it, the salt that preserves from the different, melting salt of self-pitying tears. Traditionally, irony has been Polish art's most potent mode of defence, and the site of irony is the apartment block that says Poles are all one family and yet contains myriad separate lives. Poles can no longer necessarily reach agreement with other Poles, as Wałęsa once thought. The agonized quality of much of the *Decalogue* may be read as a sign of mourning for the Poles' entry into the realm of mutual incomprehensibility, the modernity so often symbolized by apartment blocks, as the ethos of Solidarity dissolved with the dissolution of the helpfully unifying enemy, the socialist state. So although the *Decalogue* may not be a political work, the twilight of Communist rule in late-eighties Poland being all too evidently inscribed in its indifference to political demands and constraints, it offers a relentless demonstration that the totalitarian-bred habits of wearing a mask – habits delineated so pungently by Miłosz in *The Captive Mind* – still persisted in Poland.

Such an atmosphere is clearly congenial to the making of a film about killing, that ultimate embodiment of absolute distance, total noncommunication; but how can it sustain a film about love? Here Kieślowski is very canny, for his love itself is distant. At one point in *A Short Film about Love,* Tomek, the nineteen-year-old spying on the love life of Magda, an artist in her thirties living in the opposite block, rings the gas company to summon repair men to interrupt her lovemaking. His chortles over the ensuing consternation express the spirit of irony that hovers over all of Kieślowski's work. Kieślowski himself has a tendency to distance us suddenly from his films, virtually mocking our absorption once it has been achieved – as when angelic music flutes forth almost absurdly during Jacek's confession in the film about killing or when Tomek's landlady peers through the lens at *his* encounter with Magda: the moments are too grotesque to be true. (Given his interest in alternative scenarios, most apparent in *Coincidence,* these moments may be signs of an absent Other, a different version, as the director virtually crumples up his work to throw it away.) It is during that encounter that the spirit of irony takes its revenge on Tomek, now no longer master but object of the look: he runs his hands up Magda's thighs and ejaculates prematurely – even at their closest, people are vastly remote. Tomek does indeed have nobody close to him: he has lost his parents, his friend is serving with the UN in Damascus and the love of his life does not know him and is, in any case, far older than he. When the milk round he has wangled so as to be able to deliver to her takes him to her door and she opens it, asking why he is bothering her and whether he wants to sleep with her, he says there is nothing he wants. It is hardly surprising he should crush ice against his ears as he stands in solitude on top of the block.

It is possible to feel that Kieślowski's film is somewhat forced, lacking the inevitability, the harrowing tension, of *A Short Film about Killing:* less ground-breaking than the other film, it has the air of a five-finger exercise, with the conventions of the minigenre reducing the demands on the director's inventiveness and granting him the leisure to pare the finger-nails of his other hand. (He is the ironic creator described in Joyce's *Portrait of the Artist:* in both Joyce and Kieślowski, it is the irony one feels vis-à-vis one's own adolescence.) The slightly contrived air is something shared with some of the other films in the *Decalogue* – particularly numbers 2, 3, 7 and 8 – though there it is the contrivance of short-story terseness. The quotations that pervade the film imply a degree of self-consciousness, while the autoquotations can even be read as indicating a slackening in the tension of novel creation. For quite apart from the *Rear Window* parallels, there are references to *Knife in the Water* and Kieślowski's other films. The *Knife in the Water* reference concerns the boy's solitary reprise of the game whereby Polanski's hitch-hiker makes a blade dance flawlessly between his fragile fingers. For Kieślowski, love is even more remote and unattainable than it was for Polanski: the woman of an older generation is on the far side of a courtyard, not in the same boat. What is more, Tomek, clearly unskilled in male rituals, cuts a finger. And yet this vulnerability makes possible a spiritual link between him and Magda: as he licks his cut, she licks a finger dipped in spilt milk. (The red and the white are spatially separate: almost as if the Polish flag itself has been torn in two as a sign of Kieślowski's renunciation of Polish political themes.) As Magda cries, her back to us, milk slopping on the table before her, Kieślowski seems to be distancing even one of his most intense scenes by punning on the link between tears and spilt milk (the milk a metaphysical conceit for the tears – and also, in a sense, for Tomek's own subsequently spilt seed).

Yet the spiritual link is strongest in the final scene, which is also imbued with self-quotation. Tomek has returned from hospital following the abortive wrist slitting prompted by his erotic humiliation. And Magda, who has been training her binoculars on his window (with his penchant for conceits, does Kieślowski want us to see significance in her use of the binoculars that can stand for breasts, while he employs a single phallic lens?), greatly relieved at his return, comes to see him. She regrets having humiliated him to recover power over her own life, which had been drained by his interventions. He lies asleep, wrists bandaged, his friend's mother a warning Fury guarding his bed. Unable to be near him, for the other woman's presence keeps her away, Magda peers through the telescope nearby, consecrated by the cloth draped over it. She sees herself entering her flat in slow motion, spilling the milk, and Tomek in her kitchen, comforting her. If there is irony here – the image of comfort is available only in memory, and the two are in fact separate here and now, in Tomek's room – it is heartbreaking in its sublimity: Magda has been initiated into a dimension previously closed to her (the angelic dimension, perhaps, of the witness figure whose presence hovers over the *Decalogue* – his prominence in the first episode rendering him as it were the tutelary spirit of the ten-film sequence). Tomek thus becomes like Antek, whose guardian presence accompanies the same actress – Grażyna Szapołowska – in Kieślowski's earlier *No End*. There is indeed no simple ending: references echo from film to film. They extend to a still earlier work, *Coincidence*. The protagonist of that film, whose life appeared in three variants, nevertheless sank to his knees in each, as if felled, in moments of great emotional stress: and Magda does likewise when the postman tells her Tomek is in hospital. Kieślowski is clearly aware that his films form a system of correspondences.

Works concerned with surveillance are also often interested in processes of enlargement, be they the retrospective ones of the developing tray (*Blow Up*) or simultaneous with the activity of surveillance itself. For Kieślowski, however, it is not just an external instrument of vision, but one attached to and generated by the body, that alters what one sees: *tears* are a leitmotif of the work and the subject of a separate conversation between Tomek and Magda. The film's epigraph could thus come from 'Pau, später', Paul Celan's poem about Spinoza, the philosopher as lens grinder: to cut the tear to the right proportions ('Die Träne zurechtschleifen'), through a mixture of irony and empathy, is surely its aim. Hardly surprisingly, the sense of distance in Kieślowski's film is tied to its implicit self-reference. It begins with Tomek's theft of a camera lens and omits the earlier period when binoculars were the instrument of his voyeurism. The obsession with distance may also be linked to a yearning for other cinemas in Kieślowski himself: a yearning suggested by his self-transformation from documentarist to feature film-maker. Thus, the documentarist yearns to become a feature director; the Pole, for a Western cinema where the treatment of eros has traditionally been more frank than in Poland – and he achieves this self-transformation, albeit at some cost, in *The Double Life of Veronica*. The modern film-maker is fascinated by the silent cinema, borrowing its taciturnity and variable framing in *A Short Film about Killing* in particular, and here using the curved glass in the corner of the rectangle of Magda's window to suggest framing by a silent film iris. And the story-teller is obsessed by the visual effects normally prominent in avant-garde film. The remarkable visual effect that shows events in Magda's flat doubled, once in reality, once in the curved glass suspended in the window, raises questions of how events should best be framed: profoundly theoretical cinematic questions. The crisp round image is like the minted imprint of Tomek's watching lens on the surrounding space, which it sucks in magically, like a wide-angle lens: as if in fulfilment of Bazin's dreams, the excluding frame becomes *in*clusive. (It also recalls, and reiterates in another key, the round hole in Tomek's post-office counter window.) In the early scenes in particular, the visuals are almost heart-breakingly prodigal, as in the stunning moment at which Magda's reflection on the counter window appears much larger than the image of the harridan official behind it – with Tomek caught in between. Orange-coloured, Szapołowska's face floats so large across the reflecting surface, a mysterious cloud or desire-distended moon, that it suggests a sudden infusion of dream into reality – its convulsive inundation. Out of synch with the surrounding space, it is spectral, as if for Kieślowski desire itself is spectral, resistant to embodiment, a Platonic form unable to squeeze into actuality. Thus, the beauty of the final image, where Tomek is a comforting presence in memory's revision, involves the transformation of eros into philia, desire into friendship: the transmutation that underlies Platonic love. Magda, who has described herself as not good, becomes just such a tutelary presence as she imagines Tomek to have been, present yet unseen (seen by him, perhaps, in his dreams?). In the cinema, that machine for the simultaneous bridging and maintenance of distance, this may be as close as we can ever get.

Postscript

I have written here of the parallels between some features of Kieślowski's work and aspects of silent cinema. The use of masking devices and filters inter alia in that cinema can be read as implying both that a totality exists and that we are unable to see it in full: 'we see in part' is inscribed in the form of the image. The frame is humanized, and perhaps even anthropomorphized, by this inscription of a limit upon the seeable: normal vision focuses on the centre of a scene, and all is not equally clearly focused. If the cinematic frame shows 'the round earth's four corners', silent cinema lays its stress upon the *roundness.* If this awareness has generally suffered loss since the demise of silent film, it is powerfully present nevertheless in the work of two of the most interesting Polish film-makers of the eighties. Their Polishness may be relevant: the melting of ice in Poland meant that truths were being revealed, but some things still remained hidden: there was transparency on the one hand, but also enigma. Hence, in *A Short Film about Killing* Kieślowski suggestively uses filters to evoke the pressure of an iron grip on the world, which has already caused the edge of the frame to buckle. A similar preoccupation with restricted visibility pervades many of the films of Agnieszka Holland. One sees the world through slim apertures, breaking off one of the wooden slats of the cattle car in *Angry Harvest,* scraping away the ice on the inside window of a bus in *To Kill a Priest,* scratching away the whitewash on the window of the tramcar conveying one through the Łódź ghetto in *Europa, Europa.* The example from *Europa, Europa* is hallucinatory in its force, suggesting the distance of the very past it brings before us. It also permits one to grasp what Holland may have had in mind when scripting the Warsaw Ghetto scenes of Wajda's somewhat tired *Korczak.* In all these examples, one is dealing with an insider who discovers that he or she is an outsider. It is surely the experience of Holland herself – an internal exile whose exile is redoubled by her Jewishness.

This exile, however, is also legible as woman's exclusion from power: a reading corroborated by Satyajit Ray's marvellous *Charulata,* whose enclosed upper-class wife views the passing world through opera-glasses. If restricted vision suggests partial political repression in the Polish films mentioned, Ray's film – set at the turn of the century – allows one to correlate the emergence of cinema, and silent cinema in particular, with the first stirrings of speech in the sexually repressed. A woman may be unable to speak her love, but her gestures cannot help but do so – and the silent cinema captures, and even privileges, that silent speech of the body. If film allows the silent to speak, it stresses their continued silence by restricting our vision. And so we are compelled to identify with the characters: our vision is impaired in the same way as their speech. For if we only see in part, we only speak in part also – as Freud was to show.

PART TWO
Genres

CHAPTER III

Limits of our language, limits of our world: beyond the ideology of SF

Just as we cannot possess again an imagination that is past and extinguished, so we cannot picture the imagination that will animate future generations, and which may alter our current world in a manner that is unimaginable for us.

Ryszard Kapuściński[1]

Notes on the ideology of SF

Apologia pro vita futura

Science fiction has many apologists these days. The modes of advocacy they adopt are not without their contradictions. They can be inspected, for instance, in the work of Robert Scholes, who offers one of the most sophisticated apologies. He contends that 'our need for future feedback to guide present action makes writers responsible for the production of alternative models of the future',[2] adding that 'all future projection is obviously model-making, poesis not mimesis'.[3] Scholes is clearly fighting on two fronts: on the one hand, desirous of an SF that bears the prestige of think-tank relevance to the present (a trip to the future that is not just 'back to the future', a canny time-loop carrying the fiction around the current reality that might just disconfirm it), but on the other, unwilling to clip the wings of the jet-propelled Pegasus. Fighting on two fronts may also be described less charitably as seeking both to have one's cake and to eat it – the neither–norist critical strategy Roland Barthes deems quintessentially petit bourgeois.[4] A utopian longing for a morally informed fiction whose presentation of models will guide selection of the best path through the labyrinthine future is combined with a poststructuralist emphasis on poesis, the separation of sign from referent. Scholes forgets that mimesis can never be avoided entirely: a novelist's experience may inform the work's style and tenor rather than furnishing its material, but is omnipresent nevertheless, while the conscious mind that flees mimesis simply pursues a more convoluted mimesis, such as appears in dreams. In the preface to *The Left Hand of Darkness*, Ursula Le Guin, one of Scholes's preferred SF writers, terms herself a novelist, not an expert on the future.[5] Her declaration is surely prompted in part by awareness that the curse of futurity is a fatal imaginative arbitrariness – the *unbearable* lightness of so much SF's lack of the logic of compulsion of real experience, the weightlessness that renders the future's own likely verdict on the graphomaniac oeuvres of so many SF writers a negative one.

Scholes may be deemed to have confused the rhetorical strategy that sets a work in the future to suspend disbelief with the futurologist's prognostic interest in prophecy.[6] As Robert Philmus notes, 'The distinguishing feature of science fantasy involves the rhetorical strategy of employing a more or less scientific rationale to get the reader to suspend disbelief in a fantastic state of affairs'.[7] Philmus's own 'more or less scientific' similarly begs the question of the degree of SF's scientism. Meanwhile, Scholes's confusion indicates his status as genuine SF aficionado. A similar confusion underlies many SF readers' reactions to the launch of the sputnik in 1957, as described by Brian Aldiss: the supersession of imagined interplanetary flight by reality caused withdrawal symptoms, and SF magazine subscriptions plummeted.[8] Revisionists then redefined the genre in more philosophical, reality-proof terms, as 'speculative fiction' (or Scholes's 'structural fabulation' and Philmus's 'science fantasy': for all the increased sophistication, the initials SF nostalgically remain – a lifeline to the old abandoned planet, as it were). If the result was the emergence of a class system among SF readers, the unsplit audience persisted nevertheless, transferred to a different star system: that of the cinema. The gesture of SF, which fictionalizes science to create the illusion of the wide accessibility of scientific knowledge, is replicated by cinema, which similarly opens up worlds we never really enter: a possible awareness of exclusion is assuaged by the fantasy of knowledge, of understanding the often really baffling world. The cold scientist, egg-headed and hence a quasi-Martian, is the ambivalent scapegoat and saviour of post-Romantic ideology: the actualizer of our dreams, he can also bear the blame for realization of our nightmares. For SF blossoms in a culture whose increasing reverence for the idea of science spurs a general urge to be in touch with it, since its reality is the only true one, even as at the same time one suspects that the consolidation of a separate scientific elite means one's world is in alien hands already. The scientist as Other is both magician and madman. SF builds a scaffolding around this Otherness: our representatives – artists – clamber around it and gingerly inspect the slab. Their simulation of scientific language (or, in film, of the look of futuristic technology) permits us a pseudounderstanding: *mimesis* of the Other as a magical means to control it.

SF reverses the equation of modernist art, and hence may be defined as its dialectical counterpart: where the latter filters familiar events through unfamiliar forms, shattering the dulling glasses of habit, and consequently the effect of familiarity per se, SF employs the Otherness of its material as an alibi for the retention of traditional form. Any intellectual reproached with falling behind the times through reading such work can point in extenuation to a content well ahead of the here and now. Scholes laments 'the vacuum left by the movement of "serious" fiction away from storytelling'[9] (the inverted commas round 'serious' are surely demagogic) and adds that narration persists only in minor forms. There is no need, nevertheless, to resort to debased forms to achieve one's 'narrative fix': we need only become real time-travellers, ready to confront the great narratives of the past, whose preterition continually reminds us that the pleasure they afford is one history has attenuated, even as their persistence intimates that no past is ever past entirely: pockets of 'other times' litter 'the present', indicating the incompletion of the world economy's intended integration. It can be argued that such imaginative time-travel furrows up a deeper difference than the SF whose formal transparency sabotages the depiction of ostensible alterity. SF and modernism may be seen as rival contenders for the crown of truly radical imagination. If this is so, then the most valuable SF is that which transcends the doubly-bound opposition of modernist form versus modern content. Hence, it can be argued that the most challenging SF has not been produced by the permanent members of the intergalactic security council, the SF ghetto, but by novelists whose move into SF is prompted by a particular problem propelling them across its borders: one may think of Burgess, Orwell, Piercy, Lessing, John Fowles or the genre's granddaddy himself, H. G. Wells. Meanwhile, the place at which SF is still unitary may well be the cinema (its set linear form rendering it the last haven of the narrative fix?): the fiction truly dependent on science (the chemistry of the photographic plate), the Other truly Other, not the partial product of the reader's turning of the pages, but persisting in its own inviolable time, in the darkness of outer space. Could it be that the cinema is the other planet we visit in fantasy (and whose abandonment for TV and VCR betokens a growing incapacity to imagine the genuinely Other)?[10]

SF horror: beyond progress and regression

Like Rocky Balboa, the SF film is an underdog that has become a top dog in recent years. Its advance in prestige clearly owes a great deal to minority-group pressure, academic and capitalistic desires to colonize new fields and baby boomers' fond memories of the camp fairy tales told by the electronic child-minder: 'Star Trek' or 'The Twilight Zone'. As the Cold War's ice melted, the sophisticated SF message of tolerance for the Other seemed to be trickling down. Nevertheless, there are darker strains to SF. Indeed, it may well be that the evolutionary leap that permitted SF's conquest of mainstream cinema was its fusion with the horror movie, which supplements technology fetishism with a sense of the vulnerability of the body in the midst of technology. The unclean fantasy, the Other of the clean one, becomes its double and renders it realistic. SF and the splatter movie meet as demonstrations of what technology can do – the monsters it can build, the worlds it can project, the mutilation it can harmlessly inflict. The two genres can fuse because the self-proclaimedly rational man of the SF film can double as the sceptic whose unbelief provokes diabolic attack in the horror film. Horror is conservative, aligning all forms of otherness with the primal Other of the Diabolic.[11] SF, on the other hand, proclaims its progressiveness, its intellectual focus enabling it to define 'monsters' as quite normal in terms of the system that has generated them. Nevertheless, SF's tolerance may be deemed purely hypothetical and emptily self-congratulatory, untested by any reality. The conjectural nature of its imaginary worlds can render them trivial. To prevent this happening, SF can enlist the powerful structures of feeling of the horror film, themselves anchored in the viewer's apprehension of the cutting mechanism of the film,[12] to lend it greater weight. The alliance's value to horror is the provision of a retort to accusations of hysterical mindlessness. After all, what human knows what transcendental strangeness may lie in wait beyond the last nebula? The alliance of SF and horror is highly potent. Each seeks to replace national differences with a distinction between us and a cosmic them. Each thus reinforces the 'one-worldism' that is a keystone of the ideology of the multinational economy. If world unity is to come, however, it must be under the aegis of capitalism. Capitalism delivers the goods. In search of new markets, it boldly goes where no man has trod. It extirpates the bad Other, which refuses to trade, replacing it with a friendly puppet government in the interstellar economic system.

The Fly: *a virus respects no morals*

The fusion of SF and horror is both exemplified in the form and dramatized in the scenario of David Cronenberg's *The Fly*. In it, Otherness spreads like an ink-blot through the passive paper of its protagonist's mere humanity. A virus respects no morals, to borrow the title of Rosa Praunheim's black comedy about AIDS. It was hardly surprising that many reviewers saw the accelerated evolution of Brundlefly out of Seth Brundle as a metaphor for the disease's spread. Cronenberg himself, doubtless sharing others' image of him as a virus in the film industry's body, has a far from negative view of disease. He describes it in interviews as a sharing that occurs between body and virus. (Hence, the allegorical reading of his film as an extended metaphor for AIDS gains credibility when one recalls that, in Forster's *Maurice*, filmed by Merchant–Ivory about the same time, 'sharing' is the preferred euphemism for homosexual love-making.) Between the virus – the microscopic part – and the social whole, the film inserts Seth Brundle. The intermediate party, he will share the fate of the excluded middle when the film finally endorses society's binary distinctions. Horror narrative involves the conquest – and hence elimination – of all middle ground. Nevertheless, *The Fly* could well have ended differently, as Stuart Cornfeld notes:

We actually shot a stop-motion ending that was the other side of Geena Davis's abortion nightmare. After she blows Goldblum's head off, you cut to this beautiful dream: out of darkness, you dolly in on this big chrysalis and it opens up and there are these beautiful big blue wings that expand, and there's a little baby with wings who's hanging upside down. The baby kind of rubs its eyes and drops from the chrysalis and flies off.[13]

As it stands, *The Fly* shows a human organism swamped by the insect with which it has fused: the minuscule part incorporates the whole. The alternative ending reverses this process. Here a form associated with the insect world (a chrysalis) opens to disclose something human: the baby. Cornfeld states that negative audience reaction caused the ending's excision. It responds to a wish to conserve – to remain true to – the dominant system of the film up to this point: the beautiful alternative close, possible for an SF futuristically interested in redemptive children, goes against the grain of the horror system. Seth Brundle's absorption by the fly is an allegorical, concealed self-reflexive metaphor for the horror movie's absorption of SF. If the rejected ending proposes a positive reading of the assimilation of human to insect, it does so through its domestication. The only alteration of the traditional human form is the external addition of wings: there is no penetration and transformation of an entire human genetic make-up. (It is this *externality* that marks the image as nonhorrific.) The winged baby is itself highly conventionalized, reminiscent of amoretti or angels. But the discarded conclusion interestingly suggests that should the fusion of human and insect occur sufficiently early in their life cycles, the result may be the generation of a new species, not the undermining of an established one. Humanity may be retained by making concessions to the Other early on. The new life form would be the fruit of natural selection, emerging from a chrysalis, not the metal, artificial cocoon of the telepod.

The Fly may wind up a horror show, with Brundlefly catastrophically fused with the telepod and requesting the coup de grâce from his erstwhile lover Veronica (Geena Davis), but initially the absorption of Otherness enhances Seth's life. It is not yet clear that horror will win out over SF. Seth's boosted potency leaves Veronica exhausted, and he enjoys padding about the ceiling, fascinated by his new status as object of his own scientific documentation. But the human's greater size does not entail greater genetic strength than the fly. To the allegorically minded, the subtext may not just be AIDS but also Canadian–U.S. relations and species dominance of this planet. In a sense (and here the film really does resemble Kafka's *Metamorphosis,* to which it has been perhaps prematurely compared) the whole film arises out of a play on words: Seth's jealousy of Veronica is the fly in the ointment of his contentment, one his angry decision to teleport himself in her absence magnifies into the hamartia of his tragedy. Seth may voice his ambition to be the first insect politician, but the insect is no democrat: its genes overrun his. The way in which the part subverts the whole is like a nightmare extrapolation from Eliot's contention in 'Tradition and the Individual Talent',[14] that the addition of one work to the canon alters it throughout. That would seem to be Cronenberg's ambition too. His sympathy with insect amorality is apparent in the deletion of the alternative ending on the basis of audience reaction.

'Yeah, I build bodies. I take them apart and put them back together again', Seth remarks to the girl he picks up at the bar. The lines may be read as presaging his final fusion with his own machine, for the teleporter takes bodies apart and reconstitutes them elsewhere. (It is what the film has done to the original *Fly.*) Identification with the machine permits literal dismemberment of others. Seth's development of this ability may indicate a will to inflict on others what he fears for himself: just as castration anxiety may once have led him to shun girls' society, so the symbolic castration of others preserves him from the same fate. If this is so, then the fly is a metaphor for Veronica. (Horror enters SF through its traditional misogyny.) The final consequence of his surrender to Veronica (of allowing a foreign body into his life) is *his* destruction and her eventual appropriation of the phallic gun. In taking bodies apart and reconstituting them, Seth is of course the modern Prometheus known as Frankenstein. Cronenberg, however, inserts into Frankenstein himself the monster Shelley uses as a metaphor for the scientist's unconscious: horror's (in)version of SF is the colonization of inner space. Seth's tender inclination over the experiment of himself is explicitly narcissistic (so the preoccupation with doubles in *Dead Ringers* should be no surprise). Like Frankenstein, he assembles a body of a creature out of the body of (his own, and others') death, his double in the form of the Other. When Seth criticizes Veronica's reluctance to enter the telepod, to dive into the 'cosmic gene pool', he forgets that for Narcissus in particular the plunge into water is the symbolic equivalent of loss of identity. With the imperialistic objectivism of science, he thinks he can enter the unknown without suffering alteration by it. His is a pre-Heisenbergian science. Like the film audience, he would like to keep the body in which the culture is bred safely at a distance, placing the body's reappearance elsewhere under the aegis of transference, not transformation. (May not the photographic process itself balance transfer with transformation?) But, of course, something is lost and gained in the process of exchange. And that tiny something – the fly – can make all the difference.

The cinema as time machine

The emergence of time-travel as a literary theme at the end of the nineteenth century is a phenomenon one may suspect to be linked to the simultaneous emergence of cinema, with its capacity to manipulate the illusion of time. It also appears connected with two other phenomena: the growing acceptance of the idea of evolution and the rapid expansion in knowledge of the sheer size of the universe. In the work of H. G. Wells, who deemed evolutionary theory the formative influence upon his world-view, the motif of time-travel intertwines with that of utopia: time-travel is fuelled by a hope that it will enable one to miss out a stage or two of the evolutionary process and take a short cut into the future. Wells was to propose in 'A Modern Utopia' the idea of a kinetic, rather than a static, utopia. The acceptance of evolutionary theory in Wells's culture finally exploded the notion of the 6,000-year universe, transforming time into a vast field to be mapped and colonized, creating – in a sense – a domain for colonial enterprise once all the available space in the world had been taken up. The spreading knowledge of the extent of the universe, in turn, rendered it apparent that a great deal of time is required to cross it. To move with reasonable speed from one world to another (eliminating the dead time of the black intervening space, as in the shots, which never last very long, of spaceships moving between planets in SF films, while the space travellers often sleep out the time between solar systems – thereby justifying the text's omission of this time too) is in essence to travel through time, traversing light-years of distance.

The notion of the possibility of time-travel begins to be formulated as the development of the cultures of *this* world becomes increasingly uneven. Although the late nineteenth century experienced the cementing of the unity of the world economy, it was a period of continental drift in the technological sphere: cultures drift apart, as some become 'advanced' – and hence qualified for the role of 'master' and 'Superman' – while others become 'backward' and so are slated for servitude. Travel in time is in a sense travel between the unevenly developed countries of this world mapped onto the space of the universe. Hence, in the film *The Day the Earth Stood Still* the other civilization drawn to earth by the fear that the world's inhabitants may abuse the rudimentary form of nuclear power they have just discovered is defined as more 'advanced' than ours. Here we see one of the consolatory functions of time-travel in SF at work: it domesticates a feared future, dispelling our terror at the possible consequences of technological change by demonstrating that its denizens (the visiting aliens) either look just like ourselves or – if not – feel as we do. This is the rational and rationalizing version. We see the future, and yes, it works. The horror future fiction, by way of contrast (as practised, for instance, by David Cronenberg), exploits our deep-seated dread that the time that has witnessed so many profound evolutionary changes may conclude by generating another species out of humankind – Foucault's 'death of man' with a vengeance. It was this fear, of course, that prompted Butler's Erewhonians to destroy all their machines.

The idea of time-travel in the fin-de-siècle period is not restricted to SF, however. It is the motive force of Proust's mammoth work, while resemblances between *The Time Machine* and *Heart of Darkness* are less the fruit of the acquaintanceship of their authors than of the murmurings of the ideology of the era, for which the 'fourth dimension' had assumed the status of a cliché. The structure of Conrad's work replicates that of Wells's and shows the difficulty of disentangling 'high' and 'low' culture during this period: both show a journey into another culture that is also another time. Kurtz has revealed to Marlow the possibility of regression from 'civilization' to 'savagery' – that is, the movement in time from a 'higher' stage of evolution to a 'lower' one. The other country stands for another time – again, the theme of uneven development.

It is Wells's awareness of the human cost of innovation that gives his work its power. The Time Traveller mounts his machine for the first time in the mood of a suicide readying himself for his demise. The subsequent description of the actual process of movement through time – the nausea, the cinematic time-lapse effects, as day and night blur into greyness – is one of the most remarkable passages in this remarkable story. With all the aplomb of the realist novelist, Wells scrupulously considers the obstacles the Time Traveller will have to surmount. How, for instance, is he to pass through the different solid objects that will arise upon the space he now occupies but cannot reserve for himself at a future time? Time-travel itself becomes a form of Russian roulette: to halt may be to encounter the object that will annihilate one. A Bergsonian might applaud Wells's solution – the thinning out of matter at high speed, he says, renders the Time Traveller invisible and invulnerable – while decrying as a petrification of the movement of time his willingness to drop his traveller off in the future and stage a drama there. One has to admit the extreme fortune of the Time Traveller in landing in a conveniently empty space. So long as he moves, however, he can slip through matter with the ease of a ghost (ghosts being, after all, the prototypical time-travellers): he is himself the laser beam of time. Hence, Wells's Time Traveller and his Invisible Man are related figures: for as long as he travels, the Time Traveller *is* the invisible man (for we cannot see time). It is coincidental that Wells presents the 'image-movement' (to use Deleuze's term) of time-travel as that of a man dissolving against the solid background of the present during an era in which cinema, with its capacity to superimpose and dissolve forms, was coming into being?

The Time Traveller and the Invisible Man are intimate relations, for their attributes are those of the viewer of a film. The great Polish film theorist of the interwar period, Karol Irzykowski, wrote of an innate human desire to view events in abstraction from the moment of their first experience and applied this idea to cinema.[15] Thus, the viewing of an event in a cinematic auditorium, whose darkness renders one an invisible man, becomes a species of time travel (obviously so, for the events appearing on the screen are not occurring at present but have long been 'in the can'). Leaps backwards or forwards in time involve a syncopation of history that closely resembles the mechanism of cinematic cutting: the intervening events are edited out. The events left out by time-travel – as one fast-forwards the film of actuality on the editing table of history – blur into invisibility and end up, as it were, on the cutting room floor. This invisibility is of course a fin-de-siècle theme and even *episteme.* It is in part the consequence of the convergence of multiple forms of alienation: the artist begins to feel invisible to his or her audience, as the shared conventions linking her or him to a public of peers are broken down by the growth and unpredictability of the new mass audience – the fruit of the spread of literacy and the mass circulation newspapers.[16] Invisibility, however, is not simply a sign of alienation: it also has a utopian meaning. Here it is related to the idea of time-travel as metamorphosis: a travelling backwards down the evolutionary scale towards the blessed irresponsibility of the animals,[17] or of children, who should be seen rather than heard, but preferably not even seen. The look of the moviegoer – as Walker Percy notes in his book of that title – is like that of 'a boy who has come into this place with his father or brother and so is given leave to see without being seen'. This boy is the child taken out on Sunday to watch the planes from the observation platform in Chris Marker's *La Jetée:* a boy who will emerge from his invisibility through the identification with the on-screen figure, who is always *seen,* a boy who will thus come in the end to share the exemplary death of that seen figure.

Beyond the outer limits of SF

The haunting of time: La Jetée

The more time passes, the more *La Jetée* grows in stature, acquiring a resonance its mere twenty-nine minutes would hardly lead one to expect. It is worth the revisiting that gives it its theme and structure, as it evokes a world in which everything (including one's own death) has always already happened. Here, as in Proust, the precondition of time-travel is revealed to be the end of time (the sense of the fin de siècle): the protagonist has preexperienced his own death; or rather, the entire film can be seen as the unfolding of the contents of the moment of death, in which memory ranges through time in search of a way out of the present moment of imminent demise, only to return – having failed – to that deferred moment (just as the whole of Cocteau's *Le Sang d'un poète* occurs while the chimney falls). The central figure is a revenant, a discarnate spirit moving towards the embodiment of his own past. He has been pursued by a vision of the enigmatic face of a woman and the image of a man falling nearby, at Orly Airport. Only at the end of the film, which is also the end of his life, does he discover this primal scene to be that of his own death, that he is the man falling.

La Jetée begins with a world devastated by World War III. An oracular, poetic voice-over that derives from Cocteau (as does some of the film's imagery – for instance, the defaced heads of the classical statues) recounts events. And so seldom is this great film shown – its brevity and its unusual aesthetic strategies providing the distribution networks with an alibi for its scandalous marginalization – that it may be helpful to begin by summarizing these events.

After World War III, the radioactivity on Earth's surface is so intense that the survivors have had to retreat underground. Marker sardonically notes the fruits of victory: 'the victors mounted guard over an empire of rats'. The survivors fall into two groups: experimenters and experimentees. The first experiments prove unsuccessful; their subjects either die or go mad. Their purpose will later be explained to the protagonist by the director of the camp, who is not the expected mad scientist but a man who gently explains that humanity has been cut off from space and its only hope lies in time (the new domain of the colonial enterprise): if a hole can be found in time, then the present will be able to import the necessary resources from past and future. The death of space in the present is reflected in the way Marker builds up his film (or 'photoroman', to use his own term): by a succession of still photographs.

Following the initial disappointments with randomly chosen subjects, the experimenters concentrate on subjects capable of conceiving strong mental images. 'The camp police spied even on dreams', Marker notes: they select the nameless protagonist as their subject because of his obsession with a childhood image. It is their manipulation that ferries him into the past; since they use injections, it is almost as if Marker is implying that the artificial heightening of the senses by cinema is also a drug, against whose effects he practises therapeutic sensory deprivation, reducing film to its origin in a series of stills in black and white.

On the tenth day of the experiment, images begin to materialize: 'a bedroom in peacetime – a real bedroom', for example. The insistence on the reality of these things paradoxically draws attention to their status as *images.* The nameless subject – his namelessness a metaphor for the damage consciousness has suffered, but also a means of easing our identification with him, since we too are viewers of images – may see 'a happy face' from the past, but it is always 'different': no longer reality, only an image; no longer present, but framed as *past.* Other images appear and mingle in what Marker terms 'the museum that is perhaps his memory', anticipating the later appearance of the museum as the scene of the last meeting between the protagonist and the image of the girl he pursues into the past. It is as if the museum is a materialization of his dreams.

Finally, on the thirtieth day, he encounters the girl. The separation of the sexes that could well have been a motive force of the destruction of this world (one sees no women in the underground realm) is briefly abolished. He is sure that he recognizes her; it is indeed the only thing that he is certain of in a world whose physical richness disorients him. She greets him without surprise: reality is always already known. They come to inhabit an absolute present, 'without memories or projects'. 'Later they are in a garden – he remembers there once were gardens'. Again, it is as if they have materialized out of his memory – rather as whole worlds depend on the observer (*esse est percipi*) in the fiction of Borges. As he watches her face asleep in the sun, he fears that in the course of the time it has taken him to return to her world, she may have died. The imperative to annihilate time thus becomes all the more pressing. On about the fiftieth day, they meet in a museum, a place of 'eternal creatures'.

When he next comes to consciousness in the laboratory, the man is told that he will now be dispatched into the future. In his excitement he fails at first to realize that this means the meeting in the museum has been the final one. 'But the future was better protected than the past'. When he breaks through at last, he encounters 'a transformed planet', its 'ten thousand incomprehensible avenues' embodied in a close-up of the grain of a piece of wood. The people of the future have a dark spot on their foreheads in the position where mystics locate the third eye, an enigmatic echo of the protagonist's dark glasses. At first they reject him as a vestige of the past; they then give him a power supply sufficient to restart the world's industry.

As 'the doors of the future close', the man realizes that the completion of his task has rendered him expendable. Fearing liquidation by the experimenters, he responds to a message from the denizens of the future; declining their offer to take him into their society, he asks them to send him back into the past. He does not yet know that in doing so he has chosen death. He arrives on the jetty of Orly Airport. As he runs across it, he senses that the child he once was – and with whom the film has begun – must be out there somewhere, watching the planes. Death manifests itself – as so often – as the double, as the self occupies two places and times simultaneously. As he runs towards the woman whose image has obsessed him, he sees a man from the underground camp (wearing the glasses that recur in so many forms in this film, signs of the damage to sight – and cinema – that has reduced everything to stills) and recognizes that 'one cannot escape time': he himself was the man he saw fall dead on the jetty as a child.

As the sound of jets rises, echoing the beginning, the film comes full circle, to then continue circling endlessly in the minds of the spectator and of the child the man once was, who is still looking towards a future that has now closed, and of the man himself, always heading towards this future past. At the start of the film, the protagonist had wondered whether he had really seen the image that so obsessed him or had only invented it 'to shield himself from the madness to come'. The image itself, however, proves to be the madness, and his entry into it the self-splitting of death. It has left him trapped in the labyrinth of time.

At one point, the girl whom the time-traveller visits in the past terms him *mon spectre* (my ghost): like a phantom, he comes from a nameless, distant land. Strictly speaking he is both a medium (used to gain access to past and future) and a ghost (he haunts – and is haunted by – the scene of his future death; like all of us, he is so habituated to living life in a linear fashion that he can make no sense of the vouchsafed glimpse of the future, which has the opacity of the flash-forward in so many films, of the unheeded prophecies of Cassandra). His insubstantiality is that of a ghost. (As Wells has shown, time-travel calls for dematerialization – a sign perhaps that it is only *the mind* that truly travels.) It is quite deliberately that I term the film's protagonist a medium: *La Jetée* reestablishes the links between SF and the supernaturalism SF writers so often deny, desirous as they are of colonizing and domesticating the unknown.

The theme of time-travel corresponds to the notion of parallel worlds generated by the spiritualism of the late nineteenth century. In Elizabeth Phelps's enormously influential *The Gates Ajar* (1868), for instance, the temporality of the spirit world runs parallel to that of our own; the absence of the dead becomes a form of presence. The notion of the parallel world is cemented by the emergence of photography, which sifts the detached surface of one time into another like a card reshuffled in a deck. Thus, it is appropriate that Marker's film should be an assemblage of photographs.

Critics writing of *La Jetée* often begin by stating that it is made up entirely of stills. This is *almost* true – for there is one exceptional moment in the film, to which I will return later. The use of still photographs creates a sense that all that remains after the disaster of World War III are the fragments of a narrative. The very form of the film is the imprint of death – rather as the still photographs at the end of Andrzej Munk's *The Passenger* stand for the director's premature death and inability to complete the film.

In the midst of the sombre succession of stills, however, the image flickers into life for a moment as the eyes of the girl in the past are seen to blink. On occasions, Marker has varied the rhythm of his film by dissolving from still to still, rather than simply juxtaposing one baldly with another. Here the dissolves accelerate into normal motion; it is like the mysterious birth of time itself and can also be compared to Godard's wondering use of stop-motion techniques at points in *Sauve qui peut*. The acceleration indicates the presence of fantasy, of film as animation of the inanimate. As the girl's eyes flicker while she lies in bed (the eyes of the remembered mother, at the child's-eye level?), there is a sound as of a dawn chorus, the sound of a world awakening. Then the moment is cut short. The girl's eyes are, as it were, animated by love, her love for the man/child, the love that has transported him into the past. For it is this sense of the possibility of renewed movement, of the flame of life being rekindled out of the universal ashes, that draws the protagonist backwards. If the regressive magnet can of course also be seen as Oedipal, the search for the lost love doubling with the quest for the seductive mother, the unity of eros and thanatos, this in no way diminishes its poignancy.

La Jetée taps the inherent poignancy of the still photograph, that sign of an absent presence, aligning stills in a series as if in the hope that a spark might leap from one to the next and animate all the figures, thereby cheating death; the occasional dissolves are the moments at which such a hope flickers into plausibility. The elegiac quality of this film in black and white may well owe something to the threatened status of monochrome itself, about to be generally displaced in European film-making when Marker composed *La Jetée*. When the protagonist and the girl in the past walk through a natural history museum, the use of stills generates a piercing irony that is also heart-breaking: there may once have existed a distinction between the skeletons of the extinct animals and the people standing beside them, but death has rendered them all equally antediluvian: in a photograph (is it of relevance that these are the photographs of a *Frenchman?*), they cease to be 'still life' and become 'nature morte'.

Perhaps the most powerful image in *La Jetée* is the uncanny one of the blindfolded protagonist, electrodes apparently attached to his eye mask, during the experiments that employ him to break out of the devastated present. The image derives much of its resonance from the manner in which this post–World War III experiment repeats the pattern of the ones conducted in the German concentration camps during World War II (a suggestion reinforced by the German words whispered on the sound-track). A paradox of great power links the capacity to travel through time with impotence. Time-travel becomes an ironic reflection of Marker's own freedom, as he sits at his editing table, to voyage across the surface of images whose originary moments he not only is unable ever to reenter, but never even inhabited in the first place, for the process of filming them held him at one remove from them. But it also provides an inkling of the utopian possibility of actually reimmersing oneself in the moment when the image was first etched on the negative. The blindfolded time-traveller may be likened to the implicit viewer of Buñuel's *Chien Andalou:* to open one's eyes in the cinema is to lose them in actuality. (Buñuel will use the cutter's razor to open our eyes so wide that their contents literally fall out.) When visiting the future, the protagonist wears dark glasses. His damaged vision corresponds to the way the film identifies time less with the visible world of the image-track than with the audible one of the sound-track: the images may be frozen, but the words one hears are not; the images float on the sound-track like ice-floes on a river.

The time-traveller is sent into the past in preparation for his all-important voyage to solicit the technological aid of the future. He himself, however, views the movement into the past as more important: when offered the chance of permanent residence in the future by its inhabitants, he asks to be sent back in time instead – a request that clearly differentiates him from the curious protagonist of most SF and suggests that Marker would criticize much SF as in thrall to a future-mindedness he deems manipulative in the experimenters.

One could argue that time-travel into the past is a motif more emotionally charged than similar travel into the future, which involves a debilitatingly arbitrary speculative projection. Time-travel backwards becomes a metaphor for the regressive movement of imagination and desire, for the split-second resurgence of the totality of one's life in the instant of one's death. Time-travel here fuses with memory and becomes the herald of death. The life one can traverse instantaneously has already become its own ghost: it no longer offers any of the material resistance of real experience. The circle closes as the past reveals its identity (its simultaneity) with the future. The consequence is the perennial repetition of death.

The time-travel that had seemed to offer infinite possibilities is transformed into fate, the dark fulfilment of the oracle of the opening scene. As beginning and end interlock, the open linearity on which time-travel feeds collapses into a circularity that is strangely satisfying, even as it entraps us. The satisfaction is of course the aesthetic one of circular form. The trip around the curved universe returns one to base. The fact of imprisonment (the protagonist's, in the camp; our own, in the cinema) finally seeps into the dream of escape, darkening it in the moment of waking. The hope of self-transcendence that fuels time-travel crumbles into an illusion.

If Wells's *Time Machine* derives poignancy from its final reference to the Time Traveller's failure to return, *La Jetée* does so from its presentation of return as a tragic recognition of misrecognition. Only in the moment of death does the protagonist know himself; only in the moment of its demise does humanity achieve such self-knowledge. This self-knowledge entails self-destruction, in part because the self one knows is no longer there, but also because it involves the transformation of subject into object required by the science whose consequences (nuclear devastation and experiments on human beings on the one hand, self-transcendence on the other) are considered in the fictional form that is itself impregnated with science (its own antibody, whose lack of empathy it heals with the antidote of identification, whose trappings and air of precision it employs as cryptic coloration for and counterweight to its own anthropomorphism and romanticism): in the *science fiction* so profoundly and pregnantly embodied in *La Jetée.*

Visions and revisions of Solaris

When Kris Kelvin arrives at the space observatory hovering over the planet Solaris, he encounters a disorder apparently attributable to the planet's telepathic generation of hallucinatory figures from the disturbing memories of its observers. Kris himself will be haunted by a neutrino-based materialization of his dead wife, Rheya, who will return repeatedly and in the end will seek release from her increasingly human, ever more tortured condition in the annihilator one of the space station's scientists has constructed. In the end, Kris will fly down to the planet, no longer content to consider it from the comfortable abstraction of the scientist, to await the 'cruel miracle' promised by the phantoms of contact he has known.

In such terms, at least, one might summarize Stanisław Lem's 1961 novel *Solaris,* which is particularly remarkable in its dense, viscous evocations of the churning movements of the ocean planet and in its divagations on the Alexandrian hypotheses proposed by centuries of devotees of Solaristics. Andrei Tarkovsky's 1972 epic, panoramic film *Solaris* stretches some of the work's elements, compresses others, in a series of divergences it would be pedantic to consider closely, were it not that taken together they radically rethink the novel, to the intense displeasure of its primal begetter. The main elements are the addition of a lengthy prologue, set on earth, before Kris's (Donatis Banionis's) departure for Solaris and a visionary climax that may well affect the film-goer as itself a version of the cruel miracle for which Kris had hoped. In essence, Tarkovsky's *Solaris* is 'Ligeia' in outer space.

Tarkovsky begins on earth and − in a sense whose ambiguities I will weigh later on − returns to it at the close. The framing gesture rescinds traditional SF's clinical break with terrestrial habits: Tarkovsky insists that we cannot responsibly leave our own planet until we have got our own house in order first. To the extent that it is an anti-SF film, it is also deeply − albeit codedly, implicitly − critical of official Soviet priorities in the early seventies.

If Tarkovsky's choice of genre seems perverse, the poetic abstraction SF can facilitate is clearly congenial to him. In later years, influenced perhaps by recollections of the problems posed by his lead actor, he was to proclaim that nothing of value could be achieved in SF. His ability to make such a declaration may be correlated with the problems besetting his last three films, and may even betoken a lack of self-knowledge that sabotages those works' autobiographical intentions, but it is nevertheless true that *Solaris* goes against the grain of SF and of Lem's novel, paring to a minimum the theoretical reflections on which Lem lingers with loving virtuosity, fleshing out the love theme that is the most conventional element in the Polish original and turning the alien planet's mirror in the direction of earth. Scenes of scientific experiment are virtually nonexistent in Tarkovsky's version − there is none of Kris drawing and analysing Harey's (Natalya Bondarczuk's) blood (the decision to call her Harey, rather than Rheya, is something I will return to later; for the moment I will simply note how it indicates a desire to scramble the code of Lem's text even on the microscopic level) − and Kris's lengthy ruminations on Solaristics vanish. Discarding the novel's first-person narrator for its own third-person objectivity, the film accentuates the love affair, placing Harey's agony insistently before us. We cannot vanish from her presence into the maelstrom of Kris's thoughts. Only in retrospect do we learn of experiments, their results relayed tersely, without the suspense of waiting; indeed, the entire story unfolds in the retrospective mode, which it infuses with tragedy: by the time one discovers something, it is already too late. Even Tarkovsky's reference to weightlessness is intended less to add scientifically convincing detail than to enhance the air of symbolist enigma. When Harey and Kris float together in the library, the artefacts of a European culture largely absent from Lem's work swirling around them, it is both an epiphany and just the sort of thing one might expect in outer space. Even as the use of Bach suggests fulfilment, the narrative reference to an expected weightless spell removes the symbolic weight of the event. It is as if Tarkovsky wishes to disguise the scene's metaphorical reference to eros (even though there is a Venus de Milo in the library, framed with the scientist Snauth as he kisses Harey's hand), rather as Alexander's entwined levitation with Maria in *The Sacrifice* is undercut by strong subsequent suggestions that it was merely a dream.

Why does Tarkovsky adopt this double, self-undercutting perspective? The name 'Maria' in the later film offers a clue: a Maria can only be a mother. Harey is associated with Kris's mother, wearing a similar shawl and undergoing replacement by her in Kris's fevered vision near the film's end. If Harey can return again and again, it is because she is always already a substitute, even in her first incarnation: one for the mother. Undercutting the symbols of love banishes incest's spectre. The wife–mother equation is marginalized, occupying a centre position only in *Mirror*, Tarkovsky's next work. (It may well be that the decision to foreground this element in *Mirror* – whose original plan included a forty-minute interview with Tarkovsky's mother – dispelled repression and metaphor and hence contributed to the sense of aftermath pervading the subsequent films, with their insistent self-quotations.) In light of Tarkovsky's earth-centered vision, the scrambling of Lem's 'Rheya' may seem surprising: after all, in Greek mythology 'Rhea' is the earth. The force of the change, however, is again to disguise the mother's presence. In addition to this, the rearrangement of 'Rheya' as 'Harey' provides a concise icon of her disordered condition, the disorder of the earth itself and of the contemplative mind. The earth mother, once left behind, returns as blank phantom of desire, her status as object of desire being admissible only after disavowal of her identity with the mother.

Tarkovsky's film may begin on earth, but not all the opening matter is foreign to Lem's novel. Berton's account of his unsettling visit to Solaris reaches the film's beginning from the novel's middle. Tarkovsky establishes a sense of vertigo very early on, showing Kris and the aged Berton watching a film of Berton's interrogation – and then inserting Berton's own film of Solaris into the film-within-the-film. It is still

more disturbing that Berton's film should be in colour, while the interrogation film of which it is part is in monochrome. There is surely
something mysterious about a planet that seems to exert such strange
effects upon film stock. (An oscillation between black and white and
colour is, of course, central to Tarkovsky's poetics and will recur
later.)

The work's most vertiginous moment, however, is its close. We return to the lakeside dacha of the beginning, where Kris peers through
the window at his father inside, on whom water is raining. Whereas
earlier his father had castigated the destructiveness of his view of the
cosmos, they are reconciled here, son falling at the father's feet on the
dacha's steps in a reprise of Rembrandt's *Return of the Prodigal Son.*
The reconciliation reunites painting and film, as well as father and
son (a reconciliation first adumbrated when Harey grasped the meaning of Breughel's *Hunters in the Snow* through a memory-flash of the
young Kris lighting sticks in the snow in a home movie): one may be
reminded of the ending of *Andrei Rublov,* as the cinematic image slips
into the mould of a painting. Film itself, perhaps, is the prodigal embracing its denied father. Could it be that Solaris, which has extruded
this image from its watery surface, makes no distinctions between
modes of representation, thereby becoming the utopian patron of the
reconciliation of the arts? The rain dousing Kris outside at the outset
now falls on the father standing inside. Inner and outer meet in another sense also, for the camera zooms backwards to show the dacha
standing on an island in Solaris: Kris's thoughts have assumed form
'outside' him. Or have they? Home may have been re-created on the
planet – earth and cosmos reconciled – but for all the exhilaration of
the rising camera and the intense, almost pentecostal windlike rushing on the sound-track, the miracle may be cruel, connoting Kris's insanity or an absorption into Solaris whereby simulacrum replaces
reality permanently. In a sense, reality has been sucked out by the cinema. For a film-maker, the moment cannot but breathe an air of the
utopian, but it is limned with ambiguity: representation, distance,
Rembrandt may melt into the reality they once designated, but in so
doing they melt reality itself into a sign.

It is at this point in particular that Tarkovsky's *Solaris* achieves the
density of a dream, confronting us much as the planet itself confronts
would-be analysts. The language of dreams is inscribed on a Möbius
strip that folds endlessly back on itself like the planet's waves. The
dream's reverberations echo through an unconscious that is as political as it is personal. Perhaps the most pregnant example is the free-
way sequence near the beginning. On one level, the Tokyo setting taps
a Russian fear of 'the East', an element of the film whose identification
as 'chauvinism' is surely legitimate, given Tarkovsky's decision to ban-

ish the negress from the novel's survey of the visitors the planet des-
patches. On another level, however, it formulates a displaced critique
of the Soviet city: displacement being grimly necessary to preserve the
critique from actual excision by the censor. On yet another level, of
course, Tokyo's technological superiority renders it a valid representative of 'the future'. As the car flashes in and out of tunnels, consciousness becomes subject to hypnosis, intermittence. The sequence is all
the more dreamlike because unmotivated: it is Berton and the child
travelling, not Kris (who might logically need to enter the technological world symbolized by the city preparatory to his departure). In a
sense, the father–son pairing here nevertheless anticipates Kris's final
reconciliation with his father (or with the paternal imaginary). As the
music thickens to a cacophony and cars flit by with increasing speed,
the sense of upthrust almost leads one to suspect that the next cut will
transport us to the silence of outer space (the film's opening tracing a
dialectic of utopia [the countryside], dystopia [the city] and SF [outer
space]). If, for all that, we cut to Kris at the dacha *before* moving on to
outer space, the suggestion may well be that the dacha and interstellar
space are one, transforming the moment into a subliminal flash-forward
to the moment of fusion at the end.

When Rheya first appears in Lem's novel – with a surrealism that is
Felliniesque rather than Tarkovskian, sun-tanned and in a white beach
dress – Kris's first thought is, 'I was dreaming and I was aware that I
was dreaming'.[18] The words may remind one of Donne's 'The Dreame',
an association whose appropriateness is cemented by its writer's status as *metaphysical* poet: 'Deare love, for nothing lesse then thee /
Would I have broke this happy dreame, / It was a theame / For reason,
much too strong for phantasie, / Therefore thou wakd'st me wisely;
yet / My Dreame thou brok'st not, but continued'st it'.[19] Hence, on kissing Rheya, Lem's Kris can think, 'I was not betraying her memory, for
it was of her that I was dreaming'.[20] (For Tarkovsky the question of
betrayal is less one of the past by the present than of present recurrence of past betrayal of Harey; betrayal is, as it were, always already
present, perhaps because the marital love that is the displaced, sanc-
tioned form of love for the mother itself betrays her primacy.) Another
metaphysical poem, Marvell's 'Definition of Love', may also suggest itself: love was 'begotten by despair / Upon impossibility'.[21] Marvell ex-
pounds the conundrum with wit; Tarkovsky inducts us into the
despair. Lem's Kris, for his part, doubts his own sanity, and one can
understand why: the first-person narrator is very much on his own. He
performs a series of complex calculations to demonstrate his own sanity to himself. Inevitably, the third-person objectivity of film dismisses
this issue: the focus is rather on Kris's relationship with a Harey who
is a definite continual fact, and if she is part of him also it is in a more

complex sense than a mere hallucination. The phantom's objectivity, the persistent miracle of its being, is stressed by the scrupulous separation of reflection from person reflected: when we see Kris and Harey before a mirror, there is no intention to baffle us with regard to which is image and which reality (the sense of vertigo will be reserved for the end), for droplets of water dot the glass. Harey's reflections in those droplets are multiple miniature clones lying in wait to replace her. If Harey is nonidentical with her own reflection (she views a film of 'herself'; however, it is not a mirror image but rather one dredged up from the past, almost as if it were the image of herself on earth finally reaching Solaris after light-years of transmission), the suggestion is one of entrapment in the antechamber of what Lacan would term the mirror stage.

On seeing Rheya, Lem's protagonist remarks, 'My memory of her was uncannily precise'.[22] This precision can itself be the hallmark of dream – the dream of film itself. Consider the following quotation from Tarkovsky's *Sculpting in Time:*

Mysterious blurring is not the way to achieve a true filmic impression of dreams or memories. The cinema is not, and must not be, concerned with borrowing effects from the theatre. What then is needed? First of all we need to know what sort of dream our hero had. We need to know the actual, material facts of the dream.... These must be shown with the utmost precision.[23]

The precision of the filmic image, in which *everything is in focus,* radically contradicts our normal mode of vision, in which the periphery is blurred. (The early cinema's use of the iris and the masking shot betrays awareness of the disparity and a desire to mute film's uncanniness by cropping the image into an approximation of our habitual way of looking.) The equal visibility of margin and centre in film is dreamlike also: if the margin needs to be visible, it is because it is *really* central, as the exactitude of its reproduction indicates, and only the dream's censoring agency has banished it to the edge. Centre–periphery displacements betray Tarkovsky's dreamwork on the original. Thus, the novel's incidental reference to *Don Quixote* – Gibarian's face is described as 'all vertical planes', like that of Quixote – is amplified in the film, which quotes a significant passage on sleep's resemblance to death and shows the novel floating in the library during the period of weightlessness.

If a photograph is in a sense frozen water, film becomes the effort to melt the ice: it is the effort to animate the photograph of Harey that Kris seems about to consign to the fire near the film's start (fire as an image of transformation?), the effort to transform it into *film.* (One may recall Christa Wolf's remark, in her *Model Childhood,* that photographs one has considered often and lengthily do not burn well.) We will see the photograph later, on the space station; but is it a copy of a copy? Water, of course, is obsessively present in this film, as in many of Tarkovsky's other works. It is the source of reflections; the transparent, invisible image of time's invisibility; an agent of baptism and purgation; and one of the Bible's metaphors for the Holy Spirit. The recurrence of images of fire on snow (Kris in the home movie; *The Hunters in the Snow*) indicates a desire to release frozen emotions: to free the princess locked in the heart of the ice. The inundation of the town of Tarkovsky's childhood in the late thirties links childhood, water and memory. The unconscious is that which lies under water. The 'visitors' float up from the ocean planet while the astronauts sleep. In Lem's novel, Snow (termed *Snauth* in Tarkovsky's version) suggests that the planet is making awkward attempts to send them presents: Rheya is like Aphrodite, born of the waves. The film transforms that image into the Venus de Milo in the library: the image of an *incomplete* woman. If Solaris is indeed dispatching presents to humankind, then Lem's story becomes a revision of Genesis (note how the title's evocation of the sun hints that Solaris may not be so far away after all, its water a dream inversion of the fire of our sun; while the '-is' suffix recalls Genesis also): Harey is fashioned from Adam's rib by the imperfect God invoked in Lem's final chapter. If Rheya's return is destructive, however (the destruction earth's return inflicts upon SF as a genre), it is because she is less Eve than Lilith, the repressed first wife of Hebrew mythology, the vampirical Lamia who absorbs Kris's life (and so the drained look worn by Banionis, the actor who plays him, is very appropriate).

The planet itself thus becomes readable as a coded image of a dominant woman. Identifications of femininity with water and circularity are of course common, founded on parallels between lunar and menstrual cycles; in *Solaris,* however, the feminine is by no means as passive as the traditonal identification implies. By separating the woman from Solaris, the work disavows the image of dominant female, even as its separation from the Harey it generates is also *the mother's* separation from (and primacy over) the wife. Is it fabled feminine intuition that has divined Kris's memories? On one level, the film's close constitutes Kris's return to the womb – one disguised as a reinforcement of patriarchy, return to the father. Traditionally the colour of water is blue. Tarkovsky's film eliminates the red sun that alternates with a blue one in Lem's original: his aim is clearly to steep the world in water. Hence, the film's palette stresses colours associated with water: the green of the waving fronds at the start (hair as tentacles), the browns of Harey's dress, the silver of the space station, the interstellar equivalent of the silver of ice. The use of water-based, muted colours indicates Tarkovsky's holism: his desire to forge a world all of whose details could issue from, and be pigmented by, a single mind. The binarism of the blue–red spectrum disappears. That single mind is surely male, desirous of a woman who will be part of – subordinate to – man. Its inability to live with Harey's real otherness causes her multiple deaths, both on earth and in outer space. The film both embodies and seeks to transcend a form of male–female relationship that may be termed 'asymmetrical'. This is a term Simonetta Salvestroni has derived from the logic of Matte Blanco and applied to *Solaris:*

Thus, for example, 'John is the brother of Paul' formulates a symmetrical relation, 'The arm is part of the body' an asymmetrical one. . . . By consequence of the principle of symmetry, Matte Blanco emphasizes, all the elements of a class come to be considered identical in a way which annihilates such traditional logical distinctions as that between subject and object, part and whole, thought and action, and past, present and future.[24]

Solaris struggles to transform an imagination animated by asymmetry and hierarchy into one of equality (symmetry). Harey may have been defeated on earth; now she has another planet, the symbol of another order, on her side. Even under these circumstances, however, her defeat seems irrevocable: for much of its duration *Solaris* seems mired in the Nietzschean cycles of eternal return mentioned by Otto the postman in *The Sacrifice.* Milan Kundera has written movingly of the unbearable lightness of a world in which nothing ever returns; the world of eternal return, conversely, is monstrous. The moment is so heavy it cannot be passed. Whence the length, the agonized quality, of Tarkovsky's film. By its end the weight seems to have crushed the femininity so often identified with lightness. It may not be too late for the son to achieve reconciliation with a father who is still alive, but there is no chance of reunification with the dead wife. Her eternal recurrence as image is the cruel miracle that parodies the resurrection. It is begotten by despair, upon impossibility. *Solaris* is an enormous threnody.

A perpetual sense of impossibility underlies Tarkovsky's oscillations between colour and monochrome. In *Sculpting in Time,* Tarkovsky condemns the automatism with which colour film reproduces the world:

Why is it, when all that the camera is doing is recording real life on film, that a coloured shot should seem so unbelievably, monstrously false? The explanation must surely be that colour, reproduced mechanically, lacks the touch of the artist's hand; in this area he loses his organising function.[25]

His proposed remedy is as follows:

Perhaps the effect of colour should be neutralised by alternating colour and monochrome sequences, so that the impression made by the complete spectrum is spaced out, toned down.[26]

The alternation nevertheless is more suggestive of impossibility than of possibility: the image could always bear a different hue. The presence of colour cannot banish the spectre of lack, just as that of 'Harey' cannot conceal her real absence. The occasional presence of monochrome cannot revoke the film history that now proscribes its thoroughgoing use, except as the commodified signifier of nostalgia. Tarkovsky may remark that more and more films are being made in black and white, but his own merely partial use of monochrome betrays subconscious awareness of its current duplicity.

Solaris ends by quoting a painting by Rembrandt: the seamless weaving of quotation into the work that quotes it obliterates distinctions between past and present forms of art, and so becomes utopian. The final dream of a reconciliation of painting and film − a pervasive dream in Tarkovsky's oeuvre − is nevertheless present embryonically throughout in the use of the camera to create a *mobile still life.* Again and again the camera will range across a chaotic litter of objects. They cannot be dwelled on with satisfaction, only traversed; in the sense of Benjamin's baroque tragedy book, they are ruins, allegories whose key has been lost. One has to travel in search of it. Here Tarkovsky's SF displays a bias extremely common in Soviet and Eastern European thought: things do not work. Nor, in a world of extreme secrecy, does interpretation: Tarkovsky rejects the Freudian hermeneutic his works appear to solicit. Objects do not signify. The world of the ending of *Solaris* is one in which sign−referent relations have been swallowed up by a black hole. And yet there is always the possibility of their re-emergence in another universe − in colour or, conversely, in monochrome − on another planet, on the other side.

From tragedy to melodrama

For all its focus on kings, tragedy is radically anti-individualistic. Indeed, René Girard argues that tragic characters continually shift into one another's positions:[1] the ironic movement of the tragic mask yields the birth of tragedy from musical chairs. Freud's psychologization of the Oedipus myth may thus be a misreading: Oedipus did not follow Everyman's desire to murder the father and marry the mother (in fact, he left home to protect those he viewed as his parents!): he merely enacted the oracle's decree. Melodrama, however, is instinct with individualism. If its characters appear in opposed pairs, it is, as Kafka reminds us, because the presence of an enemy floods the individual with strength. The opposite's repression is like the subordination of one of the hemispheres of one's brain, yielding one's gendered identity. In melodrama, dreadful outcomes do not stem from hamartia or fate but are present from the very outset, in the primal enmity of hero and villain. Their irreconcilability is evident in the frequency with which their opposition is mapped onto that between the sexes: calumniated virtue in distress being customarily feminine. The stamp of fortuity that melodramatic disasters nevertheless often bear is simply the arbitrariness of the moment at which opposition was disclosed: it could have occurred at a multiplicity of other points. The moment of disclosure indicates the function of the melodramatic tableau, that precursor of the filmic freeze-frame. A pause in pell-mell events, it reveals the form's essential stasis. (The heroine is noble throughout, the villain unswervingly villainous, and although their companions may misapprehend their identities, the reader is never in doubt: hence, the tableau may be the moment at which the child interrupts the drama by warning the hero of the villain's approach.) Nevertheless, the work takes the apocalyptic desire to halt time *in its stride,* proceeding unabashed. The time of melodrama is *endless.* (The tableau is a publicity still, and the text's mimesis of the image that would interrupt it illustratively prevents any actual interruption: as if, for instance, the Chinese language were to illustrate itself by momentarily foregrounding its status as picture.)

The freeze-frame or tableau may also be seen, of course, as the moment at which the narrative is transfixed into a configuration by the overhead lighting of transcendent significance: and since transcendence and ending are closely related, it is hardly surprising that most films freeze frames only at their close. For Peter Brooks the perceived pressure of the transcendent upon the real defines melodrama: 'States of being beyond the immediate context of the narrative, and in excess of it, have been brought to bear on it, to charge it with intense significances'.[2] To apprehend the presence of something beyond is to begin to grasp the present moment's dependence on a system. (In the case of Balzac, from whom Brooks draws the instances that underpin his generalization, that system is not just socioeconomic, but also the array of remaining books in the 'Comédie Humaine', whose existence follows logically from the stylistic preoccupation with the beyond.)

The repetition of the effort to seize a gesture's meaning in the Balzac passages Brooks quotes indicates its quasi-religious status as the mystery that generates commentary and secretes meaning. Similarly, in Richardson's *Clarissa,* a paucity of events is accompanied by reams of commentary (whence the novel's eerie sense that everything is both in motion and at a standstill). The meaning is unclear because the regimes of gesture and language, sight and sound, are out of synch. The image cries out for a context, perhaps due to a suspicion of the photograph or tableau that lacks one; and since an imagistic context is absent, film not yet having been invented, the context has to come from elsewhere (from language or music). The search for a context mirrors the melodramatic heroine's wandering away from home, as gesture and language fail to mesh. (Marriage proves impossible.) Only at the work's end do they fuse, gesture finally becoming as transparently readable as language in the this-worldly utopia of calumniated Virtue's reward, as duplicitous Evil's smoke-screen blows away. The utopian quality of the final revelation is usually concealed, so *Clarissa's* willingness to link revelation to death indicates its depth and distance from the melodramas it spawns. Only in death can the heroine reconcile the opposed imperatives of telling her story while preserving the silence prescribed to women in general and the dutiful daughter she in particular is: her coffin and her tombstone speak for her. In other melodramas, however, both plot and image are quasi-religious rather than religious. The scenario of Virtue's persecution, misrecognition and final recognition wish-fulfillingly assigns to *this* life the Christian scenario of this-worldly persecution followed by other-worldly reward: religious structures of feeling are both tapped and traduced, upheld and secularized.

Nevertheless, the manifestation of the other reality is far from unambiguous; one has to pore over the image, seeking the clue. The tableau is a frame arrested on the Moviola, potentially significant. The clue need not be lodged in the frame, however, but may be secreted in the *melos* of the drama. Music invisibly represents the excess beyond reality: as the would-be total expressivity of gesture fails to 'say everything',[3] music strikes up to signify the ineffable. In classic film the music functions, as it were, as a subliminal performative, enacting what it designates: 'This is a villian', 'This is a climax', it says. Music serves to flatten the contours of character, the complexity of the sign, into a single meaning: in melodrama, narrative triumphs over character; the black hat slips down over the face below it. (It pulls down the visor, obscuring the eyes.) Hence, if, as Mary Ann Doane notes, 'the maternal melodrama tends to produce the uncomfortable feeling that someone has been had',[4] the effect is neither restricted to melodrama nor attributable to the single cause Doane isolates (the feminization of the spectator through pathos): it stems primarily from the insidiousness of the music, which persuades one that the image signifies more than actually inheres in it. One has been swayed subconsciously and is subconsciously aware – that is, semiaware – of the fact. Sound can manipulate so consummately because, as Julian Jaynes remarks, it is 'the least controllable of all sense modalities', since the lack of a 'point in space from which the voice emanates' increases the helplessness of the hearer.[5] Just as the protagonists of Balzac become mirrors of their environment (*their* excessiveness, that which renders them so pungently memorable, flows out into it), so those of melodrama in general are caught deterministically in their musical surroundings. The music is the Gothic prison whose walls, ceiling and floor are identical with – and hence invisible from within – the frame. The abstract image of 'man' designated by the tragic king gives way to suffocating concretion: democracy does not permit anyone to survey the whole realm but shackles all men to their specialization, their individuality. The king persists only in parodistic form, as the warder at the centre of the panopticon, a spider watching another spider's web.[6]

Big boys don't cry

In a culture which insists that men hold back their tears, the cinema is the exceptional place that allows the rule to prevail elsewhere: under cover of darkness one weeps without fear of one's manliness being impugned. If tears are valued as a sign of sensibility, and yet their display is taboo for men, cinema brings the 'female' aspect of the male to expression, even as the darkness simultaneously represses it. Thus, the viewer of melodrama is essentially ambisexual in character – as one might expect, remembering that *Clarissa*, the primal text of the genre, was written by a man surrounded by a salon of female admirers and that the 'woman's picture' has always been made by men. The contradictory nature of this viewer reveals some of the recent theories of spectatorship to be somewhat simplistic: the viewer is neither implicitly male and sadistic, identified with the pointing of the camera (*pace* Laura Mulvey), nor implicitly masochistic, passively absorbed into the work's flow (*pace* Gaylyn Studlar), but *bisexual*. The oneiric regressiveness of cinema reinstates the primary bisexuality that is also primary narcissism, for one becomes one's own other (in Jungian terminology, anima or animus) while watching. This also justifies the spectator's (often voyeuristic) exclusion from the viewed scene: the bisexual cannot intervene in events, for he/she cannot 'take sides'. Androgyny is a feature of the self that has assimilated the Other, in other words, a self extended into utopian form by the imagination. Like the grieving Margaret in Hopkins's 'Spring and Fall', in crying for the other one cries for oneself, the half of one's being with which – according to Platonic myth – love seeks to rejoin one. One can cry in the dark because one is the dark about whom one is crying for. (Similarly, Hopkins's poem is about both the girl's tears and his own projected grief.) If the sexes are reconciled within the cinematic viewer, however, that reconciliation betrays its merely utopian character when they go their separate ways on leaving the auditorium.[7]

Of the melodramas known to me, it is Kurosawa's early, minor *Quiet Duel* that most fully embodies and critiques the notion of male imperviousness to tears. Kyoji, a wartime surgeon who contracts syphilis when cut while operating on a diseased patient, is tormented by his inability to tell his fiancée why he no longer wishes to marry: if she knew the reason, the distant prospect of a cure might cause her to wait for him and so ruin her life. The difficulty of sacrifice is as central to Japanese melodrama as it is to that of fifties Hollywood (see the following section). But if certain elements of the melodramatic grammar seem to be universal and not simply Western, Kurosawa's work has a distinctively Japanese preoccupation with stasis and shame. In it the excess characteristic of melodrama is shown to embrace both the excessively constrained and the exhibitionistic. (Thus, Hegel's description of tragedy as the clash of stubbornly opposed individuals may project onto it the characteristics of melodrama, enabling one to attribute the weakness of his age's tragedies to a confusion of two forms.

Recent theorizations of melodrama, meanwhile, largely reflect the modern imperative of self-expression and focus too exclusively on the lurid and overblown.)

For most of *Quiet Duel*, the doctor's dilemma is not the one that 'says everything': rather, he is able to say nothing. Again and again he and the other main characters – his father and fiancée – stand frozen, silent, heads bent, agonized. At such moments, only the music's presence tells us time has not stopped. If melodrama is polarized between good and evil, Kyoji is paralysed by their copresence, which renders him unable to function in his melodramatic world: his closest approximation of an explanation comes when he tells his fiancée of the possibility that someone may be both virgin and physically defiled. At one pole lies stasis, excess of nobility; at the other, the mobility that is lack of control, of sexual self-discipline. It is the man from whom Kyoji contracted the disease who becomes hysterical and violent at the suggestion that he may still be ill. He grapples with the doctor, smashes a glass table-top and pours himself a stiff drink that overflows. Later, when his pregnant wife is hospitalized, he will again rampage, smashing glass – the glass that Kyoji, often shot through a window-pane, can never break through. It is emotional, not sexual, release that Kyoji finally finds in confessing his torment, in tears and rage, to a trainee nurse. His choice of confessor is significant. Initially coded as a loose woman who sees the doctor's self-administered syphilis treatment as a sign of hypocrisy, she is changed by overhearing Kyoji's confession to his father and becomes a trainee nurse who adores and aids him. When Kyoji unburdens himself to her, she offers herself as the permissible outlet of his desire. Having borne a child already, she need not fear the disease. She concludes by remarking what strange places hospitals are (they are indeed among the key sites of melodrama), for in them one can say everything in the most business-like way. Her reference to professionalism unintentionally snaps the doctor back into a professional mode, and he briskly resumes duties. The scene's emotional release will suffice for him, and he does not respond to her offer. Her self-denying devotion to him is summed up strikingly when the diseased man's wife dazzles her with light from a hand-mirror while commenting on it, and it is as if her inability to look herself in the face stems from a shame that has become the blinding light of her own purity. Meanwhile, the doctor will continue to be the selfless helper of the unfortunate, deemed a saint by the policeman who occasionally talks to the nurse. Any expectations that the fiancée might learn the truth and a last minute rescue of the love-match may be effected wither away as the film approaches its close. The nurse who was once an eavesdropper has changed – she will not tittle-tattle – and the fiancée, inwardly torn, marries another. The doctor pulls back from kissing her the day before her wedding. He will continue as what he has said himself to be – one of those who sweats things out silently. The film's motto could even be 'glad to be unhappy': the father remarks that Kyoji would never have amounted to much had he been happy. In a sense, Kyoji's world remains unchanged. He may lose a fiancée and gain a devoted admirer in the nurse, but in the end he is still uncured. This stasis, of course, is profoundly characteristic of melodrama, an often-noted feature of its primal begetter, Richardson's *Clarissa*. As in *Clarissa*, it is a stasis whose repression of action infects the few key events with violence, a repression fed by fear that occurrence is synonymous with cataclysm. That fear becomes a self-fulfilling prophecy, and this dialectic of stasis and violence will recur in Kurosawa's work, most notably in his samurai films. For all its interest in excess and extremity, the force melodrama wields derives from its being all too human: it is our failure to foresee changes that makes them catastrophic.

Modes of fifties melodrama

The Fountainhead *and the double bind*

If melodrama is the family romance par excellence, then the form of that romance – as R. D. Laing has shown – is the double bind. There can be few works richer in such double binds than *The Fountainhead*. The focus of the double bind is Dominique (Patricia Neal), who links the uncompromising architect Howard Roark (Gary Cooper) to Gail Waynard (Raymond Massey), who has built his newspaper empire on telling the public what it wishes to hear. A double bind in the literal sense, she binds Roark and Waynard as doubles. Their kinship beneath the skin becomes apparent in the latter part of the film: when Waynard's *Banner* goes against public opinion and defends Roark's dynamiting of a project where his specifications had been marred by compromise solutions, the unsold, rejected newspapers resemble the skyscrapers Roark has never been hired to build; when the court instructs Roark to rise to receive sentence, Waynard rises simultaneously; and when – incredibly – Roark is pronounced innocent and the film's unconscious, well aware of his guilt, exacts sentence through Waynard's suicide, using the double as scapegoat (the man whose death will make no difference, for his alter ego will survive). If, for all Tooley's rabble-rousing accusations, Roark is paradoxically self-sacrificing (giving up Dominique to Gail), the surrender of the object of desire is also illusory, for at the work's deepest level (repressed by the final *ascent* of the skyscraper), he and Gail are one. The left hand may be ignorant of the deeds of the right, but both belong to the same invisible hero.

The double bind between Roark and Dominique becomes apparent when, on meeting him in New York and recognizing in him the worker whose gaze from the quarry had transfixed her previously, she concludes her confession of love by vowing never to see him again. Her rationale — a rationalization — is her inability to look on as the world destroys him, as it destroys all greatness. She proposes, on the condition that he renounce architecture. As he refuses he adds that she must learn not to be afraid of the world. She cements the double bind by marrying Waynard, who will come to resemble Roark ever more closely as she prepares to leave him. The film never shows her having to make a conscious choice between them (in the depths of the melodramatic consciousness, the other is simply the other hemisphere of one's own brain, and so is never so much rejected as just set aside, for later recovery): Waynard is simply absorbed into Roark, and even the monument to him is another enormous Roark building.

Dominique has a mixed ancestry, for she also descends from the femme fatale of film noir, the perverse rich bitch who does not know her own will. In the individualistic world advocated by Roark and depicted by Vidor, characters never truly meet: their unfulfilled, perverse desire generates the hysteria pulsing in the music, beneath the apparently monolithic simplicity of the narrative surface. The double bind is resolved by an echoing that disentangles things by translating spatial deadlock (the world of the architect) into temporal successiveness. Whereas Dominique begins by arguing that reality destroys beauty (and so, in the arresting moment of her first appearance, she is seen dropping a statue from her apartment window, shot from below, as if she will fall down after it: the camera angle discloses the suicidal meaning of her remark, which identifies with the reality principle, and also adumbrates the motif of the substitute death that will save Roark), Roark will teach her that destruction can be turned against the ugly: she plants the bomb for him in the marred Courtland. By planting the dynamite she brings under control the explosions that had detonated random and distant in the quarry where she first met Roark (the explosions representing the unacknowledged trouble in her desire).

On first encountering Roark, Dominique is shown looking down on him, whip in hand (the rich bitch slumming as a recurrent motif of fifties melodrama — slumming as the impossible, taboo effort to bridge the polarities of society): at the end she rides the elevator towards him as he stands triumphantly atop what is now the tallest building in New York. The perverse, Strindbergian sexuality of the double bind gives way to normality, as the echoes rewrite the antinomies: if contradictory emotions paralyse the person in whom they are present simultaneously, the echoes place them at different points, generating time — before and after — out of the hysterical stasis that has characterized melodrama ever since *Clarissa*. Thus, the story is able to end; it eschews the endlessness of the serial. As this happens the pattern of melodrama is ruptured. At the beginning of his acquaintance with Dominique, Roark speaks of the pressure exerted upon marble by the foreign elements that enter it: it is a metaphor both for his own gradual acceptance by society and for the way the narrative pressure infiltrates change into the unchanging. In this film obsessed with tall buildings, it is also the pressure of phallic masculinity whose entry into the female liberates her from the dungeon of unexpressed desire. At the end, Roark and Dominique need not sacrifice themselves any longer. What began as a double bind is happily translated into having things both ways.

Reader's Digest *religion:* Magnificent Obsession

The structure of melodrama is one of displacement, and hence also — as *The Fountainhead* suggests and *Magnificent Obsession* makes explicit — one of sacrifice. To start with, one has the displacement and camouflage of the Oedipal scenario underlying Sirk's film. It is no deliberate aggression on Bob Merrick's (Rock Hudson's) part that causes Helen's (Jane Wyman's) husband to die for lack of the resuscitator in use to revive Bob himself after his reckless motor-launch ride. (After all, Bob can hardly be blamed for an event that occurred during his black-out — even though, of course, it is while one is unconscious, during sleep, that illicit desire speaks in the language of dreams.) The doctor's death permits Bob to step into his shoes: to adopt his selflessly philanthropic way of life, and even turns of phrase; to become a doctor himself; to operate on Helen to restore the sight she had lost (again, in an accident he had caused); and then, presumably, to become her husband as well as lover (a denouement left unrepresented, perhaps because it would too clearly complete the Oedipal pattern, thereby betraying its repressed presence).

The displacement of Oedipal motifs is apparent in the fact that blindness afflicts Helen, while Bob suffers no ill effects from his spill. Although he ought to, for his arrogance is begging for a comeuppance, nothing happens: in the film's leitmotif, the debt is paid by *another*. The substitutive sacrificial chain is almost unending: Phillips dies to effect Bob's moral regeneration (deliberately, as if his is the unseen providential hand behind the narrative, his invisibility a metaphor for his identity with the omnipresent, self-congratulatory director?); Bob sacrifices himself for Helen; and Helen in her turn flees Bob at the height of their happiness (cf. Dominique's confession of love for Roark in *The Fountainhead*), to prevent others from pitying him for marrying her. ('If you love me, don't try to find me', she writes in her farewell note.) Because the waxen acting combines with Sirk's compositions to lend equal weight to people and things (we see rooms before people enter them, and colour schemes force people to cede pride of place to sick-room flowers), things constitute an adequate sacrifice for people: both exist on the same plane. Thus, in what is perhaps the film's finest and strangest sequence, Helen, anguished by the dashing of her hopes of a sight-restoring operation, gropes her way towards her hotel balcony. (Open earlier, we sense that she will go out onto it.) The swelling music intimates disaster. Yet the premonition has the vagueness of music itself, whose meaning is never clear: it both conveys and muffles premonition. Because Helen's intentions are not spelled out, existing only on the inchoate level of the music, and because the film has cherished her – a cherished doll in a doll's house – up to this point, we cannot conceive of her committing suicide. Hence, when she displaces a flowerpot, which crashes to the ground (cf. Dominique's statuette in *The Fountainhead*), it seems as if it has always already been destroyed in her stead.

The film's fundamental displacement, however, involves Christianity. Doctor Phillips's onetime best friend, a painter, extols the virtues of secret philanthropy to Bob and says that once begun it will become a magnificent obsession. Nevertheless, the price to be paid will be high: a man who once lived this way died on the cross at the age of thirty-three. Thus, Christ is described simply as the follower of a way, not its initiator. The Christian ethic is despecified into a wisdom of the ages, generalized into the practise of self-sacrifice. The painter may mention the power-house one has to tap to let one's light shine, but the word 'God' never crosses his lips. This displacement then permits Bob's romantic obsession with Helen to be dignified with heavenly choirs on the sound-track. Is he not Christ-like in his sacrifice?

Displacement conceals motives. The motives for Helen's blinding surely include a wish to maintain her in the safely subordinate position fifties society prescribes for women. The possibility of change limns the horizon, however: her blinding, like that of Samson, responds to fears of her potential strength. She must be as subordinate as a film's music is to its images. Because she is sightless, one can feast one's eyes on her without any fear of a challenging look back; it is as if the male onlooker is guiltily aware, however, that to objectify woman thus is to mutilate her. Like Bob, we may want to make it up to her. Yet the suffering that accompanies her blindness is minimized (one's sense of guilt is kept in check): 'I always dance with my eyes closed', she tells Bob. One can be blind and still dance. Sirk's glacé, glossy style distances all suffering, all violence. Hence, crisis is depicted as always already overcome. One of the best examples of this occurs when Bob proposes to Helen. Before doing so, he asks, 'Could you forgive anything now?' 'I think so, yes', she replies. 'Even Bob Merrick?' When she answers, 'Yes, Bob, of course', it becomes clear that she knows his identity even before it is confessed. One never learns when she first recognized him: 'I don't really remember when I first had the feeling'. The crisis is already past: in the world of displacement, everything is always elsewhere. The bland air of reticence intimates the director's tasteful superiority to his material. But he does not risk compromising himself by attempting anything more demanding.

Written on the Wind: *class relations and double standards*

It may seem as if I have been not quite fair to Sirk: after all, it is not upon *Magnificent Obsession* that his apologists' case for his work rests. *Written on the Wind* is a very different sort of melodrama from the women's pictures with which he is usually identified, closer, in fact, to *The Fountainhead* than Sirk's other films. In juxtaposing the sexual problems of the rich with oil wells that are (a) the source of the wealth that induces impotence, (b) mocking parodies of the phallus and (c) signs of the dirt beneath all sexuality, it even adjoins on the territory of *Touch of Evil* (the common factor being a shared producer, Zugsmith). Sexuality is a problem for rich boy Kyle (Robert Stack), the gun under his pillow an alienated phallus alienated still further when Lucy (Lauren Bacall) throws it away after their marriage. (She is doubtless aware of the dangers of life under the classical narrative economy, whereby a gun once introduced is bound to go off eventually.) Like *The Fountainhead*, *Written on the Wind* doubles the rich boy with a poor one (Mitch – the Rock Hudson role).

Sirk uses the double to have things both ways. On the one hand, the poor boy Mitch never actually makes love to Lucy either for or against his rich friend Kyle; on the other, Lucy becomes pregnant. The ambiguous behind-the-scenes implications establish a conversation piece that is really a gossip piece, the atmosphere of innuendo that shrouds 'Lives of the Rich and Famous'. The film demonstrates that Mitch always finishes what Kyle starts, while showing at the same time the destructiveness of Kyle's belief that this is invariably so: aware of his own impotence, he is convinced Mitch must be the father. The film operates a double standard, separating the classes absolutely – the rich are spoiled, alcoholic, impotent and dangerous, whereas the impecunious are potent, natural and virtuous – and yet also claims that they can fuse – hence, the rupture in logic when in the end Kyle's bad-seed sister Marylee (Dorothy Malone), who had sought to blackmail Mitch into marrying her by claiming that he murdered Kyle, has a change of heart and tells the truth in court. In a paradox that encapsulates the film's hypocrisy, she reverts to the values of the riverside retreat where she and Mitch exchanged childhood vows and carved their names on a tree trunk, *but* does so by renouncing all claims on Mitch, the poor boy graciously assumed into the rich family (doubtless to rejuvenate it).

A double standard also operates with regard to Mitch's symbolic centrality. Rich and poor may seem to meet in him, the imaginary reconciliation of real opposites representing the ideological form of utopia, but in the end the rich are eliminated as the rich boy–poor girl (Kyle–Lucy) marriage collapses and the possibility of a Marylee–Mitch union is sabotaged by Mitch's departure with Lucy. (The K, L, M initials indicate just how closely – how almost incestuously – implicated the characters are.) As this happens, Mitch loses his utopian mediating role. Since the rich are going to die out, there is no need to maintain any link with them. Mitch and Lucy drive off, leaving Marylee alone, clutching a model oil derrick before a painting of her father doing likewise: the fetish stands in for the sexual satisfaction she is denied. Ideologically, the film defines sex as the recreation of the poor. 'There's nothing wrong with *Lucy*', the doctor has told Kyle, whose response is to cast an envious glance at Mitch dancing with her. Dissolving opposites on one level (Mitch as ideal hero, fusing rich and poor), it reinstates them on another. The meeting of nature and culture, outdoor and indoor, Mitch and Kyle, is not an ideal moment but an indicator of crisis: the moment of disaster, given twice for its double significance, in which leaves blow into the mansion as Kyle returns home thirsting for revenge. In fact, the film is a petit bourgeois revenge fantasy in which the power of the rich is expropriated; the rich must be left behind as Americans once abandoned the lands of corrupt European aristocracy (Sirk as the inversion of Henry James?). The poor boy recovers the girl he once had to cede to the lord of the manor, and Marylee remains alone with the cold comfort of the model derrick.

If displacements dot melodrama, the decadent rich are for Sirk the scapegoats whose demise preserves his own decadent style. Paradoxically, in placing people and things on the same plane, he himself looks with the reifying evil eye of the rich. Formalist populism, his work mingles envy (the rich are other) with camouflage (he himself resembles them). The flattening of character in his films, whose protagonists are lurid playing cards, is no Brechtian alienation device, however, but typically melodramatic. I have argued that melodrama subordinates character to narrative. Whereas in traditional melodrama this resulted in black-and-white characterization, in post-fifties, postmodern melodrama it entails a violent oscillation between black and white within the same characters. With the same actor or actress performing continually, the contradictions between their actions are not always patent and are, in fact, veiled. The internal oscillation hollows out character from within. In the end the characters are only character functions. The extreme case is the late 'Dynasty', in which different actors and actresses play a Stephen or Fallon, and no one on set is seen to bat an eyelid. (Interestingly, the series' lynchpins, Blake and Alexis, remain unchanged.) The family becomes akin to a football team (there always *has* to be a quarterback), a stable, self-regenerating system: the Hydra only low ratings can defeat. It is as if the real star is less the individual than the system itself, which subsumes all apparent change into its self-identity.

Conclusion

It should be apparent from *The Fountainhead* that fifties melodrama embodies an aporia of individualism. Individualism may be the American way, and melodrama may promote that individualism by insisting on the irreconcilability of opposed characters, but each depends on the other's existence for confirmation of its own. Moreover, as Garry Wills notes,[8] the final incarnation of the individualist is the terrorist. He becomes the capitalist's double and henchman: destruction makes possible construction. That is why the system can use Howard Roark. The degree to which capitalist and terrorist in fact work hand in glove should indicate that fifties melodrama is far removed from the militant bourgeois contestation of feudal oppression found in eighteenth-century melodrama. America's lack of an aristocracy turns its melodrama into shadow-boxing, the films of Sirk, for instance, being as fascinated by the eminent rich as they are critical of them. A problem of identification arises: the audience may deem the rich corrupt, but it yearns to be like them also. Is there not a royal road from the log cabin to the mansion? Is not classlessness the U.S. reality? Such beliefs repress class awareness into the shadows of hysterical undertone. In fifties melodrama, the opposites coalesce, and the hero–villain antagonism evaporates: contentment with the system checkmates the possibility of real contestation. The melodrama of virtue in distress, a staple of the inevitably highly gestural silent cinema, shades off into the woman's picture (in the forties) and then, in the fifties, ceases to specify any victimizing force. This indicates the degree to which power's operations have become invisible. Such films as *Caught* and *Rebecca* are the last gasp of Gothic melodrama. Whereas such traditional melodrama appealed to men through its display of the image of suffering femininity (having asserted in imagination the male power that is fading in reality, one can then soothe one's conscience by rushing to woman's aid), fifties melodrama appeals to a 'feminine audience' that includes *males feminized by their sense of powerlessness.* The message now is that all *anyone* can do is suffer.[9]

Melodrama: black and white

Narrative and repression

Melodrama, the epitome of premodernist narrative form, represses our awareness of the conditional basis of point of view. (The bridge from melodrama to modernism may be *style indirect libre,* in which questions of point of view are raised, though only obliquely.) The work's point of view dictates variations in style: 'good' characters are presented more or less realistically, negative ones expressionistically (think of Mrs. Sinclair in *Clarissa*). Melodrama represents the extreme instance of a point-of-view structure's simultaneous omnipresence and concealment: although recounted from the point of view of the 'good' characters, it masquerades ideologically as 'objective'. Apparently positioned 'outside' both good and evil characters, it in fact views the world from the perspective of the good alone. The good, of course, is that which survives (e.g., the rising bourgeoisie). Stories are told by survivors, and outlived characters and castes may be condemned. The guilt of the survivor is repressed: history, or the character's own villainy, caused his or her demise. Here film may be particularly formally ideological in its eschewal of the past tense, the illusion that everything is occurring *now* obscuring the degree to which the story has been framed after the fact to vindicate 'the good'. Use of voice-over would thus constitute an attempt – sadly quixotic, for the sound-track itself is repressed into subordination – to impregnate the image with pastness. It is hardly surprising that film noir, with its complex sense of the mutual imbrication of shadow and light, should employ voice-over often. It is barely ever a feature of melodrama.

It is possible to define the logic of popular cultural narratives as one that plays itself out between melodrama and the picaresque. The structure of melodrama is one of dualism, repression and disavowal: all evil is projected onto an ever-menacing Other. The alternative mode of narrative organization in popular culture may be termed picaresque: where melodrama moralistically upholds categories of good and evil, the picaresque positions us amorally to identify with one mercurial character and his or her meteoric ascents and descents through the social hierarchy. The premium late capitalism places on mobility and adaptability means that the structure of feeling of contemporary popular culture owes more to the picaresque than the melodramatic, as a glance at virtually any U.S. TV miniseries will show. Hence, Frederic Jameson's insistence that we discard categories of good and evil is a call for something already achieved in U.S. popular culture. The protagonist of melodrama tends to be immobile, held at bay (whence the form's emphasis on domesticity and entrapment, the house as primal scene and prison, marriage as dungeon); the protagonist of the picaresque is socially and geographically mobile. When melodrama seeks to cross-dress as picaresque, one has the ridiculous globe-trotting of 'Dynasty' in its late-eighties dotage.

Melodrama and its double

It seems that there is melodrama and melodrama.[10] Jack Zipes, for instance, criticizes *The Lost Honour of Katharina Blum*, by Schlöndorff and Von Trotta, in the following terms: 'The melodramatic devices prevent the disclosure of how the relations of power intrude not only into the victims' but also the victimizers' lives. The network of relations that cause violence and violation of human rights remains impenetrable because evil is personalized.'[11] Earlier, however, he quoted Thomas Elsaesser's influential case for the utility of melodrama:

Melodrama, at its most accomplished, seems capable of reproducing more directly than other genres the patterns of domination and exploitation existing in a given society, especially the relation between psychology, morality, and class consciousness, by emphasizing so clearly an emotional dynamic whose social correlative is a network of external forces directed oppressingly inward, and with which the characters themselves unwittingly collide to become their agents.[12]

The degree of qualification here ('at its most accomplished, *seems* capable' – my emphasis) is clearly cognizant of the possibility of such objections as Zipes raises and may indicate repressed doubts concerning the actual compatibility of melodrama, which does all the work for us, with a modernism that compels us to work. So when Zipes complains that 'the viewer *cannot* make up his or her mind about the narrative sequence of events',[13] he is not lamenting any lack of clarity, but rather the viewer's deprivation of the freedom to come to conclusions: as if, by the logic that sets a thief to catch a thief, melodrama had to mimic oppression in order to combat it more effectively. Paradoxically, however, the problem with the Schlöndorff–Von Trotta film may be an insufficiency of melodrama, an internal inconsistency.[14] For although its heroine's name denotes purity in classic melodramatic fashion, the music subtending the film (Hans Werner Henze's atonal score) places shifting sand under the film's seeming certainties, creating a melodrama whose aura of art indicates a lack of the courage of its own convictions and sows the seeds of the very doubts Zipes voices. The Schlöndorff–Von Trotta pairing of melodrama and art cinema is another version of Fassbinder's attempted synthesis of realism and formalism ('contentism' and 'sensibilism', to use Michael Rutschky's terms).[15] Melodrama becomes a half-way house between realistic social statement and neo-Brechtian formalism, though the upshot is arguably paralysis. Indeed, it seems as if the effort to transform melodrama goes so thoroughly against the grain of the genre as to destroy the wood; placing dualism 'under erasure' makes the scenario go flat.

If there are negative and positive versions of melodrama, the former may be defined as employing the pressure of the unseen upon the immediate as a limiting, allegorizing factor that subordinates characters to their cipher-like roles as heroes or villains – while in the latter that pressure functions to laminate an entire world with mystery. The former tactic may be seen in *Fatal Attraction*, seeming initial realism transmogrified into horror film hysteria; realism gives way to melodramatic dualism in the same way as the country at first contained in the city, in the form of Central Park, secedes from it and becomes opposed to it. The latter characterizes the work of Georges Franju, which uncorks a mysterious genie from the bottle of melodrama and always discerns the forest *underneath the city*.

Opposites attract?

On one level, *Fatal Attraction* is simply ludicrous: the absurdity of the image of the rampaging woman in white is compounded as she resists death and rises from the bath-tub (shades of *Les Diaboliques*) to menace her lover and give his wife a chance to share in the joy of dispatching her. And yet it is the margin (none too wide) by which the film exceeds the formula of slasher movie with a role reversal that has caused its enormous success. It seems in fact as if the overwhelmingly popular work is the one that possesses undertones of which its authors were probably blissfully unaware. The excess of significance in the work intrigues by making it hard to know what kind of work one is dealing with: initially 'realistic', it spins rapidly into the dehumanizing dualism of Gothic melodrama.

The main body of the film is purely ideological, projecting all irrationality onto Alex (Glenn Close), the demonic career woman who can be destroyed with a clear conscience. The film camouflages the degree to which the irrational is already inherent in Dan (Michael Douglas), the lawyer whose one-night stand with Alex precipitates the narrative's entanglements. Yet it carries hints all the same that the problem is as much in Dan as in Alex: she asks him why he spends time with her if he's married. The question goes unanswered. The narrative does not clearly formulate Dan's problem, though there is evidence to suggest that he is a victim of overcompartmentalization of experience. (The collapse of the compartments then causes chaos.) The main partition separates wife and lover, tame marital affection from animal extramarital sex. Near the start we see Dan's wife Beth (Anne Archer) in panties and T-shirt, about to dress for a party. Beth's near undress is alluring, but the come-on frustrates, for it is simply a prelude to dressing up further. After the party she retires to sleep with her daughter – and we follow Dan's hangdog glance through the door. Later still she will sit scantily clad before her dressing table mirror: this time the telephone short-circuits Dan's advances. Wife cannot be lover; subliminally, the film is establishing adultery as a necessary evil.

Dan's firm then asks him to work the weekend. An office meeting brings him into closer contact with Alex, a fleeting presence at the party who now appears as an editor at the publishing firm he is representing legally: law and the lawless (A-lex) fit together snugly. Beth's weekend absence permits their atavistic coupling. The brutality of Dan's intercourse with Alex is accentuated by the sharp cut from their restaurant pleasantries to him backing her up against a sink whose tap spurts water in a ludicrous sexual metaphor. When Alex later complains that Dan has treated her like a prostitute, we are cued to read her as overreacting. Nevertheless, she may indeed legitimately resent Dan's association of intercourse with dirt, transforming her into the dream whore one relinquishes on waking. When Alex proves to be pregnant, she ceases to be the safe place outside the law, becoming instead a rival for Beth's maternal role. One may wonder whether Beth had no desire for a second child (whence the impossibility of sex). Conversely, Dan's resort to Alex may betray yuppie terror of the responsibility of an extra child. The film's inadequacy comes from prompting such speculations while withholding the evidence needed for any sort of answer; it thus becomes an ideal conversation piece.

If Dan's actions are indeed symptomatic of repressed desire for a second child, it would surely be a son with whom he might establish a narcissistic symbiosis paralleling the one between Beth and her daughter. Beth's narcissism is signalled by her association with mirrors, which echo in one of the film's key long-distance imagistic rhymes: in an early scene Dan approaches Beth from behind, and we see them side by side in the mirror; when Beth wipes steam from the bathroom mirror near the end, she renders visible the knife-wielding image of Alex. This nightmare spectre is a conventional slasher-movie trope, but the reprise of the earlier mirror image suggests that the murderous Alex may be the reality concealed beneath Dan's surface-sweet reasonableness. But although the subtext hints that Alex embodies

Dan's disavowed violence, it seconds the disavowal by defining Alex as a separate character, rather than a split-off materialization of Dan's denied libido. Dan's own destructiveness is shown as sublimated, be it into sex with Alex or into rabid defence of the family. The film's thrust is to justify the paranoia that says one false step can plunge one into the abyss. Even casual, jokey details reinforce the sense of sexuality's danger: the presence of the theme even in the work's margins is a sure signal of paranoia. For instance, there is the case of Bob, who dislocated his neck while making love to his wife. The detail is ambiguous, for if danger resides in the marital bond, Dan's step outside it becomes understandable. His neck now rigid, Bob can only look towards his wife, with no sidelong glances at other women. Another multivalent detail is the blood above Dan's heart as he struggles with Alex at the end: he is indeed a bleeding heart, too weak to dispatch her alone. Indeed, how could he do so, for she is in a sense his double? It is Beth who has to deliver the coup de grâce. As in Dostoyevsky, shared guilt is the best cement for relationships. The ending is happy because it proves that Beth can be just as deadly as Alex; indeed, the division between them dissolves, as each is dressed in white and the editing leaves it unclear just whom Alex's knife is wounding. (We may recall her attempted suicide by slitting her wrists.)

By the end, all sympathy for Alex has evaporated as surely as the steam from the pot where she boiled the family rabbit. Surely the family ensconced in the country will be secure from the demonism of city dames. She becomes the symptom of a pathology whose roots remain untouched. As that which abolishes distinctions (she wears black and white dresses alternately, brings water and fire together to boil the rabbit or create the steam that shrouds her presence), she has to be abolished herself. But if she is most dangerous when wearing white, we should perhaps be leery of all appearances of innocence. Thus, when the camera slides away from Beth and Dan's final clinch to a photograph of them standing behind their white-clad daughter, the dress suggests that she is also in a sense Alex's child: the horror motif of irrepressible evil. The film may not be happy with this undertone, but in summoning the spectre of the horror movie in the bathroom scene it has rendered it inescapable.

The slipperiness of *Fatal Attraction* is most patent in its ambivalence with regard to high culture. To juxtapose images of Alex mournfully listening to *Madama Butterfly* with scenes of Beth and Dan bowling with friends is both to promote sympathy for her and to insinuate a relationship between her solitary pathology and high culture. (It is, of course, a *popular* high culture the audience may be assumed to recognize; as such, it can the more easily be dismissed.) Popular culture, meanwhile, brings people together. Alex should surely have watched the TV set whose hum surrounds Beth and Dan with the ambience of home. Yet at least at first, the film recognizes that there is good reason to switch off the set, and not just because one needs to go out in order to see *Fatal Attraction* itself: the first image to bloom on the TV screen is of a woman doused with multicoloured paints. Dan's daughter may revel in the spectacle, but Dan places his hands before her eyes. Does the gesture betoken incipient identification with the female whose aspirations to independence are so often denigrated? *Fatal Attraction* itself participates in the denigration, however: Dan's sympathy with the outsider woman is a dubious quality and has to be rooted out. Since it is never too early for a woman to learn her real place in the world, perhaps he should have let his daughter watch on undisturbed.

Franju: Caligari meets Judex in the forest of the city

Franju's films are a witchlike fusion of melodrama and expressionism. When we watch a Franju film, eyes stare soulfully out of the screen at us. They belong to men and women in an iron mask: to the heroine of *Eyes without a Face,* whose scientist father abducts young girls and lifts their faces in an effort to repair her ruined mask; to Thérèse Desqueyroux (Emanuèlle Riva), betrayed by curiosity into a rural bourgeois life that shuts like a prison around her; to François Gerane in *La Tête contre les murs,* consigned to an asylum by a father outraged by his motorcycle-boy defiance. Only in *Judex* is the concealment of the face the sign of liberation: and its hero is the superhuman masked man of popular fantasy, Fantomas, the French outlaw Batman; liberation is a beautiful dream. With their lilting music, Franju's films are dark fairy tales in which people seeking to become themselves are rendered vulnerable by their hesitancy and suffer transformation into puppets by a bad sorcerer, a poetic version of the melodramatic villain. The girl wandering tentatively down a corridor, that key Franju image, is the soul trapped in a Gothic labyrinth expressionistically darkened by the impossibility of redemption. Only the eyes behind the mask tell us this person was once 'one of us'. As in German expressionist films, the mask is a trap glued to one's face by society, the father – in short, an authority whose insanity is evident in the blank rigidity of the eyes at the heart of *its* mask. Franju's heroes bang their heads against the asylum walls in an effort to dislodge the cage affixed to their faces. Like Francis in *The Cabinet of Dr. Caligari,* they have made a trip to the fair that ended in a prison house.

The expressionist element in Franju's work is fused with the Proustian. As Thérèse Desqueyroux reviews her memories in a slide show in the car window, retracing the steps that led her to poison her husband, Bertrand, we see that she was drawn to him by his association with a forest that stands for her own unconscious. As in Proust's *Recherche*, people are coloured in cryptic, chameleon fashion by the places they occupy. (His is a poetic version of melodrama's naturalistic determinism.) It is this that makes their images so treacherous: one cannot see them for the superimposed place, which functions as a mask. The forest is, of course, as Canetti has noted,[16] an essential archetype of the German imagination, and Franju himself is a German film-maker disguised as a French one. Only when walking in the woods is Thérèse able to talk freely. In a telling alteration of the original Mauriac novel, the young Portuguese Jew with whom she strolls in the forest states his preference for Chekov's *Three Sisters* over her favourite, *The Seagull*. *Three Sisters* ought to be Thérèse's preference: the sisters dream of Moscow as Thérèse does of the cosmopolitan world of Paris; and at the film's end, banished to Paris by Bertrand's family, she will realize that the city was the true forest of her aspirations. Her choice of the 'wrong' Chekov play parallels her disastrous choice of husband. In *La Tête contre les murs*, François seeks refuge in Paris following his flight from the asylum. Like Thérèse, however, he walks into the trap society sets; although warned against staying with his girl-friend, since her apartment will be the first place the authorities' bloodhounds will visit, he nevertheless does so. As if under the long-distance spell cast by a Dr. Mabuse, Franju's protagonists walk automatically to their doom; the light in their eyes dies out behind the mask. François can no more justify this move than can Thérèse, who says that only people like Bertrand have a reason for every action. The spell they are under, however, is that of their own unconscious. As François gravitates towards his girl-friend's house, he sleep-walks into another Franju film: the girl-friend, living alone, reminds one of Thérèse, free and wild in the stony Parisian forest. (It is not just a joke when Thérèse stamps out a cigarette on the Paris pavement and Bertrand reminds her of her failure to do so when bestriding his own far more combustible woods; it indicates that for her Paris is the true forest, which she has no desire to burn down.)

Images of headlights dancing eerily over speeding trees recur in Franju's films; they remind one of *The Testament of Dr. Mabuse*. The forest means liberation: François and his epileptic friend will pass through it, drawing strength from it, before their escape attempt; François is told to hide there when his later get-away attempt succeeds. The forest is thus an image of a fairy-tale underworld: Franju has a profound empathy with Robin Hood figures, masked men who inhabit an alternative society remote from the civilization that outlaws them. For him, as for the Young Turks of the Nouvelle Vague, popular culture is the shifting site of that alternative; though, unlike them, he

draws on the popular culture of France rather than one made in the
United States. It is surely a misinterpreted dream of such an alternative that lures Thérèse into the ogre's den of a provincial Catholic family, whose sole motive for saving her from indictment for attempted
poisoning is to avoid scandal and exercise its cherished right to inflict
its own punishments, placing Thérèse under virtual house arrest.
Thérèse's dream that the forest might still be a place of refuge is an
anachronistic one, more reminiscent of the Middle Ages than the present day, but Franju sympathizes with her temporal dislocation. His
own film was to be criticized for anachronisms of detail. Raymond
Durgnat has defended Franju spiritedly against this charge in his fine
monograph, though without grasping the function of anachronism in
the work of a man whose film debut came late in life.[17] *Judex*, for instance, with its Ernstian feel for the surrealism of late Victorian iconography, is utterly anachronistic, as is Franju's fascination by the
melodramatic scenario in which innocent daughters are plunged into
distress by their fathers' nefarious actions: the melodramatic pieties
are subverted by a modernism that has no faith in knights in white
armour. (The only knights are indistinguishable from members of the
underworld: Judex dresses like a cat burglar.) Franju's anachronisms
testify to the intensity of his empathy with the forest's medieval dream
world.

In *La Tête contre les murs*, François is, as it were, a tree isolated
from that forest. He has no effective allies: civilization has felled the
surrounding trees. The anarchist is a figure of heroic defeat for Franju,
who savours his own pessimism, finding a Nietzschean joy in the
knowledge that he has the strength to contemplate the worst. That isolated tree is the key image of *La Tête contre les murs*. Opposed to the
conservative asylum director is a humane psychiatrist who speaks of
the value of creative therapy for patients. They begin by fashioning circular shapes and can be considered cured when they produce images
associated with life, such as a baby in a cradle or a tree standing up-
right. The moment after this, Franju cuts from one of the patients'
sculpted trees to its original, a real tree standing in a circle of lawn
that echoes the other circles found in the film (e.g., the patients linked
in a ring). This tree stands within the asylum grounds. The cut is
poker-faced, ambiguous and yet devastating. The tree that transcends
the rounded shape is itself enclosed in the circle of entrapment; the
symbol of life is part of the asylum, Eden as prison. In other words,
society and the asylum are coterminous. That is why there is no escape for François: even as he flees at night, a statue points back to the
asylum. The conservative director who works hand in glove with the
paternal system of oppression is right after all: madness and sanity
are indeed hard to tell apart in a world in which François's father can

be deemed normal. Perhaps only a close interrogation of the eyes –
blazing fiercely behind an iron mask in the young – can reveal who is
truly healthy. Yet the anarchists and dreamers are helpless in the face
of their own externalized unconscious dreams, forms of the social superego feeding on their ids to immobilize the young with their own alienated power, turning them into their own worst enemies. The asylum
head says his primary objective is not to heal but to protect society.
The things from which society has to be shielded include the doves he
keeps in a cage. If ever they broke free, there would be an apocalypse
to rival that of Hitchcock's near-contemporaneous *The Birds.* Only in
Paris – which, as Péguy reminds us, belongs to no one – can caged
dreams go free. In a world where nothing is what it seems to be, the
city is the true forest.

Postscript: *La Signora di tutti*

At the opening of this essay, I reflected briefly on the separability of the
melos and drama in melodrama. I would like to conclude with *La Signora di tutti* by Max Ophuls, one of the most interesting – and frustrating – of melodramas, for it flirts with explicit consideration of the status
of the melos in its own drama – only to fail to follow through. We begin with its heroine, Gaby Doriot (Isa Miranda), film star and singer,
having attempted suicide; a flashback on the operating table unfolds
her past life. It begins under the aegis of music: as she sings in a
school choir, the suicide of the music master besotted with her is an-
nounced. The proximity of his suicide and her suicide attempt suggests the hovering of a fatality simply conjugated differently according
to one's gender. Gaby swears that nothing happened between herself
and the master, and is backed up by her plain sister, but she is ex-
pelled from school nevertheless, and rumour further isolates her. Her
later attendance at a concert at La Scala, escorted by the husband of
an aristocratic lady whose loneliness her visits have assuaged, ends in
her discovery that the husband, Leonardo (Memo Banassi), is ena-
moured of her. Like the music master, he cannot live without her: in
each case music is the facilitator of eros. 'Our song is playing', he tells
her in the garden as the radio his wife has turned up echoes outside.
Ironically, it does so only because she has smashed the window with
her cane: seeking to corroborate her tumultuous suspicions of the pair,
the wheelchaired Alma (Tatjana Pavlova) tumbles down the stairs that
carry so many uncanny associations in this film; she is killed.

In a sense Ophuls's film uses music as a scapegoat: it provokes
eros. And yet there is no real sense of blame attributed: the pervasive
romantic atmosphere causes us to sympathize with the seductiveness
of music. But anyone desirous of assigning blame finds music avail-

able to receive it: after Alma's death, Gaby smashes the radio. Yet film itself is surely equally to blame: the notion of a looking that is not touching is central to cinematic stardom. After release from jail for malversation of company funds, Leonardo – down and out now – wanders inappropriately amid publicity photographs for Gaby's latest film and is ejected by the doorman. Are not Ophuls's own famous tracking shots guilty too? Near the film's start, when Gaby's manager goes in search of her and the camera tracks from room to room towards the bathroom, that movement combines with the manager's prominent cigar and cajoling repartee to lead us to expect an erotic image as the camera's goal (only later on, when Gaby's loneliness has become a leitmotif, will we grasp the implicit irony of the manager's leering suggestion that she might not be alone): we are as shocked as he to see a woman seemingly dead (significantly, the cigar drops out of his mouth), but are also shamed into recognition of the nature of our desires. The film may deconstruct its own romanticism in miniature here, but it is far less explicitly self-critical as a whole.

The cinematic spectator can look but may not paw the goods. 'Nothing happened' between Gaby and the music master, we are told – an assertion that gains credibility when she later prevents Leonardo from kissing her while Alma is in the next room – but can we be sure? The film may stress Gaby's rectitude, but the combination of the indirect conventions for representing love-making during this stage of film history and the still more important fact that glancingness is the dashing sign of romantic delicacy means that the omission of scenes of a certain kind does not necessarily mean they never occurred. It is as if the film is far from determined to *prove* that nothing happened: it wants Gaby as both calumniated victim and femme fatale. Victim she may be, but she tells Leonardo in the garden – nature as the romantic site of love – that she knows what she is doing is wrong. Embraced by the older male, she hardly resists; she is the music subordinated to the film. Both male and female succumb to the curse of beauty. Giving way is indeed the essence of the film, embodied in the melting multiplication of dissolve upon dissolve. Music's fatal force is later sentimentalized when Gaby tells Roberto (Federico Benfer), Leonardo's son, that certain episodes in her life recur like a melody, and this is beautiful. One may be sceptical, for melody's recurrence can be far from beautiful. On returning to Leonardo's home from a world tour and finding everything chillingly unchanged – Alma's portrait traversed by the shadow of a cross that suggests the tomb before which Gaby lays flowers – as she watches the fire she imagines the radio's music still playing. Since it continues to play on the sound-track when she runs out to the garden, how can we be sure where aural hallucination begins and concludes? The conventions for the use of on-screen and off-screen music are exploited to create an ambiguity that hovers between romance (music prompts our identification with the storms of passion) and expressionism (only one character, who is distanced from us, is hearing this). The sole resolution of the problem is the destruction of the source of music – of Gaby herself. Only thus can her sense that she is completely alone – her suspension between solitude due to victimization and incarceration in hysterical delusion – be overcome. When that happens the film production process that relentlessly prints her photograph even when her life is in the balance (the relentlessness of Ophuls's film itself?) finally grinds to a halt: the frame freezes, as it were. And yet Gaby has been always already dead throughout, not just because the film is played out in the flashback that justifies nostalgia: she begins, as she ends, as an object mechanically reproduced, as a record around which male hands gesticulate. It is perhaps the separation of record and photograph, image and sound, that heralds her death.

Mary Ann Doane has written powerfully of Gaby's abstraction, though she links it to the process of mechanical reproduction, rather than to the disembodiment of music, as I prefer to do.[18] For it is the abstraction of music that motivates Gaby's isolation – and music's wide appeal that makes of her 'la signora di tutti'. This may be why we never see the putative film-within-a-film of that title: only the heroine *of a song* can elicit such generalized desire. It is as if music is the art horrified by the danger its beauty means for others. Gaby may at first be dangerous without knowing it, as her oppressive father puts it, but in the end that knowledge reaches her, transforming her into a Lulu who is martyr to the conscience that drives her to suicide.

CHAPTER V

Doubles and male fantasies

This essay considers two of the most pervasive cinematic male fantasies of the century, the Western and film noir, as well as the ground onto which they have to move to then collapse. It falls into two halves, each treating two films: in each case an example of a genre's shaky, partially subverted persistence is followed by one of its disintegration. If the Western persists under a question mark in *The Searchers,* and film noir does likewise in *Out of the Past,* the genres are folded over into near unrecognizability and unforeseen dimensions of paradox by *The Man Who Shot Liberty Valance* and *The Singing Detective,* the former in particular being remarkable – for all its artistic unevenness – as a critique of the genre by one of its long-time practitioners, John Ford. If the male fantasies of film noir still survive in pastiche, it is because its urban world is still with us, but also because its often self-parodistic voice-overs seek to defuse female challenge by partial identification with the aggressor (the femme fatale). Playing hard-boiled is playing dead in an effort to survive. In *The Man Who Shot Liberty Valance* and *The Singing Detective,* the genres are dislocated definitively by the explicit introduction of the double. When the male sees himself as the other sees him, he has to step out of himself.

Doubling and the crisis of the Western

As late-nineteenth-century realism entered the crisis that was to issue in modernism, it began to throw up doubles with increasing frequency. The double's eruption betokened self-consciousness concerning the real location of a self that could be in more than one place at once – consciously here but unconsciously there – and was to split the realistic notion of character, replacing it with a quasi-Freudian, expressionist interplay of ego and id. Before the final split occurred and expressionist modernism emerged, however, there was a period in which the subterranean doubling of characters was hinted at, but not made explicit. Given the time-lag separating developments in high culture from parallel occurrences in popular culture, it is hardly surprising that this should not take place in film until the late fifties. In the Western, the best example is John Ford's *The Searchers*. A sure sign of implicit doubling is the shift in the protagonist's personality towards the film's end. Subsequently, in *The Man Who Shot Liberty Valance*, the doubling becomes explicit and the Western collapses. Ford may seek to define this catastrophe as somehow marginal, by filming it in monochrome. But his gambit revealingly parallels Hitchcock's tactic in *Psycho*, that near-contemporaneous work of genre melt-down. In each case the director seems to be using black and white to repress his own awareness of the revolutionary nature of his undertaking: the work thus becomes as deeply impregnated with the unconscious as the figure of the double itself, which thereby gains in weight and necessity. And why is it that the double is so disturbing? The harbinger of death, he tells the Westerner he is no longer his own man. Doubling mounts a crushing assault on the redoubt of the hero.

I have already mentioned the internal fission in the protagonist of *The Searchers*. The inconsistency in character logic subverts narrative logic almost as effectively (if unwittingly) as the New Hollywood filmmakers so devoted to Ford's film. *The Searchers* begins with a question in the song on the sound-track: 'What makes a man to wander?' It is arguable that we never discover why; or if we do, the answer is provided less by the narrative than by the expectations we have come to associate with John Wayne. A man wanders because he is a man – the lone wolf incarnated in Wayne. The narrative will throw up many other unanswered questions – some formulated by the characters (George's 'Why didn't you come home before now?' following Ethan's early remark that the Civil War ended three years ago) and some by ourselves (where did Ethan learn to speak Comanche?). George Wilson accounts for Ethan's wandering by stressing his suspension between white and Comanche norms; on scalping an Indian, he realizes how his preferred form of revenge makes him quasi-Indian himself. Consequently, 'the realization that he makes entails that he cannot cross the threshold that Debby and the others cross. He knows himself to be caught between, and alien to, the two cultures that are internalized within him'.[1] There are problems with this account, however. For Ethan, to scalp the scalper is simply poetic justice. The main problem nevertheless lies in Wilson's use of the verb 'knows'. There is no hint that Ethan ever achieves knowledge; his initial view that 'a man's only good for one oath at a time – I took one to the Confederate states' frustrates possible acknowledgement of his own duality. It remains repressed, unconscious, and Ethan himself a somnambulist in his own life: the bigot whose virulence towards the Other is unwitting violence against himself (most apparent in his relationship with Martin, whose

Indian blood compromises him in the eyes of Ethan, who nevertheless permits him to accompany his quest). If it is hardly surprising that this avowed racist should have fought on the side of the South, Brian Henderson is surely wrong to see 'Indian' in *The Searchers* as code for 'black'.[2] 'Indian' seems rather to mean the Other within the particular generic context of the Western. Its appearance within the Western, with its outworn setting, is less a coded reference to current racial problems than a way of implying that such problems lie in the past. And if redskin is bad, might not the film's 1956 date make it equally likely (or unlikely) that red equals communist? Wilson's explanation, meanwhile, may be a good hypothesis, but it rings false in ascribing to Ethan a capacity for self-doubt and self-knowledge. When Ethan walks away at the end, it is simply because that is what the Western hero does. He is by definition a man one can search for forever, the diehard individualist who has no desire to be found.

Although *The Searchers* addresses the question of how one man can be two, be doubled, both Indian and white, it fails to answer its own question. The answer arrives in a subsequent Ford film, *The Man Who Shot Liberty Valance*, which uses flashbacks to unearth the unillumined, invisible past that festers underneath *The Searchers*. (Its investment in the flashback is underlined by the monochrome that renders it also a flashback within Ford's own career.) *The Searchers* may cohere stylistically (e.g., with tracks in and out of doors that link beginning and end, and Ethan lifting up Debby at start and close), but this form of coherence is a smoke-screen before the narrative incoherence caused by the inaccessibility of Ethan's past. Similarly, all disasters occur off-screen – Lucy's death, Brad's failed attempt to avenge her – while Ethan makes many references to unwillingness to confront horrors. It is as if the film's neurosis regarding open showing is shared by its main character. The inability to disinter the past may in turn be a consequence of Ford's refusal to question openly the image of power Wayne projects. That reluctance may even persist into *The Man Who Shot Liberty Valance*, whose introduction of the double may be the inadvertent effect of double billing (John Wayne plus Jimmy Stewart), but to double power is inevitably to lose it by inserting a gap that becomes the disparity between image and actuality.

Where *The Searchers* seems to be amenable to the structuralist analysis that would define the hero as the mediator of opposites, *The Man Who Shot Liberty Valance* unmasks reconciliation as an illusion: 'unhappy the land that needs a hero' might be its Brechtian motto. It presents the hero less as spatial and fixed than a bridge in time, a man of the moment, socially required to negotiate a transition (in this case, from Wild West to small-town civic virtue) but expendable afterwards. The text's retrospectiveness is a matter not merely of the use of flashback (and then of flashback within flashback, indicating how deeply hidden trauma lies, when the perspective shifts and the voice that speaks belongs to Tom, who recounts *his* role in the shooting of Liberty Valance), but also of the rehearsal of old Ford themes, particularly ones from *The Searchers*.[3] *Liberty Valance* may thus be designated the metatext of earlier Ford texts. Where *The Searchers* may be accused of duplicity (e.g., by Henderson),[4] *Liberty Valance* takes duplicity as its subject. It is the duplicity of the historiography of progress, which seeks to abandon the past and speaks of movements from one zeitgeist to another, in this case from an age of lawlessness to one of law. (In the form of Ranse, Law enters Shinbone to a whipping and returns as a senator.) In actuality, of course, law and lawlessness are interwoven dialectically as they are within Ranse (the Jimmy Stewart role of lawyer); for the public, the legend the newspaper has to print is that of progress. But the utopian historiography of progress unravels into ideology as Ranse recounts his story: 'the man who shot Liberty Valance' is nameless, the nonexistent gap between nonexistent eras.

In *The Political Unconscious,* Fredric Jameson transforms the semiotic rectangle of Greimas into a model of the logical possibilities inherent in all texts – some of which suffer repression or simple elimination through authorial bias, choice or the text's historical moment. By tradition, texts of popular culture tend towards a melodramatic polarization that obscures how each of the main oppositions in play will cast a double shadow: a maleficent Other who exists on the hero's own plane of fantasy, and an ineffectual sidekick whose presence imparts a legitimizing realism to the fantasy. *The Man Who Shot Liberty Valance* begins to make this structure explicit by allowing two figures to slide across the slot assigned to Rance's Other: they are of course Tom Doniphan, the John Wayne figure, and the sadistic Liberty (Lee Marvin) himself. Furthermore, the nameless status of 'the man who shot Liberty Valance' makes of him a shifter allowing both Tom and Ranse even to occupy the same position (e.g., both shooting simultaneously at Liberty). Hence, contradiction is shown to exist *within* characters and not just between them: Ranse, the man of peace, shoots a man; Tom, who has a stake in preserving the lawlessness embodied in Liberty, in which he himself thrives, and who is thus himself in a sense a throw-back, prompts historical progress. The structuralist narratology that proposes the rectangle as a model of oppositions and their shadows seems to break down when applied to works that employ doubling, for Ranse, Tom and Liberty are not just opposed but also partially overlapping figures.

Although the plot's primary level polarizes, for instance through the Tom–Ranse rivalry for the same girl, the polarities themselves are united by the anonymity of 'the man who shot Liberty Valance'. The Ranse–Liberty opposition, meanwhile, is compromised by the fact that Ranse's seeming shooting of Liberty belongs to Tom. If Tom can shift back and forth between Ranse's side and that of the order of Liberty, Ranse himself resorts to the law of the gun at the text's crucial moment. There is thus a Tom 1, potentially allied to Ranse, and a Tom 2, on Liberty's side; and Ranse himself is similarly dual. In traditional texts the primary characters represent intransigent opposition, whereas the subsidiary ones enter into combinations; they lack the absolutism of the main ones, the dignity and irreconcilability of the principles those figures incarnate. They also parody the unyieldingness of those principles, furnishing melodrama's unreality with a realistic substratum (a chorus incorporated into, albeit still marginal to, the main protagonists' drama). In Ford's film, however, the term 'the man who shot Liberty Valance' insinuates into the primary level the element of substitution normally reserved for the secondary one. (Ranse is a hero, and hence primary, but he is really secondary to Tom, the true dispatcher of Liberty Valance.) Since it is the hero's absolutism that grants him heroic status, making him both admirable and appalling, the dissolution of the hierarchy of upper and lower levels destroys the notion of 'the hero'. His dissolution involves the self-erasure of the Western itself. Nevertheless, the process may in fact be one of self-transcendence: the ironic, wrenching dissonances of *The Man Who Shot Liberty Valance* are those of classic tragedy, in which everyone fails. To all the interlocking causes of the Western's demise – the studio system's confusion and then collapse, the passing of a generation able to recall America as nature, the shifting of the frontier into outer space, the compromising of the masculine ethos of strength and silence in Vietnam – Ford's film adds perhaps the most important of all: systematic doubt in the nature of representation and agency. The passing of the Westerner makes him the phantom of Liberty. It is not the senator who represents us, but the man who shot Liberty Valance – a dreamed reconciliation of lawlessness and law, John Wayne and Jimmy Stewart, a man who never was.

The voice-over and the mute: *Out of the Past*

Feminist critics have pointed out the frequency with which film voice-overs (like so many other positions of authority) are ascribed to men: 'The capacity of the male subject to be cinematically represented in this form aligns him with transcendence, authoritative knowledge, potency and the law',[5] runs a typical statement. Such critics have a point. It is indeed interesting that in *Sleeping with the Enemy* a female voice-over emerges only momentarily, after its female protagonist (Julia Roberts) has escaped her abusive husband (Patrick Bergin) – and is silenced for the remainder of the film, which stresses the husband's continued power of horrifying menace. It is the male voice-over's implication that whatever happens the speaker will survive that fatally blunts the immediacy of the threat of war in Oliver Stone's *Platoon:* we know the greenhorn soldier (Charlie Sheen) will come through his Vietnam ordeal. (A Freudian might read the reassurance as signifying a desire to assuage castration anxiety.) *The Man Who Shot Liberty Valance,* however, may shake the feminist generalization with which I began: Ranse tells the story at the side of Tom's coffin, but he is hardly its hero (law is not potency here); indeed, he may be all the less heroic for awaiting his rival's death before doing so. The association of male voice-over with power is undermined more thoroughly still in Jacques Tourneur's *Out of the Past* – a film that overturns the usual noir scenario by pushing it to the point of tragedy.

Where the classic noir scenario sends the woman to perdition and allows the male to survive – often chastened, in jail – *Out of the Past* doubles the image of woman and so allows one girl to survive. On the one hand, there is the dark lady who pulls Jeff Bailey (Robert Mitchum) back into his past; on the other, Ann, his small-town lover, who survives him. Elements of the noir ideology may persist – Kathy (Jane Greer), the girl from the past, is a destructive force, but her apparent condemnation is mitigated. (This may be in part because she has incorporated some of the features of the Anne of the original novel, *Build My Gallows High,* who smokes and has a yen to go to Los Angeles or Reno.) When Kathy and Jeff echo one another and say they deserve each other, it is hard to disagree, given Robert Mitchum's aura of indolent sleaze. Jeff's repetition of Kathy's words accords with a general feature of the film, whose protagonists tend to reiterate, with only slight modifications, lines that have just been said to them. Bailey's habit of doing this corresponds to an inability to escape the terms laid down in the past, which in this case is the previous moment. But there are other reasons why he and Kathy belong together. Although one level of *Out of the Past* establishes an opposition between the small-town world of nature and the corrupt one of noir, another erases it, switching signs on the psychic map so one no longer knows where one is going. Thus, Kathy, the femme fatale tracked to Acapulco by Jeff, the hired detective, first appears in unexpected white, coming out of the sunlight. Jeff's voice-over says she came in out of the sun – speaking of later assignations, he will say she came in out of the moonlight. The two phrases are conjugations of 'out of the past' and indicate Kathy's power over realms of both night and day. She too is associated with nature, albeit

primarily the one steeped in dark, in noir. In Acapulco, Jeff only
meets her in bars, at night, whenever she chooses to materialize.
She is the dream girl; and it is appropriate that he should first see
her from a table in a cafe, swayed perhaps by the music from the
movie theatre next door, or that he should later await her opposite
that theatre's flashing lights. It is as if Jeff is the viewer whose movie
dream has come through the frame of the door. Thus, Kathy smears
together the two terms Jeff would like to separate so as to come out
of the past: the eros of the love-scene in nature, the thanatos of
night. On finally conceding their inseparability, he drives through
the night with Kathy to his death. Whereas, earlier, he had begun
telling his story to Ann in darkness, concluding it in light, here
there is only dark; the echo of the earlier image of him seated
alongside Ann is ironic.

Kathy unites opposites in another sense also: a figure of control,
she nevertheless insists that she had no choice but to return to Whit
(Kirk Douglas) after leaving Jeff – and yet Whit speaks of her whim-
pering to come back. 'The real Kathy' seems to be nonexistent. Her ambiguity surfaces again just before leaving with Jeff, having killed Whit:
she takes Jeff out on the terrace and shows him a view of nature,
claiming never to have ceased loving him and to want now to recover
the natural idyll. What she is showing Jeff is, however, only a view:
nature as object from which the subject is separated; it is not a scene
in nature, like the ones with Ann. She has just killed a man and talks
of regaining innocence. Yet is there not also a sense in which her murders – of Fisher, then of Whit – have been forced upon her by Jeff's
inability to kill? After all, only killing makes it possible finally to
leave the past, silencing it; and that silence supervenes for the film
itself when it ends with the deaf-mute boy. Kathy's possession of the
gun surely points to a deficiency in the languorous male, with her actions his disavowed ones. (Here, as so often, the prototype of film noir
seems to be *Macbeth*.)[6] Jeff's lack of control, his inability to kill, entails the guttering of his voice-over midway through the film. The film
too goes out of control – chronically so in the San Francisco scenes
surrounding the killing of Eels – but in doing so it shatters the frame
of film noir ideology. It can do this in part because the borders of the
genre are themselves unclear; noir cuts across genres.[7] Hence, the
story is haunted by a continual sense that the next room – the neighbouring story one would like to enter – is as important as the one one
can see: it is the room from which music floats as Jeff awaits Kathy in
Acapulco or watches her phone the caretaker at Eels's apartment
building. The *absent* is all-important, as Jeff leans back again and
again, dreaming the story: 'I never saw her in the daytime; she seemed
to live by night'. His head in shadow, he stands in for the anonymous

viewer attracted to the absent through the death-wish for which Jeff alone has to suffer – rendering Mitchum's laid-back languor readable as acceptance of one's own demise. Hence, it perhaps does not finally matter whether or not he rang the police while Kathy was collecting their bags – we do not see him talking, and road-blocks have already been mentioned – since to go with her is to respond to the charm of la belle dame sans merci.

In *Out of the Past,* the urban night-world of noir is infiltrated by its opposite, the nature that beckons beyond the labyrinthine interiors and their complex betrayals. It issues the poignant summons to Jeff to attempt to escape his criminal past. Ann's sweetness and the attempt in the voice-over section to set a seal on the past conjure up the mirage of success. Our expectations are horribly undermined. On catching sight of the road-block, Kathy accuses Jeff of a double-cross, shoots him and is machine-gunned herself. Had Jeff foreseen this, choosing death in the knowledge of the past's inescapability – or did he miscalculate? The title neatly reflects the equivocation: one may be perennially on the verge of emerging from the past, but it always dispatches an emissary to recapture one. The final scene is harrowing. Although we know that Jeff did not commit the murders for which he was framed and told Ann as much, she is finally denied full knowledge of him (a sign of her inability to enter his life as deeply as would have been needed to draw him out of the past?). Accompanied by her cipher-like childhood sweetheart, she asks the deaf-mute boy, who can lip-read and is the film's final repository of truth, whether Jeff was leaving with Kathy when he died. The boy nods. Could it be that he (or the film?) wants her to be deluded, thus rendering it easier for her to forget Jeff and start anew – or is *he* in the dark about Jeff's motives too? The possibility that truth may never emerge darkens noir into tragedy. Or is it just that the *whole* truth is too complex to tell? The children of light depart to the small-town haven's antiseptic travesty of the promise extended by nature earlier on. The very last image shows the deaf-mute, who has worked at Jeff's garage, looking up at the sign that still bears his old employer's name. It is an ambiguous, temporary tombstone, a *mute* sign that tells one nothing of the true identity of the person it designated. (His real name was different.) Since the voice-over, with its air of male control, had embraced only part of the film, its conclusion with a deaf-mute is logical. Loss of voice means loss of male authority, of the sexuality Ann's sweetheart so patently lacks. The boy, meanwhile, is debarred from possession of the voice that betokens authority. The implication is not only that Jeff will never speak again, but that his name will never again be spoken. Ann will think Jeff abandoned her, and the boy is a mute. The sobering bleakness of the end reveals the degree to which most films noirs are but patriarchal pipe-dreams.

Lazarus laughs: *The Singing Detective*

Dennis Potter's *The Singing Detective*, filmed by Jon Amiel, is a whodunnit with a difference. The body that gives evidence of the crime is not dead but alive – and is in the end, arguably, that of a Lazarus who laughs. It is the devastated psoriatic body of Philip Marlow (Michael Gambon), a hospitalized crime fiction writer whose complex mental and physical healing the film slowly plots. And 'whodunnit?' here means who or what brought Philip's body to its appalling current state? The mystery ramifies into further questions clicking in and out of vision in the work's kaleidoscope, including: Who killed the drowned woman in the story Marlow reviews in his mind's eye? Who did dirt on the desk of the nagging school-marm of his childhood? Who is to blame for his mother's death? And who uprooted Philip's aspiration to praise God and made him a crime writer instead? (Was it the omen of the nomen or was it something else?) Unfolding over six hours, *The Singing Detective* uses indirections to find directions out, like the psychoanalyst fencing associative word-duels with Marlow: it is after all very hard to outmanoeuvre oneself and one's fantasies, to step out of one's blind spot and see oneself as one's double, the singing detective who wears one's own face but is also in a sense one's crooning father. And did not Novalis describe the long cure as the lasting one? Beginning with the linear, Oedipal logic of the detective story in ruins, with multiple enigmas apparently inextricably intertwined, the work patiently – an immobile patient in reverie – seeks to find meaning in the linear time that carries one forwards and is a far better healer than hospitals or psychoanalysts.

'Let's be economical', Marlow remarks at the outset: blood can also be lipstick. Likewise, any one of the work's elements can lead in reverie's melt to another story-plane. Ambiguity becomes systematic. The whore in the river is the mother who betrayed one's father and is also one's wife (Janet Suzman); the criminal is oneself, as one frames the class's fat boy for one's misdeeds, later discovers that he went mad and nevertheless gives his name to the villain one portrays in cahoots with one's treacherous wife; and the singing detective wears one's face but is also one's father as forties balladeer. Uncannily, nothing is what it seems to be. The overdetermination gives the lie to Marlow's statement that 'you can't do *three* things at once'. It is the Freudian world where there are always at least four present wherever two are gathered. (The couple cannot banish fantasized others from the scene.)

Perhaps we never do learn who killed the woman whose naked corpse emerges obsessively and repeatedly from the river – but it does not matter; for we have found the cause of 'her' death on another story-plane, and whatever transpires on one level trickles down into all others: we discover that Philip feels guilty of his mother's death, for she killed herself after hearing that he had seen her 'shagging' another man in the woods. 'You always hurt the one you love', his singing father had crooned. Philip's guilt stems from the child's belief in the omnipotence of thought: one hates someone and she dies. The world in which this occurs is of course the fictional one, and one prolongs it pathologically by becoming a writer. This is economical indeed – for the scene in the woods is a version of the Freudian primal scene (though the image of the father is preserved for idealization, for narcissistic investment, through removal from the primal scene, whose male protagonist is given the face of another man), and it is arguably the scene's contamination of Philip's tree-top trance that prevents him becoming the kind of writer he could have been. The exaltation of all-encompassing vision, identification with God, gives way to an obsession with the sexuality down in the depths, on the forest floor. This is hardly surprising given Potter's Freudianism. Where, as Freud notes in his analysis of the Wolf Man, a high tree symbolizes scopophilia, Philip's tree-top position metonymically represents the primal scene it simultaneously represses, unwilling to concede that its 'height' is complicit with 'depth' (and that, in this dialectically Freudian context, to posit 'height' is to create 'depth'). That desire to cover the tracks of one's scopophilia also dictates Marlow's transformation of the private *eye* into a *singing* detective. It is this sublimation, perhaps, that allows an identification with God to persist, however degraded: one is the maker of mysteries (the dirty mystery of the faeces deposited on the school desk). One may be a detective only in fantasy, not in reality, as one had vowed, but the dream's shadowy persistence conjures up the possibility of its achieving substance.

At one of its levels, Potter's reverie on degradation muses on the career of Raymond Chandler, the begetter of the Philip Marlowe of whom Potter's Marlow is the stunted double. (Degradation is compounded by an inability even to match a degraded prototype.) Potter seems to suggest that in Chandler's case, as in Marlow's, a British writer's identification with an American genre entailed masochistic self-entrapment, enraged self-hatred. The detective story, a fast read, becomes a rush to judgement that humiliates justice itself; so Potter slows things down, rendering them poetic, multilevelled, even Wagnerian, with a plethora of exquisite transitions between the interlocking leitmotifs. At the same time, however, Americanism has a utopian dimension: ambivalence is the source of one's fixation upon it. American speech may provide a classless alternative to the polarized speech of England, where young Philip's dialect marginalizes him. One may flee one's tongue because of the traumas associated with it – as in the case considered in *Le Schizo et les langues*. Philip's traumas are both class-based and private, and are hence more complex than the largely class-based ones that underlay British thirties and forties working-class writers' debt to American hard-boiled fiction. The foreign speech that is nevertheless one's own tongue has utopian features: the self–other split is always potentially curable – hence, the possibility of the healing work *The Singing Detective* records (and performs?).

The healing is itself problematic and multilevelled, however. No longer the sort of mystery Marlow loves, all clues and no solutions (the sort of mystery that refuses to advance beyond fixation), the work seems to be headed towards a safe haven when fantasy erupts in the final scene, a sick-room shootout in which the singing detective, who wears Marlow's face, kills the heavies who have wandered in from Marlow's musings upon his novel *The Singing Detective* and for good measure plugs the bedridden Marlow himself. The detective then strolls out with Nicola, Marlow's wife – her adultery redeemed by transformation into affection for an other who is one's virile alter ego. The recurrence of the fantastic at this point implies that resolutions on one level are bought through repression on others. Thus, the ending's unpredictability may be only apparent: banished for so long, fantasy – like the repressed – is bound to return with a vengeance.

If Marlow's problem is solved in the end, it is not so much by the singing detective as fictional character as by Potter's text, *The Singing Detective*, which has demonstrated the falsity of Marlow's conviction of the incompatibility of popular fiction and *symbolisme*, high culture and low (the forest floor and the tree-tops), for it has brought them together. And if low culture survives, it is through its representation by the singing detective who is the idealized son of the idealized father, the singer of the forties Tin Pan Alley songs Potter so clearly loves. The double who walks away is the father, resurrected, recovered, yet transformed in the body of the self. Complete destruction of the Oedipal riddle-solving trajectory of the detective story requires elimination of its content also: father–son oppositions dissolve into magical synthesis within the singing detective. The separate narrative planes come together – the singing detective steps out of Marlow's head and enters his room – and so collapses the textual system. As so often in modernist works, doubling is catastrophic; this time, for a change, the apocalypse is redemptive. The private eye finally unmasks the criminal double, one's misanthropic, misogynistic self – the other who can perhaps be dispatched only because the doubling of a British culture by an American one, the father by the son, makes an elsewhere always available within the oppression of the home (the fatherland, the mother tongue). The double permits one to die and yet defeat death. This ending seems to mean the end of a writing that is linked convolutedly to sexual problems; and in killing the writer in himself, Marlow is on one level completing the self-destructive process begun when he decided to become a crime story writer in the first place – though he does so in order to recover the fantasy of an ideal relationship with a woman. Romantic fantasy defeats the hard-boiled one. (Love-songs and Vera Lynn overcome the crime story.)

The singing detective shoots Marlow wearing the ironic disguise of an element of popular culture, but he executes the high cultural verdict upon himself passed earlier by Marlow. The creature turning on his creator is of course poetic justice – and is also popular culture's cry for respect. If the town is not big enough for the two of them, there will have to be some of what the singing detective calls 'pruning'. It is a pruning necessary for growth. Potter's metafictional text suggests that metafiction arises when the splitting that generates separate and opposed characters (good girl versus whore, for instance) dissolves, and private pain invades the conventions. The work of repression breaks down, and as the symptom that once took the form of a book scars the writer's whole body, a new book becomes possible, free of repression: not Philip Marlow's misogynist *Singing Detective*, but its double, written by Dennis Potter, which traces male fantasies through the labyrinths of rationalization and mystification, fear, rage and self-pity that sustain them and exorcizes them by reconciling mass and high culture.

PART THREE
Dark continents

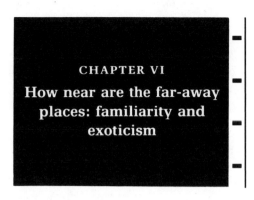

CHAPTER VI

How near are the far-away places: familiarity and exoticism

The journalist in the jungle

In recent years, several much-acclaimed Western films not only have taken Third World countries as their backdrop, but have offered to examine their politics. Such is the project of *Under Fire, The Year of Living Dangerously* and *The Killing Fields.* In each case we are invited to identify with a Western journalist as he penetrates an alien terrain whose language he never speaks. It is clear why: the journalist's professional mobility means that to identify with him is to be able to leave the country in question at the film's end with the same lack of compunction many actual journalists display when the story has run its course and their noses – or new assignments – take them elsewhere. The implication is that Western involvement with Third World countries is only a passing phase: when the Westerner leaves, they will be able to proceed with their business as independently as before penetration or colonization. The backwash of their problems will not tarnish Western shores. The ongoing dependence of the Third World on what the First World chooses to do – or not to do – is obscured. Western audiences have no wish to be reminded of their own role in the generation of the political, economic and even ecological disasters that beset these countries. The Third World setting remains an exotic backdrop, for all the appearance of analysis, often selected because labour costs are so much lower, workers so seldom unionized. Directors such as Werner Herzog and Peter Weir may be drawn to the Third World by its mute otherness, but its filmic registration translates into a metaphor for these film-makers' own mystical alienation from society. The otherness becomes an enigma we are under no obligation to comprehend. We are free simply to *look:* the scopic drive receives its fullest gratification through contemplation of the bright colours, the strange vegetation and – yes – the noble savages. Hence, in Herzog's *Echoes of a Dark Empire,* when newsreel footage of the Bokassa regime interleaves the interviews with its survivors, it is accompanied by classical music – Bach, Schubert and Shostakovitch: the political world of the twentieth century is married to the otherness of the music of the past, and Africa's otherness becomes our own. That otherness in turn becomes an objective correlative of the otherness of past art within the present. Herzog has things both ways: there is both otherness and familiarity (each 'alienates' the other); both past and present are both alien and familiar. Otherness and familiarity fuse in the disgraceful final image of a gorilla smoking a cigarette behind bars. Is this intended to be a metaphor for Bokassa himself, still in prison? Even if not, it is questionable, mordant Disney: it is no wonder the accompanying journalist asks Herzog to stop filming. There is a sardonic cuteness and mock innocence in the absence of the image's implied referent – as if Herzog were unaware of the familiar racist tradition that speaks of black apes or of the metaphorical use of animals in Eisensteinian montage. The image brazenly refuses responsibility for the connotations with which it flirts.

Herzog's excursions to the Third World are suspiciously akin to ways of gaining cheap access to the crowds he likes to confront with charismatic leaders. Weir's *Year of Living Dangerously*, meanwhile, is kinder to the noble savage, sentimentally idealizing the journalist's Asian guide (Linda Hunt). (In this respect it resembles *The Killing Fields.*) Their pairing involves a splitting: the companion is the guardian of the humane impulses the journalist's trade often forbids him to follow, an alienated walking conscience. When the Asian is lost as the journalist (Mel Gibson) escapes, the self-disgust and mourning the latter feels are less for the devastated country he has left behind than for his own lost innocence.

Of the films in question, only Roger Spottiswoode's *Under Fire* eludes most of my strictures. One suspects this is because the greater degree of physical similarity between Nicaraguans and Caucasians renders it harder to employ the stereotypes of noble and ignoble savagery. Nicaragua is not simply an exotic far-away place. One need not share the arrogant imperial view of it as 'North America's backyard' to grasp that it is not all that far away. *Under Fire* does not divide innocence from experience but shows their painful interlocking: the photographer agrees to the rebels' request that he photograph their leader's corpse as if he still lived. 'Innocent' in sustaining the right cause, he simultaneously forfeits innocence by faking the evidence. He has realized that no news report is ever innocent: the journalistic ideology that deems it possible to reflect events impartially in the mass media is absurd. Even without the proprietor's or editor's intervention, the observer's presence alters the phenomenon, at the very least. One now waits for Western film-makers to extend this awareness to countries more remote, more easily forgotten, than Nicaragua.

If 'our hearts are especially at ease over that exotic land about which we know nothing, from which no tidings ever reach our ears except the belated and banal conjectures of a few foreign correspondents', as Alexander Solzhenitsyn writes,[1] in Volker Schlöndorff's *Circle of Deceit,* by way of contrast, the conjectures are neither belated nor banal. *Circle of Deceit* transposes into a different key the concern with West German press ethics animating Schlöndorff and Von Trotta's *Lost Honour of Katarina Blum.* 'I don't mind living a lie' are the first words spoken by Laschen, its journalist protagonist. Tolerant of falsity, he is nevertheless our delegated truth seeker – even as his utter detachment from his environment, his 'I only work here', is itself the lie, the bad faith, preventing him from recognizing that the other that attracts him is a cipher for the home he cannot have. And so his flight from a divided Germany leads to a divided Lebanon. Schlöndorff emphasizes the parallels visually: a shot through bars above a river near the film's start is accompanied by a mention of the barbed wire dividing Germany; in Beirut there will also be shots through balcony bars and barbed wire. The lie is the notion of the exotic itself. In an utterly interdependent world, true otherness is a chimera; and this is surely why the potentially surreal sequences in the midst of Beirut's mayhem have no surreal feel (e.g., the mannequin tugged across the street after the shooting of the old comb seller): they are all too familiar.

The protagonist unafraid of duplicity is of course quite prepared to live a double life. In Beirut an air of invulnerability somehow undercuts the imminent possibility of his death. It is as if the journalist's profession insulates him from reality: ignored by street fighters, as if invisible, he becomes the on-screen incarnation of the double life we ourselves lead, simultaneously present and absent from the scene, part of the documented world, yet excluded from its fiction. Only when Laschen remains behind after the departure of the rest of the press, and then kills a man in a bomb shelter, does he feel involved. Even at this point, however, he retains the invulnerability of the first-person voice-over with which the film begins and ends: already outside the realm of tangibility and visibility, he has mocked death by mimicking it. The invulnerability is linked to his continual accompaniment by a photojournalist (Jerzy Skolimowski). They are one person, split in two to foil the marksman. 'He sees what he sees and leaves the doubts to me' is the division of labour. The journalist might die, but his partner would survive, and vice versa. 'What words can accompany these images', Laschen asks himself, and the film dramatizes his inability to find them: his story defies the newspaper format. Hence, when in the end he walks out of the editorial office, parodying its deliberations on the number of pages he'll need (three? ninety-eight?), as colleagues jeer that perhaps he intends to write a poem, their derision backfires. The piece he is about to write could be titled 'Dichtung und Wahrheit'.

Not surprisingly, Laschen's duplicity extends to his love-life. He leaves his wife Greta in Germany and in Beirut pairs up with Ariane (Hanna Schygulla). Yet even as he makes love to Ariane, he sees images of Greta. He can hardly complain of her subsequent betrayal of him. In the realm of duplicity, 'betrayal' can only appear in inverted commas. In Beirut, and Laschen's experience, betrayal is normality. All the same, such duality is also derangement, and Laschen's mental state finally reproduces the irrational violence of Beirut: his stabbing of the man who falls on top of him in the bomb shelter is irrational, explicable only as the delayed venting of his murderous feelings towards the Ariane whose 'betrayal' he has just witnessed. Killing the man seems to kill love itself: thereafter, his flashbacks will be to Germany, not to Greta.

Circle of Deceit seems to me to be the finest of Volker Schlöndorff's films – a lucid probing of the dialectics of self and other. The concern with duality extends into Schlöndorff's mise-en-scène: the recurrent medium shots bestow equal weight upon individual and environment, preventing any overwhelming investment in the carrier of the fiction. His habitually crisp yet unobtrusive editing muffles shocks and so reinforces our identification with Laschen's sense of invulnerability. Similarly, should the fiction break down, the documentary about Beirut offers a fall-back position, while the documentary for its part repeatedly subsides into fiction. Schlöndorff's film clearly embodies a more honourable form of the split consciousness of its protagonist: he fears the possible obscenity of superimposing a fiction on the horror of Beirut, yet the making of fictions is his metier. A radical self-questioning pervades the film, which lacks the American compulsion – apparent even in *Under Fire* – to distinguish good guys and bad guys. There are only other perplexed human beings, whirled in a vortex of vendetta, where no right way of acting exists.

Under Western eyes, to Western voices

Voice-over has traditionally been one of the major resources of the 'poor cinema'[2] – be its poverty that of the avant-garde or the Third World. Among other things, it veils the frequent absence of 'production values', indicating to those who have ears to hear that poverty in one respect may denote richness elsewhere, the partial diversion of resources and emotional investment from the image to the sound-track.[3] It may conduct a reverie upon the image or suggest a level of coherence beneath the surface discontinuities of the editing. (And so directors who have a particular interest in editing often have a passion for the voice on the sound-track – from Welles to Resnais, Godard or Kidlat Tahimik.) The withdrawal of investment in the image may even signify suspicion of superficial, mendacious or unrevealing appearances (the photograph of the Krupp factory, Brecht famously reminds us, telling nothing of the economic nexus *behind* it). The film may criticize itself as it proceeds – like so much of the work of Godard – or formulate an implicit criticism by retaining the words of the book it used as a point of departure – like Fassbinder's *Effi Briest*. The following will consider the function of voice-over in relation to the exotic in *The Saga of Anatahan, Notebook on Cities and Clothes, The Perfumed Nightmare* and *Mosquito Coast*. I begin with Von Sternberg's *Saga of Anatahan,* whose implicitly self-critical use of voice-over is simultaneously vitiated by its unabashed chauvinism.

The voice on the sound-track in *The Saga of Anatahan* overtly questions the legitimacy of the look (perhaps so as to justify its own presence – presence in Derrida's sense too – and aggrandize its territory in the war of the senses). On several occasions the narrator says we cannot imagine events as they actually happened, only reconstruct them in model form – whence the blatant *typicality,* the extreme overfamiliarity, of the characterization. He adds that the sole justification for looking at the lives of others is that it may aid in comprehension of our similar fates. Voyeurism is strictly punished: the sailor who peers at Keiko and her husband through the window of their hut comes to a sticky end. (The camera eliminates its rivals.) Interestingly, although the narrator repeatedly says 'we' and refers to himself as a member of the group of survivors stranded on the tropical island, we never have the feeling that we are seeing *him:* he is purely and simply a voice. He never gives his own name, and we are unable to align him with any one of the on-screen figures. Image and sound are subtly, but profoundly disjunctive. Since the film ends with a close-up of Keiko, who has stayed behind at the airport after the crowds gathered to greet the survivors of the island ordeal have dispersed and who then salutes the ghosts of the men who failed to return, one may even conjecture that *she* may have been the narrator. After all, did not Sternberg once say he *was* Dietrich? Her position is of course a privileged one – the position of all women in Sternberg. As the sole woman on the exotic island, she is clearly a bone of contention for the dozen or so Japanese soldiers stranded on it, unaware that the war has ended. She dominates the imagery, often placed at the top of the hut's stairs as assembled men ogle her from below. In a cooler clime she would wear the furs that would reveal her kinship with Dietrich. In many respects, however, *Anatahan* breaks with Sternberg's fetishistic earlier work with Dietrich. The tone of the voice-over is that of a tough-minded Conradian narrator impervious to female blandishments; once bitten (*The Devil is a Woman?*), he stonily resists their charms. The voice moralizes relentlessly on top of the untranslated Japanese dialogue. This nontranslation renders the contours of the action all the more emblematic and corresponds to a gestural heightening that may recall silent cinema. This is silent film with a difference: its intertitles are read out over the images. It is perhaps a chauvinistic savouring of the fact of Japan's defeat that prompts the film to override Japanese thus. By robbing words of their intelligibility (for although he can present the alibi of having given his sound-track over to one of them, one is never able to identify the speaker with any of the Japanese shown on screen), Von Sternberg suggests that little yellow men are closer to the jungle, less individualized, than Westerners – whence the loftily recorded typicality of their fate. The alienation device is complicit with racism. The attitude may suggest a cruder Bresson: the Bressonian sense of the inevitability of human degradation is made explicit through the cynical voice-over, rather than remaining implicit, unvoiced, infusing events with enigma.

Wim Wenders's *Notebook on Cities and Clothes,* for its part, could well be described as an exercise in seeing one's other in the mirror, that other being a composite of the notebook, video, fashion, woman and, of course, Tokyo and the Japanese. For Wenders – unlike Sternberg, but like Tarkovsky in *Solaris*[4] – Tokyo connotes the vertigo of futurity, as it does in Toyo Ito's *Dreams* contribution to the 1991 'Visions of Japan' exhibition, where overlapping waves of images run across walls, pass below onlookers' feet and dissolve their sense of balance. *Notebook* is Wenders's second cinematic essay on Japan; the first, *Tokyo Ga,* focused on Ozu. The degree of liberty the cinematic scrap-book offers seems to have increased in the course of Wenders's career. Where *Lightning over Water,* his first such exercise, fought desperately to banish Oedipal emotions from the transcription of the last days of the spiritual father, Nick Ray, the more recent film is devoid of father-figures and the dynamics of parricide. Yohji Yamamoto, its subject, a Japanese fashion designer who is a near contemporary of Wenders, is closer to the director's mirror image. The mirror sometimes inverts, sometimes replicates, the to and fro powering the film's dialectic. Thus, there is inversion: one sees Yohji dressed in black while Wenders himself appears in white in the mirror in Yohji's atelier, filming him but also filming himself. This moment directly follows – and interacts in an extremely complex manner with – Yohji's monologue on his preference for black, which concludes when his talk of how dipping everything in black is a sort of crumpling, a hysterical emotion, itself collapses into quasi-hysterical static. Then there is replication: Wenders likens Yohji's work to a continual decoupage (designer and director both wield scissors) and shows Yohji and his entourage watching a video of their Paris show before departing for Tokyo. Here Wenders may be accused of special pleading. He intuits resemblances between Yohji and himself that do indeed exist (the concern to be international rather than national – the Pompidou Centre, which commissioned Wenders's film and where many of Yohji's interviews take place, becoming the architectural point at which Paris folds into the futurity associated with Tokyo; the parallel between Yohji's interest in black and Wenders's own penchant for black-and-white cinema; and Yohji's repeated signing of the blackboard outside his boutique, before achieving a signature meriting preservation as the shop's sign, like a director's repeated takes, posing the Adornian question of how to render essential the ephemeral – though Wenders is blind to the irony whereby the final expression of personality becomes identical with exchange value, the store sign). Nevertheless, his conscious efforts to formulate them smack of contrivance. For if Yohji resembles a director, the film he watches is embarrassingly unlike Wenders's own: it displays the fashion show with all the classical concern for symmetry theoretically rejected by Yohji, who terms it ugly. (Wenders endorses this preference by framing Yohji's face asymmetrically as he says this – though one may then wonder why Yohji parts his hair centrally.) And although Yohji's disquisition on black as the end and consummation of meaning (whence his calm during the show) recalls the investigation of the links between monochrome and the death drive in *The State of Things,* Wenders makes nothing of this and may not be conscious of the potential echo. When the two discuss the idea of 'the true shirt', it is clearly Wenders's idea. Yohji may say he likes it, but he is tentative, noncommittal. Where Wenders is almost Platonically obsessed with relations between originals and copies, Yohji appears oblivious of the distinction. (He doesn't, for instance, worry that his original garment may be the 'true' one, and the boutique copy 'false'.) Wenders is seeking to align Yohji's position with his own romantic existentialism, and there is just enough common ground for him to think the effort might succeed: Yohji's ascetic clothes do indeed make him seem the representative of antifashion, not fashion. In actuality, however, black is fashion's consummation in autistic cool.

At the beginning of his notebook, Wenders distinguishes between film, which depends on negative and positive, and video, in which everything is a copy. To frame the distinction thus is to betray a nostalgia for film, since it could just as easily be argued that in video everything is the original. Wenders juxtaposes film and video again and again. We often see Yohji's videoed interview on a screen in a filmed hand. There is wit, but also concealed chauvinism, in the idea of miniaturizing the Japanese interviewee – miniaturization being so 'Japanese' an enterprise. Wenders suggests that video is peculiarly appropriate for the filming of Tokyo. Does this mean that the urge to truth is frustrated in a foreign city, where all is equally unknown, pure surface, and hence beyond true and false? It is as if truth depended dialectically upon falsity, the positive–negative duality. Filmed images certainly breathe a clarity video lacks, and their greater perfection may make them seem 'truer'.

Of all the points of contact Wenders discovers between himself and Yohji, perhaps the most pregnant is a passion for August Sander's photographs. Leafing through an album, Yohji reflects that they embody a time when a person's profession was inscribed in his face or clothes; he tries to guess them without resort to the captions. Nineteenth-century faces were calling cards. (Sander's photographs may seem rather like *playing cards*.) In the present, however, all faces look the same (one may recall Wenders's concern with the homogenizing force of Americanization in *The American Friend*): Yohji's perspective, like Wenders's, is that of one who is foreign everywhere. It is as if Sander's images crystallized at a historical moment at which photography was still partly impregnated with painting: some of the interiority of portraiture adhered to it still. With the dissolution of the link, one is left with pure surface, the world of photography. Yohji, meanwhile, hopes that his own clothes might be worn as one wears a heavy coat in a wintry climate: out of simple necessity. There is an almost Marxist nostalgia – though since this is the fashionable world, Marxist terminology is eschewed – for use-value. Wenders himself romantically describes Yohji's clothes as re-creating indeed the effect of those of the past (he ignores the possibility that this may be an expression of postmodern pastiche): he says he feels as snug inside them as a knight in his armour. Does Wenders thus – like the knight, or like Yohji – become the servant of women? Yohji's preference for black stems from his interest in silhouettes (the clothing patterns he cuts), and he mentions finding a book of photos with Western working women charmingly grouped in dungarees in front of a factory. Wenders wittily combines the two remarks and photographs a group of women silhouetted against bars separating them from the Louvre courtyard. It is one of the inexplicably pregnant moments that crop up unexpectedly in Wenders's films, where the line of unremarkable time suddenly knots. (Another in this film would be the conjunction of the collapse into static at the end of Yohji's monologue on black with the appearance of Wenders himself in white in the mirror.) The bars may recall Wenders's earlier likening of style to a prison and his 'trade mark' difficulty in conceptualizing women. Here they are faceless, no more than silhouettes.

Yet the use of the silhouette simultaneously identifies with Yohji. The Wenders of *Wings of Desire*, who dedicates this film to Solveig, may well yearn for a relationship with women as easy as that of Yohji, who is continually in their midst. Yohji speaks of dressing European women, of growing up fatherless in a female household. He is boyishly coquettish in expressing his fear of the high-heeled, silk-stockinged women who seem older than he even when younger. Boys live only in imagination, where women inhabit reality. His ease in their presence might well be envied by the Wenders protagonist. And yet there is a darker tonality to all this. Yohji's passion for black may be tied to his disinterest in the future: as he speaks of his wish to age very fast, we see a shot of a cemetery. One is reminded of *Tokyo Ga:* the Ozu whose tombstone bears the character for nothing is strangely like the couturier whose ideal is black. The designer who once wished to make clothes for people who do not exist ('not Japanese, not French, not American') is in a sense cutting cloth for the dead, the no-longer-present subjects of August Sander's photographs. He is the Rilkean angel who does not distinguish between the living and the dead.

Where the voice-over in *Anatahan* is hard-boiled and rather unpleasant, and Wenders's is intimate and philosophically meditative, that of Kidlat Tahimik in *The Perfumed Nightmare* is witty and poetic, a marvellously inventive form of special pleading for the bricolage of his film. Like the early Russians, Tahimik – who made the film for a mere $10,000 – shows how scarcity stimulates resourcefulness. Here the voice-over, spoken by the director himself, serves to assimilate a multiplicity of unrelated images to one another: a shot of Filipino children crowding to the camera in his native village, as children everywhere flock to any attraction, can be accompanied by the voice of Kidlat himself reading a VOA reply to one of his inquiries about space travel. The children are transformed into members of a Wernher Von Braun society, of which Kidlat is the ostensible founder. Space travel provides the work's organizing metaphor. It is Kidlat's enthusiasm for space travel that draws him to the high-tech West. Everywhere images of rockets and levitation present themselves. Kidlat's German wife photographed him sitting at the window of a French chateau's tower, and as she did so her hand shook. Where another director would have discarded the faulty take, the sparseness of Kidlat's resources compels him to see if he can find a use for it. And so the wobbly tower becomes a rocket shaking during lift-off. The repaired cupola that is hoisted onto the tower of a Bavarian church defies gravity similarly. Indeed, the whole film systematically seeks to overcome gravity's pull, transposing the real world's weight, and the many obstacles it threw in the way of the film's completion, into a weightless zone of fantasy. Kidlat may not be able to become an astronaut in fact, but as a poet he can conquer gravity already: the wit he brings to his editing table magically transforms the causal details of his Western peripeteia into signs of a great collective human project to dislodge the defining weight of origins. It is the most unlikely SF film ever. As everything is moulded into metaphor, only metaphor comes to matter. And yet for all that, Kidlat Tahimik is well aware that his devotion to metaphor (the bridge making that is one of the film's obsessive themes and organizing principles) is compensation for the impoverishment of the real: reality is the Filipino village he leaves for the West, that realm of metaphor and unreal wonder. The village bridge he crosses at the film's outset leads him from the Third World to the First, the home of cinematic technology.

Kidlat's attitude to the First World is as sceptical as it is admiring. He has to doubt the value of the progress vaunted by the American who hires him to service his Parisian bubblegum empire with refills. The last vestiges of artisanal labour are disappearing: the Bavarians lament that the uplifted cupola will be the last to be repaired by hand; the American rejoices that the departure of Kidlat's old street-seller friend releases an additional parking place. The question of the usefulness of the small is of course vital to Kidlat, for it is the question of his own usefulness. Practising his French, he notes, 'La maison est grande – je suis petit', and asks, 'If the small markets work, why supermarkets?' Small can be insignificant as well as beautiful. 'Why is everyone staring at me – I feel I am becoming smaller', he remarks in the West. Part of him strives to overcome the sense of insignificance through identification with the West. Western progress, however, is often illusory: as the radio voice of Kissinger intones its pious thoughts about the importance of progress in Africa, his words' repetitions, engineered by Kidlat, betoken an absence of real progress. The small replicates the large and enters into dialectic with it. Kidlat says his sister Alma is smart, for she goes her own way when selling ice in the village: in going her own way, she, the smaller one, is like her big brother Kidlat. Kidlat himself announces at the film's end: 'I am not as small as you think. Nothing can stop me from crossing my bridge'. And so, just as he had crossed the bridge from his village in a jeepney, at the film's end he blows into the chimney of a Parisian supermarket and transforms it into a rocket. It is a coming of age, replicating the gesture with which his father blew away numerous American soldiers before they killed him for trespassing on U.S. military property. Once small, he becomes big, like his father: the sleeping typhoon blows and 'the butterfly embraces the sun'. One can imagine little Alma (her name showing her to be Kidlat's soul sister) doing likewise in the future, changing the given forms of the world – as the villagers transform army jeeps into taxi jeepneys – so that they become the vehicles of one's desires.

In *The Perfumed Nightmare* impoverishment reveals its other face – its self-confident richness – as it stimulates the imagination to re-create reality. In the negative space of the imagination, Tahimik's riches are enormous. Self-transcendence – pulling oneself up by one's bootstraps – may be impossible in the real world, but it can be done in the weightless zone of imagination. There Kidlat somersaults gaily, hands clasping those bootstraps like an astronaut, redeeming technology by recovering its utopian meaning as material embodiment of the human dream of self-overcoming – even as he rebukes the West for having prostituted the dream to an economically ruthloo progress.

If the fabulous value ice acquires in a tropical climate is a somewhat trivial link between *The Perfumed Nightmare* and *Mosquito Coast,* a more significant one is the presence of voice-over in both films. In *Mosquito Coast* it belongs to Charlie, son of the inventor Fox (Harrison Ford), who transports his family to the jungle in search of the primal American pioneering dream. Rather as in Skolimowski's *Lightship,* the son's voice is full of ambivalence: past mixed feelings about his father, ambivalence on surviving him. As often, the voice-over bears the words of a survivor compensating for the guilt of survival through modest retreat to the sound-track. He is hiding his face, for the true hero of *Mosquito Coast* is Fox, and the film is a disquisition on the correlation of autarky and autocracy. The inventor seeks total control over his environment. He wants to see his inventions valued – his ice a form of jewel – rather than contribute yet more superfluous gadgets to the consumer society. (He can thus be seen to stand in part for director Peter Weir himself, who wants his art to count rather than be diminished to simple entertainment.) And so he leaves the United States (the autocrat abandons the breakfast table, dishes piled unwashed in the sink) and travels in time and space to the land of 'savages' (the word he applies to the black who becomes the family's best friend, Mr. Haddy). On arrival he sets family and natives to converting jungle wilderness into civilization. 'Ice is civilization', he enthuses as he completes his enormous ice-machine, his secular church. The network of huts and appliances is mustered as evidence of a conquest of the Third World's material resistance even more impressive perhaps – and certainly less dubious than – the ship in Herzog's *Fitzcarraldo.* In Weir's film, unlike Herzog's, the interest in construction reflects a desire to erect habitable alternatives to modern society. (In *Witness* Harrison Ford helped build a barn; here he conquers the jungle; he must be keeping fit through Weir's films.) But as in *Witness,* the realm of seclusion is invaded. Weir is weakest in his presentation of this invasion: the three gun-toting interlopers from the jungle are stock melodramatic heavies, their aims and provenance conveniently unexplained. Weir's hysterical characterization justifies Fox's homicidal reaction to them: he billets them in the ice-machine and activates it, freezing them to death. The intruders spoil the scheme's neatness by doing something unexpected: they use their guns in an effort to free themselves. The bullets pierce the ammonium cylinders that run the machine, initiating a fiery chain reaction that engulfs the whole settlement: a sign of the sheer excessiveness of Fox's rage.

If fire destroys Fox's first settlement, the next one succumbs to water: the hut built without the dubious assets of modern chemicals is sited too close to the sea. Fox refuses to heed Haddy's warning against the high tides that can wash it away. When a storm does precisely that, transforming the hut into a skeletal ark, the family sails upriver to land beside a church presided over by the hell-fire preacher the film casts as Fox's chief ideological adversary. Both men have total world-views. The film's schematism concludes with Fox being shot in the dark while escaping from the church, which he has torched to ensure that the religious church suffers the same fate as his own technological one, the ice-machine of Geronimo (the fateful name of the village he had purchased to settle).

Weir's presentation of Fox's encounters with alien forces is steeped in demagogy: low-mindedly compelled to will the destruction of the opposition, we periodically lose sight of Fox's complexity. Attention is diverted from his dividedness, and that of the family, by the intrusions that unite them for war. And this is a shame, for much of the film offers a finely tuned portrait of the simultaneous attraction and repulsion Fox exerts on his family. In Fox's world he alone is permitted creation; others are merely the executors of his conceptions. Initially wife, children and natives submit more or less happily: their traditionally submissive roles prepare them to do so. But gradually Fox's failings become glaringly apparent. He is so desperate for sole authority that he will lie of North America's devastation by nuclear attack to strengthen his position. Where would the family be without him? He forces them into a physical extremity where he alone has power. Whenever another male (the preacher, the three interlopers) approaches his territory, he lashes out. The supreme irony of the film, embodied in the voice-over, is that this dedicated survivalist should be outlived by his dependents. It is equally ironic that Weir's critique of the colonialist mentality should oscillate intermittently into an apologia for it. In each case, the dream of the world's renewal depends on a destruction that rebounds on the dreamer.

Bringing it all back home: *My Beautiful Laundrette*

While tracing the centuries-long opposition of country and city, Raymond Williams at one point makes a visionary leap and describes its current transposition onto a global scale: the Third World is now the country, the First World the city.[5] The logical consequence, of course, is that the microcosmic migratory movement to the city will be repro-

duced in the global macrocosm. This development, under way for decades, intensifies along with the *misère* of the Third World. Ryszard
Kapuściński remarks of Los Angeles, arguably the vanguard of the
First World, 'If one can assume that the Third World means coloured
people, then at the beginning of the next century Los Angeles will be
one of the largest cities in the Third World'.[6] This is not a condition
that awaits Los Angeles alone. Kapuściński notes elsewhere:

Perhaps what awaits humanity is the world's 'Third-world-ization'. If this is
actually what is to happen, then a trip to the countries of the Third World today would not be a trip into the past, in search of history's first links (Morgan,
Frazer, Malinowski, Mead, Lévi-Strauss), but the reverse – a trip into the
future.[7]

In the resultant environment it is less particular racial groups than
racism that runs riot. Racism may be defined as a failure in logical
typing: the individual is conflated with the class. (A similar failure afflicts melodrama – an individual is made to personify evil – and so the
linkage of racism and melodrama, forged cinematically in so incendiary a fashion in *The Birth of a Nation,* is hardly surprising.) Racism is
thus a form of unwarranted generalization (and so, incidentally, there
is a sense in which Claude Lanzmann's *Shoah* is racist in its treatment of Poles): an aggrieved member of one race sees the cause of its
grievance in every member of another one. All blacks, Latinos and
whites look alike to him: consequently, the perpetrator cannot be
found, and the thirst for justice can be slaked only by making all suffer. Racism fires buckshot, not bullets. Its generalizations may even be
seen to involve a death drive, a wish to have everything over and done
with, an end to variety and possible future difference: a world of tautology, where blacks are blacks, whites are whites and everything
knows its place.

De Tocqueville notes the proliferation of generalizations in a democratic society:

Men who live in ages of equality have a great deal of curiosity and little leisure; their life is so practical, so confused, so excited, so active, that but little
time remains to them for thought. Such men are prone to general ideas because they are thereby spared the trouble of studying particulars; they contain,
if I may so speak, a great deal in a little compass, and give, in a little time,
great return.[8]

Since the speed of events also fosters generalization, as they blur
into a single mass, its increasing rate augments the propensity for
generalization: the particular is lost in the mass. Hence, the democratic equation issues naturally in racism. Representatives of other
cultures are seen as the thin end of a wedge: pullulating masses will
soon overwhelm our own more modestly reproducing ranks. The other

race serves as a scapegoat for social changes beyond our control; and so something frustratingly abstract is lent the semblance of immediate presence. The return of the Third World within the First is one of the repressed, evidence of past crimes spewed out by a toilet backing up.[9] One's lack of the ability to shut the door on the monstrous Other who is really our double can well engender panic.

It is in *My Beautiful Laundrette* that the dialectic of racial power and powerlessness in modern Britain finds its most complex embodiment.[10] The Frears–Kureishi film is clearly *Mona Lisa's* rival for the position of best British film of the mid-eighties; a host of its fresh and razor-sharp scenes linger in the mind. It turns on a succession of paradoxes. The erstwhile colonized – the Pakistanis – dominate the former colonizers – the native British (and since the British punks in this film resemble a tribal Our Gang, the word 'native' is exactly right) – at the margins of a decaying London. And yet their dominance is itself relative, dominance *at the margins*. Meanwhile, its leading character, Omar, who renders the run-down laundrette a thing of beauty, is himself a subordinate within his family. He is thus the focus of a contradiction – both dominant (employing his old friend, the English punk Johnny [Daniel Day-Lewis], to refurbish the laundrette) and dominated. If he has our sympathy, it is because he is still a small-time operator and is consequently more appealing than the nastier bigger ones, such as the gangsterish Saleem, some of whose cocaine he sells independently to raise the capital to do up the laundrette. The film leaves open the question of his further development.

There is another sense in which we are 'on the side' of Omar: the literal sense of our placement regarding the screen. Omar and his lover Johnny are positioned like cinema-goers in relation to the laundrette's one-way mirror, which, like a cinema screen, permits them to see while remaining unseen. It screens them as they make love – just as the darkness of the auditorium screens the lovers in the back rows. When Omar's uncle Nasser and his English mistress Rachel arrive, interrupting the love-making (Omar and Johnny hurriedly button up), they may be read as emissaries of the mental censor. In preventing the scene from going so far as to tip the film's rating to X, or beyond, they have the crucial additional effect of forestalling any revelation of who exactly occupies the dominant position. The timely interruption thus allows the film to present the relationship as utopian, transcending the questions of dominance that beleaguer life elsewhere. But although at this point Frears and Kureishi offer a hope that the determining forces of economic and power relations may be overcome, they recognize the strength of the odds against such equality. (They align them with the ones against homosexual love.) There is a cartoon air – redolent of irrelevance – surrounding all the figures who are not on the make: from the comically frustrated British punks to Omar's father Hassim, with his lordly sigh that the working classes have been a great disappointment to him – or Johnny himself. They are cartoon figures because they are *harmless.* Only the Pakistani businessmen – the mock-amiable big sharks like Nasser; the lithe, dangerous, youthful ones, like Saleem; and the little ones still cutting their teeth, like Omar – have the solidity of the real. They alone are real because only they are fully compatible with the poisoned climate of neo-Benthamite, Thatcherite Britain. Omar's uncle, Nasser, remarks that whereas in Pakistan religion has begun to interfere with the making of money, 'in this damn country, which we hate and love, you can get anything you want'. The concordance between the views of that arch patriot Margaret Thatcher and this cynical Pakistani is richly ironic.

CHAPTER VII

White noise

Gentlemen and blondeness

Even as *The Blue Angel* was warning us against blonde women (given its place and date of production, it ought also to have warned against blonde *men*), on the other side of the Atlantic Anita Loos was arguing that gentlemen prefer blondes. Her analysis of the ascribed preference was to become a musical booster rocket for another blonde, whose starry trajectory would eclipse that of Dietrich, even though her singing would be just as flat (its breathy seductiveness rather unlike Dietrich's acrid and Germanic determination to push through to the song's end, disdainfully ignoring the notes' failure to come out right). But do blondes prefer gentlemen? Anthony Burgess has asked. The Monroe film's answer is a resounding yes: gentlemen = diamonds (and the best and most gentlemanly gentlemen, those whose age and marital status preclude excessive importunity, even have diamonds for heads); and these, we know, are a girl's best friend, the financial safeguard of the single entrepreneur and married security in a wedding ring. Gentlemen do not so much prefer blondes as blondes who sing badly. Their bad singing shows they will be unable to earn a living on their own (the blonde needs her brunette partner), while adoption of the designation 'singer' indicates intimate acquaintance with the euphemistic codes of gentlemanly dissimulation.

Gentlemen Prefer Blondes: the title was possible only in the interwar period, before it was contaminated by the echo of Nazi mythology. Its use as the title of an American film made a mere eight years after the concentration camp gates had opened is a sign both of American innocence and of American crassness, those Janus facets of U.S. imperviousness to the world. If the Aryan ideal is the blonde woman, the United States shows one how to achieve it painlessly: the only liquidation necessary is the dyeing of dark hair. In the United States, dye technology has a utopian air. (One may contrast it with the German dystopia of IG Farben, suggestively analysed by Pynchon in *Gravity's*

112

Rainbow.) The old world, however, is tied to its roots and cannot see the utopian possibilities of peroxide. The American blonde stands for possibility, for she used to be a brunette (Marilyn herself, or Madonna). One may be sceptical nevertheless of her offer of the best of both worlds, brunette fire beneath blonde respectability (was this the dream that drew Hitchcock to the United States, as his films with Tippi Hedren or the make-over of *Vertigo* would suggest?): the incompatible elements are just as likely to cancel one another out.

If blondes stand out ('Blond ambition!'), since most of the world's women have dark hair, peroxide comes in a genie's bottle that offers leadership by fiat. Blondeness from a bottle becomes the American ideal as the country assumes the mantle of world economic leadership: the blonde as an advertisement for the virtues of renouncing one's origins, the siren message of Americanism and colonialism. Monroe may have been sold as one in a series of Liberty Blondes, but – as Billy Wilder among many others noted – her glamour was limned with extreme vulnerability. She is the standard bearer of an imperialism that radiates good intentions; if disaster ensues, the culprit is simply neurosis. The Liberty Blonde is vulnerable because she has sacrificed the stability of roots. Her return to Paris in *Gentlemen Prefer Blondes* is almost like an effort to reclaim them. Late in the film, when Monroe's character is about to be tried in Paris for refusal to surrender Lady Beaty's diamond tiara (it was, after all, recompense for services rendered), her partner – played by Jane Russell – takes the stand in a blonde wig, impersonating her soul sister. The brunette who wishes to return to her origins cannot employ peroxide; recourse to the artificial aid may make one artificial forever. She has to use a wig. But the transformation reenacts Monroe's own: Jane Russell is less the scapegoat for her singer friend than the parodist who seeks to strangle at birth the emergent myth of Monroe (1953, the year of the film, was to be her breakthrough year). Russell's bewigged appearance in the dock argues that to become a blonde by any other means is to lose touch with oneself. The argument will be that of the gossip columnists and agony aunts who nod sage heads and wag fingers over Marilyn's neuroses. She becomes Marilyn's double, the rational self she lost to an obsession with diamonds. In the context of the film, however, as opposed to that of the logic of Monroe's subsequent career, the transformation shows that inside the blonde schemer is a natural home-town girl struggling to get out. And so in the end Monroe's character, a girl from Little Rock too, is prepared, like her brunette partner, to settle for the little rock embedded in the wedding ring on her finger.

'I just hate to be a thing', Monroe was later to complain to *Life;* 'That's the trouble – a sex symbol becomes a thing'. In other words, the brunette who believed one could become whatever one likes and traded in her identity for that of a blonde is henceforth in thrall to the laws of exchange, of reification. Monroe objectified herself before anyone else objectified her: to be 'photogenic' is to identify with the camera (at first, with the camera one projects behind the mirror) as the exhibitionist identifies with the voyeur, thereby partaking of the other's pleasure. *Gentlemen Prefer Blondes* accentuates Marilyn's blondeness by casting her opposite a brunette, but the pairing and doubling also distinguishes between sexuality and its image. Bleach blondeness sublimates sexuality into merely an image (hence Monroe's *innocence*): that is why it is preferred by gentlemen, who feel no need to paw the goods. The resultant hyperblondeness is surely also a response to U.S. whites' fears that the stronghold of their whiteness is less secure than it may seem, that it has to be heightened artificially. (One's simultaneous yearning for a good tan is a sign of unconscious identification with the black Other.) Peroxide blondeness stands for the fifties on the verge of the sixties, the era of civil rights turmoil; it was hardly an accident that Mailer, the writer most obsessively concerned with the transition between the two decades, should have been interested both in the white negro and in Marilyn, and should have put the two together in *An American Dream* associating Cherry – southern funkiness – with its denied underside, the funkiness of blacks.

As Richard Dyer has noted, Marilyn is 'desirable' rather than a femme fatale.[1] If she manipulates men with her body, that body manipulates *her* also, laying her open to the double entendres that transform her into beautiful victim. The split within her generates comedy as well as narcissism: the dumb blonde may not be so dumb after all (as her lover's father remarks in *Gentlemen*). There is a trompe l'oeil: who is one seeing? Marilyn, or her image in the mirror? And yet there is a sense in which she genuinely is dumb. The girl whose blondeness is unfurled as the banner of possibility seemed to think it possible to pass from funny-bunny roles to Method acting; Miss Lonelyhearts journalists, and even sharper writers who ought to know better (such as Norman Mailer), made the same mistake when musing how she might have fared as Grushenka in *The Brothers Karamazov*. The stupid–sassy dialectic of the dumb blonde sees character as sharply defined and then deals out opposed cards with snappily witty speed. Method acting is the reverse of crisp: character is drawn forth slowly like the entrails the character seeks to read, weakly mumbling after seppuku. Method acting had little or no place for female roles: the self-disembowelling of the psychodrama was primarily available to males, self-analysis the metaphorical equivalent of an envied childbirth, in this case: the self-birthing of the existential, Oedipal self. For women there was only the hysteria of Maggie the Cat: the reenactment of a male-prescribed role (hysteria as the required lot of the childless), no labour of self-discovery. *The Misfits* is a sadly apt title for Monroe's expedition into the Actor's Studio.

Consideration of the dialectic of blonde dizziness and ambition should make it apparent that what Richard Dyer sees as an inconsistency in the characterization in *Gentlemen* – Lorelei Lee (code for MM) may scheme, but 'Monroe doesn't play the part as if she is a manipulator'[2] – is to be expected and should cause neither critical consternation nor condemnation of the film's alleged incoherence. Lorelei is her own double, a status signalled in the repetition of her initial. (MM, meanwhile, is an image of the multiple breasts of the ancient love goddess.) That is why she can be doubled in Jane Russell and why, when the two step down the aisle together at the end, the connotations are both of them marrying each other and of Marilyn marrying herself (her narcissism). The symmetrical assault of their opening scene[3] – Kracauer's 'mass ornament' in miniature – is repeated in another key: one has to be integrated before one can marry. And yet 'the show goes on'; nothing is lost, for one is not losing a show-girl, but gaining a daughter.

At the start of this essay I paired *Gentlemen Prefer Blondes,* originally a work of the late twenties, with another iconic figure of the same period, Marlene Dietrich. I will return to Dietrich in a moment. First, however, I must consider *King Kong,* for if gentlemen prefer blondes the most famous interwar embodiment of such a preference was to be found in the saga of the great ape. Kong is perhaps a gentleman by default: the impossibility of his consummating his passion for Fay Wray crowns him with sad dignity – and he can stand, among other things, for the fan whose enormous desire shrinks the star into a mere pinprick, a small dot of light in the heavens.[4] He is gentleman as gentle man: he does Fay no harm. In *Blonde Venus,* meanwhile, which can be paired with *Kong* to form the thirties' most pregnant diptych on black–white relations, Dietrich the night-club performer clambers out of an ape suit sporting a *white* afro wig. The white woman is, as it were, rescued from, disgorged by, the black, who vanishes as easily as sloughed skin, and yet the black remains present, albeit repressed, in the afro wig dyed white. Blackness is repressed still further, of course, in *Gentlemen Prefer Blondes,* where even the brunette is white. Paris is no longer redolent of Josephine Baker. In fifties Hollywood the startling allegorical narrative of *Kong* – and the still more arresting sequence from Sternberg's *Blonde Venus* – are clearly no longer possible.

Meanwhile, the blonde that real fifties gentlemen were to prefer, the show-girl who won the prince, was of course not Marilyn but the exquisite Grace Kelly. Where Marilyn chases jewels, in *To Catch a Thief*

– set so close to her future kingdom – Grace Kelly herself is defined as one. In the seduction scene whose daring the intercut distant fireworks highlight with leaden, leering pedantry, she holds out her necklace to Cary Grant. He, the ex-burglar with expertise, may call them imitation, but she trumps him by adding that *she's* real. Nevertheless, for much of the film she *is* an imitation in a sense: an imitation of 'the cat' whose thefts imitate the ones Grant once committed, but which he redeemed as a Resistance fighter. John Robie, the one-time jewel thief renowned as 'the cat', is widely suspected of recidivism; he determines to prove he's a reformed character by catching the copy-cat thief, a task he alone is like-minded enough to perform. The film's opening intercuts elderly ladies wailing in consternation over empty jewel boxes with images of hands spiriting valuables away and a black cat stealing over tiles. Unacquainted as yet with Robie and his sobriquet, we see this start as both a witty literalization of the term 'cat burglar' and sly play with and against the Soviet montage that juxtaposed humans with animals metaphorically. (Indeed, film allusions are perhaps the major initial source of interest, as the birdcage beside Grant and Hitchcock in the bus flashes forwards to *The Birds* and the rooftops presage *Vertigo,* allowing us to peek just over the horizon of Hitchcock's mid-fifties intentions.) It is of course both: the John Robie of the present both is and is not the cat. He must become him again to cease to be him in others' eyes: one sets a thief to catch a thief.

The proverb Hitchcock's title truncates is also an allusion to amorous stratagem: one has to become a thief to entrap Robie. Both the girls courting him – the French Danielle and the American Francie, the Grace Kelly character – propose participation in a heist to John, and it is hard to know which one is more serious. At first one may suspect the new cat to be Francie herself: she swims up soundlessly to Danielle and Robie at the off-shore raft, and her love of danger is shown by her seizure of the initiative by kissing Robie and by her fast driving. She purrs with pleasure, eyes narrowed, as her car whips hair-raisingly round impossible bends. Is she the real cat? (On hearing of a jewel theft, she tells her mother 'you're next' – and she is.) But her status as imitation cat is revealed by the back-projections that show the real safety of the dangerously taken curves. Although she clearly bests Danielle in verbal sparring, those back-projections declaw her, getting both her and Robie off the hook. Her later loss of poise and control – her dishevelled anger at Robie after her mother has been robbed – may seem at the time like consummate acting, part of a plot to make John the scapegoat for her thefts, but in retrospect its reality shows her no true feline. And that blackness means substitution is spelled out eventually at the fancy dress ball where the insurance agent in blackface doubles for Robie. The true cat is Danielle: like Simone Simon in *Cat*

People, the foreign woman is the cat woman. Any suspicions that we might have underestimated the French girl by failing to see the cat in her are undercut by the realization that she was acting for her father, whose wooden leg precluded climbing. She is no true imitation of the cat, lacking his feline independence. Unlike her, Francie has no living father, so Cary Grant becomes the father figure as potential lover – like Clark Gable, the CG of Marilyn's fantasies. She steps dutifully into the shoes of the mother who is so taken with Robie.

Where feline means feminine, the black cat cannot be a man. The black cat that accompanies Robie is merely warming a place for the girl he will win. And yet it cannot be his prospective spouse: gentlemen prefer blondes (and who is more quintessentially the gentleman for the fifties than Cary Grant?). She can only be the dark lady, the French girl who has no lasting call on one's affections, who betrays one while professing love and whose desire to flee to South America with one is suspiciously suggestive of kinship with the Nazis one fought as part of the Resistance. Frenchness may be suspect – Bourbon is the only drink, Francie's mother avers, far preferable to champagne – but is not 'Bourbon' an eminently French name? What better place than France for the American bon vivant? One will make one's home there after all, having things both ways, rejecting a French girl for another called Francie. Her terms are indeed too generous to refuse. And for the audience that can only hope to have and hold imitation jewels, the imitation is the real thing. Dark ladies are too real to inhabit the white screens that highlight blondes' hair with the silver thread indicating real currency in this world: the world of Hollywood, the imaginary – of the bleach blonde.

The Rocky body show

Whereas in the sixties radical thought placed great emphasis on the body, as part of its general project of putting rationalization, repression and the petit bourgeois intelligentsia in their places, a stress on the body was – ironically – to become a keystone of eighties ecumenical ideology. It was an ideology that presented itself as postideological. Where mind is dismissible as a source of undecidability and confusion, deconstruction and weight-lifting become two sides of the same false coin. One may no longer know what the right political line may be or which politician is lying, but anyone can tell if a body is in shape. What you see is what you get. The emphasis on physical prowess, whose more explicitly left-wing version focuses on black mastery of break-dancing, indicates the continued viability of democracy. Would-be democrats haunted by the injustice with which biology has distributed intelligence are heartened by the reflection that anyone (even the proverbial weakling who gets sand kicked in his face) can up his or her physical achievements by working out – or taking steroids. Not only is physique clearly visible and quantifiable: it is far easier to alter than an IQ already largely determined by the time of adolescence's arrival. As people seek to slim down in the real world, it becomes the sign of a martyrdom to art to allow one's body to balloon, as De Niro's does in *Raging Bull*. Anyone sceptical regarding the pseudoequalizing effects of body culture need only recall Deep South colleges' uncanny eagerness to integrate talented blacks into their football squads. It is hardly surprising that Don Siegel's *Invasion of the Body Snatchers* should have been remade in recent years: loss of *body*, the sign of one's virtuous regime of self-improvement, is feared above all else. (Nor is it surprising that this film's director, Phil Kaufman, in his version of *The Unbearable Lightness of Being*, eliminated the ugly bodies of Tereza's mother and Franz's wife, leaving only beautiful people to parade naked across the screen.) In a body culture you may as well forget about soul. The blacks' assertion of exclusive rights to possession of that commodity may be a response to those who disdain them as merely beautiful bodies, but it also points to their continued exclusion – the exclusion of soul itself. (And so later, in the postmodern pastiche of Vanilla Ice, even the signs of that soul are appropriated and commodified.)

Writing of Muhammad Ali in *Existential Errands*, Norman Mailer notes that 'if he were Narcissus, so he was as well the play of mood in the water which served as a mirror to Narcissus'.[5] The emergence of Rocky, meanwhile, is a symptom of the trauma Ali inflicted on white narcissism. Since Ali was the boxer as actor, it then became possible to limit the damage by having an actor turn boxer. (A confusion of image and referent also exploited in the late seventies by another actor headed for more than symbolic office.) In the realm of the imaginary, Stallone reasserts a white supremacy long since lost in the boxing ring. The remakes are in fact rematches and show him to be really a world champ honour-bound repeatedly to put title and physical fitness on the line. Genres having virtually collapsed in Hollywood, the single film becomes a genre in its own right. But Rocky cannot enter the series of imaginary rings until the real Ali has left them: insofar as this is true, the imaginary is well aware of the demands made by the reality it seeks to repress. The racism of the project to efface the memory of Ali, 'the white negro', is partly veiled by Rocky's Italian stallion status: like the black, he is a stud, albeit a sublimated one, and a member of a visible minority. In effect, WASPs hire a member of one minority to destroy another. The sticky friendship that develops, in the later stages of the series, between Rocky and the Ali figure, Apollo Creed, is a smoke-screen before the repression of the real Ali; it embodies a dream of successful domestication while demonstrating that for the white Establishment, all minorities are alike.

It was Ali's aim, Mailer theorizes, 'to get a public to the point of hating him so much the burden on the other fighter approached the metaphysical – which was where Ali wanted it'.[6] Garry Wills remarks on how the conflicts said to exist 'behind' fights are used to dull our awareness of the brutality we ourselves display in permitting one man to belabour another so ruthlessly: 'It is as if the *art* were not enough to redeem boxing's violence, all that cruelty inflicted on the face – so we prefer to think the loser is being destroyed for some deeply ideological reason'.[7] (And whites may indeed be happy to watch blacks mauling *each other*.) When the issues have been inflated thus, the fatality that dogs all fight descriptions sets in. As Mailer puts it: 'Sooner or later fight metaphors, like fight managers, go sentimental. They go military'.[8] An unkind critic might deem Mailer well equipped to recognize this sentimental militarism, having been himself so often its purveyor. The *Rocky* cycle reaches this stage in *Rocky IV*, which is also a *Rambo* remake. Here the remake is less a repetition than the widening of a circle, to encompass the whole world (and then ... the universe? Rocky Meets Alien?).

But the threats Rocky and Rambo confront do not simply issue from other races: they also involve the menacing of the body by castration and machine. In Rocky and in Rambo, as in so many musclemen, phallic narcissism is displaced onto the whole body. American males circumcised at birth are profoundly conscious of the possibility of loss of the penis. It is hardly surprising that the specifically Jewish neuroses of so many of Freud's patients should have become normative for a large proportion of American males. The endangered organ is hidden by transforming the whole body into the penis – showing that the totality of one's energy is engaged in its protection. The displacement conceals the fact that the body's muscle-bound ballooning is itself the consequence of emasculation. One reenacts – or forestalls – one's actual emasculation by performing it symbolically on oneself. The emasculation, the down-playing of the physical that Rocky and Rambo so fear, is in part the work of the factory machine whose continually increasing sophistication throws their class out of manual work. Then there is the war machine whose development has the same effect. (One may speak of one's enemy's possession of a war machine, but one's own missiles are the ones that strike with inhuman accuracy.) Soldiers may fear lest war's mechanization undermine the value of military virtue. Stallone replies that mentality is more important than mechanism: Rambo downs helicopters with superarrows. One can be disadvantaged technically – as the paranoid generals fear really is the case – and still win.

Rocky is of course a populist figure. When he fights Drago (Dolph Lundgren) in the USSR, the mute Russians receive their voice, shouting so lustily for him that the general secretary of the Communist Party is compelled reluctantly to rise and second the applause. The populist cults of recent years (Reagan, John Paul II) seek to replace conscious recognition of ideological difference with a bland all-purpose benignity: the face of the Grandfather, who transcends social oppositions defined as part of an Oedipal power struggle. The process conceals the contradictions between rich and poor (justifying laissez-faire callousness, dispelling any fears that it might return to haunt one as the spectre of revolution) and among superpowers (assuaging the fear of apocalypse so as to free the libido for the work of self-enrichment). The result is democratic fascism. Unity is achieved through the adoration of a leader figure whose struggle is always situated in the past. As this occurs, Benjamin's feared 'aestheticization of politics' is realized in the contradiction-free realm of patriotic kitsch: the flag papers over the cracks in the social structure. 'In the end', Adorno notes, 'glorification of splendid underdogs is nothing other than glorification of the splendid system that makes them so'[9] – and never more so than when the underdog becomes top dog. In identifying with his fantasy image of ourselves, we imagine ourselves victors over the system that defeats us in reality.

Rocky IV is an iron-pumping version of David and Goliath. Just in case we missed the allusion (though no one does, so we can congratulate ourselves on our superiority to those who *might* have done so), the ringside commentators at the Moscow bout point it out. Rocky's adversary, steroid-enhanced mechanical man, Ivan Drago ('Ivan', because that's what all Russians are called; 'Drago', because a long Russian name would induce an inferiority complex in a U.S. public unable to pronounce it), is thus the dragon to be slain. The nonidentity of 'Drago' and 'dragon' suggests someone whose dragon nature is partially hidden, like the *drugs* he takes; the missing 'n' symbolizes the things he lacks, which include humanity and sexuality. The resemblance to a dragon is cemented by his apparent possession of three heads: he first appears in triplicate on a poster; after a round with him Rocky says he keeps seeing three of them out there (Paulie [Burt Young] says to hit the one in the middle); and as he appears continually flanked by wife (Brigitte Nielsen) and manager, the sense of his subhumanity is reinforced by the suspicion that they must always be on hand to wind up the robot. Their unholy trinity parodies the good one of Rocky, Paulie and Adrien (Talia Shire). Stallone repeatedly shoots Drago from below (the Rocky-eye view), as well as from the side, his face all hard edges and slow, menacing reptilian turn – a Red Dragon with a dragon-lady for a spouse (as Stallone himself was to discover later – life imitating 'art'?). The pastiche of David and Goliath involves moral rearmament through a return to nature and simple verities. When Captain Drago – a Martian disguised as a human – arrives in the United States to challenge all comers, Rocky's friend Apollo Creed picks up the gauntlet, deeming Drago an upstart. As Ali figure, however, Creed himself is defined by the film as the embodiment of a cock-sure United States whose glitz hides an absence of substance. Drago and his entourage are not the only ones stunned by his Vegas prefight appearance as star-spangled Uncle Sam; Rocky too lifts his eyebrows sceptically. This is 'Living in America', the James Brown song tells us, an America that needs to return to its roots. Its current decadence becomes apparent when Drago, having earlier pushed over a cardboard cut-out of Creed, finds that the real one offers little more resistance. Nevertheless, the U.S. flag hangs behind the cardboard Creed, nemesis waiting in the wings for the godless opponent. Since the Russians schedule the Moscow match for Christmas Day, Rocky is clearly fighting the paganism of the evil empire – a paganism compounded, for good effect, of Nazism (Drago is the Aryan ideal, and the match-up recalls the Joe Louis–Max Schmelling bout on the eve of World War II) and Communism. Rocky holds the dead Apollo in a Pietà position; prays before his fight; and on winning, preaches peace on Christmas Day. 'Greater love hath no man' is the alibi for 'vengeance is mine'. Apollo's paganism was surely encoded in his name also. The Apollo Creed is an American credo that idolizes pagan deities and places its trust in such space-age machinery as the Apollo rocket, rather than the bedrock values Stallone represents. Whereas Drago will snarl that he fights for himself alone, Rocky battles for friend, God and country.

With the stakes so momentous, it is no surprise that the film is full of portent. The white gloves of the credits revolve, with the menacing motion later to be associated with Drago's head, to reveal the U.S. and Soviet emblems imprinted on them. They explode on contact. Any illusions one may have had regarding the relative harmlessness of sporting conflicts are rapidly dispelled: the explosion shows this is no substitute for war but the real thing. The portents mass – with freeze-frames as Drago's punches are measured and pronounced destructive of concrete, to say nothing of human flesh. As Rocky eyeballs the image of Drago posted on his mirror, the music is dissonant. In a reprise of Drago's earlier toppling of the cardboard Creed, Rocky rips the photograph up. Its removal leaves him alone with his own mirror image (it is tough at the top, with only oneself for company) – muscle-bound narcissism incarnate.

Rocky IV argues that only a recovery of basic values will permit the United States to checkmate the fabled technological superiority of the

USSR. Stallone agrees with Drago's manager: the United States has become weak (weak enough to allow a black to represent it). Simple verities are of course what one should expect of a boxer whose brain has been pulped innumerable times. Rocky goes back to nature for his training. If Drago is iceman as well as dragon (the embodiment of Nazi ice philosophy, as well as the red peril), Rocky steals the icy fire by jogging through the snow, beyond the reach of his KGB chaperones' limousine. (Nevertheless, there seem to have been other chaperones – or how could the camera have spun around him as he stands on the mountaintop, shouting ecstatically? It must have been a KGB helicopter, for we all know of the dangers of illegal penetration of Soviet airspace.) Rocky's wood-chopping regimen is intercut with shots of Drago sweating in harness to high-tech instrument panels, with a big close-up of a drug-bearing needle emphasizing his unfair advantage. Drago is machine-tooled, a stiffly shuffling robot. His meeting with Rocky (Frankenstein meets Superdwarf) dispels all memory that boxing was ever deemed an art. That which was once sublimated into 'art' is de-sublimated into the pure aggression for which it had once been a metaphor. Drago is animal predator as well as machine, baring teeth and/ or black gumshield as he fights. His grin is animal exultation over prone prey. His status as villain is firmly consolidated by the film's refusal to give him a life beyond fights and training. Rocky may term himself a born scrapper, but he takes time off to play with his son and give anniversary presents to Adrien. (They've been married for nine years, and since the first *Rocky* emerged in 1976, the parallel with real time is meant to enhance verisimilitude.) Heavies are never family men: to show their families, their reasons for acting as they do, would render their demonization impossible. All Drago has is the ice-maiden who is his ring-mistress, and whose resemblance to him can suggest the troglodytic, incestuous perversity of *enfants terribles* dreamed up by a Soviet Cocteau.

Rocky IV depicts a technological disparity between the United States and the USSR that is both quantitative and, more importantly, qualitative. The film has things both ways. On the one hand, the Soviet Union is credited with superior offensive capacity (and a more offensive disposition); but in case this might imply U.S. technological inferiority to the great adversary, we are shown Rocky's home bristling with *peaceful* gadgets. Drago, the violent mechanical man, is countered by the sweet-voiced female robot slave – a Stepford wife – Rocky purchases for Paulie. The United States specializes not in weaponry but in video cameras (Rocky junior wields one already, doubtless training for the filming of a future installment – perhaps even the next one, subtitled *Look Who's Filming*), watches and fast cars. Robots are there to serve man – which is why they are female. In giving Paulie a girl robot, the film nicely – and unconsciously – verges on the pornographic. Not surprisingly, it orders the black chauffeur around. Unlike the Americans, the Soviets – evil materialists that they are – confuse man and machine. They need a Rocky, with his Christmas message, to save them from themselves. But with peacemakers like Stallone, one may wonder if anyone needs Doctor Strangelove.

Spiking the joint

Emerging from *Do the Right Thing*, dazed by the Dolby stereo sensation of having been bounced around inside a boom box for two hours, the audience may be forgiven for wondering just what the right thing is. Spike Lee's film is clearly of two minds on the subject. For much of its duration, two opinions jostle each other, with neither achieving dominance; in the end they deadlock, as a quotation from Martin Luther King unconditionally condemning violent protest is followed by one from Malcolm X justifying it, and the two men are shown in a beaming handshake whose utopian promise is mocked by all that has preceded it. Unable to sort out the relative value of opposed strands in the black heritage, Lee concludes (making a mockery of his own title) by refusing to choose.

Spike Lee, acridly gifted writer, producer and director, is also the central actor: Mookie, Dodgers fan and delivery boy for Italian-run Sal's Famous Pizzeria, is a slouching, diminutive stone face whose tormented eyes belie his stoical set expression. His seeming impassivity is a holding action against the immense tension of furiously opposed forces. These are teased out in the film's kaleidoscopic aesthetic, which alternates a quasi-pastoral image of summer life on a Bed-Stuy block, where old-timers exchange cracks and gently wafting soundtrack music diffuses a *Porgy and Bess* atmosphere, with the jagged passion implicit in expressionistic canted angles, red-painted walls and threatening wide-angle low shots of Radio Raheem's face as his overpowering boom box pours out Public Enemy's vitriolic gospel of 'Fight the Power'. Raheem's image is profoundly ambiguous: if the wide-angle lens relays the white view of him as part of an urban horror flick, the stylistic brio also conveys an impressed directorial identification with the monster's power, which makes him a fit opponent for the power of The Man. His boom box pumps out the sound of the young, whose frustration has reached a pitch at which it can no longer be vented in such self-deprecating jokes as 'I'll kick your black ass for you'. To be self-deprecating is to identify with the racial (racist) enemy.

Throughout the film, these two strands shuttle back and forth. Calculatedly sweet scenes between Mayor, the block's aged and exquisitely mannered inebriate, and Mother-Sister, who snipes at him from her window but grudgingly admires his brave, fleet rescue of a child from an oncoming car, are diced with moments of sheer cacophony, as contentious voices drown one another out or the boom box crushes every other sound like an empty beer can tossed in the gutter. The sweeter scenes are associated with the old, who share Sal's (Danny Aiello's) belief that the races can subsist in harmony, even if they do have an occasional propensity to unbottle frustrations in murderous harangues. (In an amazing tour de force of insult, at one point four of these violent monologues are bunched together and flung at the camera.) Some of the young, however, are edgier, more dangerous. Their animosity towards other races can be expressed jocularly or with menace. Property owners – mostly Italian – are fair game, for instance. As the barometer bubbles, an Italian with a large antique car drives down the street, prefacing his arrival by warning the black youths toying with a fire hydrant that dousing his car will mean trouble. They duly douse it. Lee sets the Italian up as a blow-hard who deserves his comeuppance and identifies (at least at *this* point) with the cops who mock the man's complaint. It is a poetic justice that is profoundly unjust: one law for the hip and one for the square.

The injustice becomes glaring, however, when the ante is upped and this watery destruction turns fiery at the film's end. Radio Raheem and Buggin' Out, a black radical who insists (often to the amusement of other blacks) that black heroes replace the photographs of Italian Americans on Sal's Wall of Fame, march determinedly into the pizzeria, at the end of a long day, to avenge past slights. When Raheem makes up for his earlier capitulation in turning down his radio (the precondition of the purchase of a slice) and refuses to do so this time, the infuriated Sal belabours the machine with a baseball bat. The subsequent melee is broken up in the street by police, who – in doing so – strangle Raheem, apparently inadvertently. Panic-stricken, they make themselves scarce. When the neighbourhood confronts Sal, muttering vaguely, it is Mookie who starts the riot by hurling a trash-can through Sal's window.

It is at this point that the film falls off the rails. It is not that a riot has not been on the cards as a possible denouement. A riot *sparked by Mookie,* however, is extremely problematic. Self-hatred and self-justification collide in Lee's decision to let the character he himself plays cast the first stone. By insisting – in a grim mea culpa (retracted in subsequent interviews, which somewhat disingenuously assert a total separation between himself and Mookie) – that he himself is far from innocent, he counters the potential reproach that his sweet comic moments are Uncle Tomism. Destroying one's place of employment can be an act of solidarity with unemployed brothers. There is a sense in which Mookie trashes the pizzeria in order to save himself from alignment with Sal's racist elder son: each has proposed 'Get a job' as a panacea. (Mookie's motives also include a brooding suspicion of Sal's sweetness towards his sister.)

The next morning Mookie trudges in his characteristic marching-through-mud fashion to the burned-out pizzeria, where he demands that Sal pay him. This action is so unexpected (one blinks mentally) that when Mookie awakes and says he is going for his money, the implied air of normality may prompt some in the audience to speculate that the previous night's events are about to be reclassified as a dream. (After all, the film had begun with him rising the day before.) In a sense they are right: Mookie hurling the trash-can through Sal's window *is* a dream, Lee's dream of committed art, but he pulls back from it at the end, with the helpless, scrupulous moralism of its juxtaposed quotations. The quotations identify the two tonalities percolating through the work as simply love and hate. Radio Raheem – in a steal from *The Night of the Hunter* – wears rings spelling LOVE on one hand and HATE on the other. Love seems finally to be identified with the older generation: with Love-Daddy, for instance, the 108 FM DJ whose music varies as the day goes on, cooling things down with soft music for lovers rather than broadcasting a single unrelenting note, like Radio Raheem. But Love-Daddy is screened from the violence by the glass, seeing everything, yet able to keep cool – and keep his cool – by virtue of his distance. Love is the sugar of daddyhood, and here Mookie is right where one would expect him to be – on the fence: he has a child but does nothing for him, leaving the upkeep and upbringing to his girl-friend Tina. Sal, too, is a love-daddy, proud that the block's kids have grown up on his pizza and firmly planning to stay in the neighbourhood – for all the cops' sceptical jeers and his eldest son's hatred of blacks. Yet the rising heat has transformed the American melting pot into a cauldron. Lee's remedy is a variety of apartheid: in a world in which everything belongs to foreigners (the pizzeria to Italians, the corner shop to a Korean who protects his business with a broomstick), it is all too easy to raise a rabble by pointing to relative deprivation. One had better, perhaps, keep the races apart. After all, it is hard to celebrate the joys of idling in the sun when they are leavened with a bitter sense of being out of it. (Drugs are absent from Lee's black neighbourhood, so the riot becomes the community's high.) 'I got plenty o' nuthin' ' becomes a rather ambiguous self-definition. So when Lee himself throws the trash-can through Sal's window, he is only a step away from black national socialism (with Italians the scapegoats instead of Jews) – and he both knows it and seeks to repress the knowledge. Lee headlines his film 'a Spike Lee joint', but it might more accurately be termed a spiked joint: one inhales something apparently mild (snapshots of summer-time, when the living is easy) and ends up on an extremely bad trip. The anger that fuels the comic machine finally fouls it up.

Mona Lisa and the dark lady

Generally speaking, the most imaginative recent transformations of film noir iconography have come not from the United States or Hollywood-based directors, but from foreigners, for whom it has the suggestiveness of a dream of another place as well as another time. Perhaps the best is *Mona Lisa,* by Irishman Neil Jordan. Here the dreams take the form of the fantasies that a small-time London gangster, George (Bob Hoskins), projects onto Simone (Cathy Tyson), the 'tall thin black tart' his paymasters assign him to chauffeur from client to client. They are dreams in which his search for Simone's child-prostitute friend becomes confusingly resonant, for it is undertaken not simply as a way into Simone's favour, but also because George semiconsciously identifies the girl with his own daughter. For much of the film, George is very confused (in the end the depth of his bafflement becomes somewhat unbelievable), thrown off balance by the Gioconda's enigma. A punk just out of jail, where he took a rap for his boss, George is also a dreamer, and the film is both harrowing and comic, haunting and smoky, as plies of different emotions fold over one another in the manner of the best films of the *nouvelle vague,* which also had a love affair with Hollywood iconography. The mood is one of film noir transformed into baroque. The film is rich in moments that can only be called conceits, and as they yoke opposed emotions they tear one apart. Near the end, for instance, there is a scene on Brighton Pier, to which George and Simone have fled from his boss's vengeance for the rescue of Charley, Simone's girl-friend and lover. George sports a tourist's star-shaped sunglasses, and yet, ridiculous as he is, one senses the pain behind them as he wrestles with Simone, and she, after at first fleeing him, lays her hand compassionately on his. In their subsequent headlong flight from the henchmen of George's boss, they knock over a series of red hearts lined up on the ground. The baroque texture then thickens as they pass a group of dwarfs: George has spent much of his time discussing with his friend Thomas (Robbie Coltrane) the details of a detective story involving a dwarf murderer, and now the mind boggles as real dwarfs appear. Thomas, meanwhile, inhabits a caravan with a fridge bearing a reproduction of the Mona Lisa on one side. The multiple echoes are more than just literary. They stand for the absurdity of experience and for the power of the imagination to transform the literary into the actual – either by projecting archetypes of love onto real people or by projecting blatant symbols into physical reality. It is hardly surprising that an Irishman should have made a film whose hero could have taken as his motto Yeats's 'In dreams begins responsibility. And so, in another literary reference – appropriately enough, to the period of the baroque – George becomes an incarnation of Don Quixote: his story, like that of the Knight of the Sorrowful Countenance, is the tragedy of a ridiculous man (or, to borrow the title of one of Jordan's novels, *The Dream of a Beast*). Thomas is his Sancho Panza (and so one has a baroque doubling and comic inversion, for George himself has the misleading build of the Sancho Panza type). As he chauffeurs Simone to and from her assignations, George asks her if her clients ever fall in love with her. 'Sometimes they fall for what they think I am', she cannily replies. The way her image in the driver's mirror is superimposed on the procession of King's Cross whores shows her to be both one of them and different – the spatial dislocation causing George's disorientation. George is, as it were, drawn into the sort of detective story he would normally read: and so, at the very end of the film, one sees him under a car, alongside Thomas, doing a repair job and recounting his experience in the third person. In a further baroque turn of the screw, the film becomes his own vision of himself. Even at the end he is deluding himself by casting his life in the form of a preexistent story (and this is the justification of the extreme *self-consciousness* of the film).

George's worst delusions concern women. This is hardly surprising; after all, he has been out of their company for seven years. He sees the realm of sexuality as one of confusion and, in the end, evil, the sphere of perversion presided over by his terrifying boss (Michael Caine). George falls in love with Simone's reflected image, not her reality, which he fails to perceive; he does not grasp that her girl-friend is a junkie and that they are lesbians. The film shows his growing knowledge of the depravity of the London underworld, which lengthy absence permits him to gauge. George's odyssey among the peep-shows and brothels in search of Charley is harrowing but leavened by marvellous comic detail. (The peep-show girls are making tea when he comes by.) The insistent dislocations of the film are part of its fundamental, and very Irish, theme: homelessness. Beginning with George failing to enter his own home (his wife shuts him out and he flings dustbins around angrily), the film ends with him living in Thomas's caravan – hiding out from gangland revenge for his boss's shooting. As he lies under the car we see a pair of legs approaching and wonder (with some trepidation) whose they might be. They belong to George's daughter. He may be without a home, but he has the consolation of knowing that this girl, the piece of home he most values, is with him rather than her mother – as if the meeting with Simone had existed only to foster this exchange, as if (in a final wonderfully literary convolution) the rescue of Charley has meant symbolic salvation (in the novel in his head) for his own daughter too.

On the brink: *Grand Canyon*

At the end of *Zabriskie Point* – another American film that confronts human efforts with vast barren nature – Daria Halprin, on hearing that police have shot her student-lover, explodes an American home in her mind's eye. In a sense, *Grand Canyon* executes a similar operation, taking the material of a TV movie about interracial reconciliation and exploding it so that the dislocated parts float into new and strange constellations, as they do in slow motion in Daria's mind. Despite one's awareness, at the back of one's mind, of the material's banality, the formal operation redeems and restores meaning to it. The panoramic fresco of Los Angeles life becomes a collage. On paper, *Grand Canyon*'s plot elements look dreadful: when a middle-class white driving on the wrong side of the tracks hears his car engine die and faces the menaces of a truculent black teenage gang, he is rescued by Simon, a lanky modest black tow-truck driver who resembles the D. W. Griffith 'good negro' and Abe Lincoln rolled into one; Mack, the white, then helps Simon's sister relocate away from her bombed-out, blood-stained neighbourhood and fixes up Simon with a black girl from his office, Jane. The shades of paternalism are inescapable. Meanwhile, a cynical exploitation flick director who has been jolted out of his habits when shot by a mugger returns to justifying his films as reflections of the violence and rage at work in the land; worse still, he travesties nature's majesty and the film's own title by speaking of the rage's enormity as emerging from a Grand Canyon. At the film's close, Mack and Simon stand with their families before the Grand Canyon and say wonderingly, 'It isn't all bad'.

So how does Kasdan rescue this scenario? He does so by presenting it as an exploded dream. No longer quite believable, it can be treated simply as material, rather as the auteurist of Sarris's theories redeemed studio stereotypes with formal innovation. The film's richness and mystery, however, come from the persistence of narrative coincidences that are now inexplicable and seem to point to something beyond themselves: too good to be true on certain occasions, they are like events in a dream, and this combines with the oneiric quality of much of the film to suggest the possibility of an invisible author. This author should not be taken as an image of Kasdan himself – *Grand Canyon* is not self-referential – but rather as the source of miracles. There are repeated hints that Los Angeles may indeed be the city of angels, though Kasdan's refusal to go beyond hints preserves a numinous quality, rescuing the plot from banality. The pressure of the supernatural is elusive, a now-you-see-it-now-you-don't thread that nevertheless *must* be there to hold everything together. The dream of reconciliation is poignant and deeply affecting precisely because its status as dream – not reality – is emphasized throughout: the soundtrack often breathes dread, the simmering of the unexpected before it erupts (preshocks before the earthquake): one's home may be machine-gunned, a mugger may shoot one in the leg, an earthquake may hit as one makes dinner, a running passer-by may shatter a girl's car window when she halts. The danger of Los Angeles life lends the American dream – the dream of the melting pot – the haunting quality of afterlife: Kasdan is a man trying to paste together the slivers of a shattered heirloom. It is not he who explodes the dream, but his knowledge of the reality of modern America.

Grand Canyon ought perhaps to be titled 'Los Angeles': it is about how people are to become angels for one another and how strange and improbable it is, nevertheless, when this occurs. Characters wonder if the good things are luck or fate: as Simon and Mack drive away from potential disaster, Simon says, 'We just got lucky'; Jane and Simon wonder if their meeting was fate. And Mack for his part muses about the identity of the girl who once pulled him back from the path of a bus; she wore the cap of his favourite team, the Pittsburgh Pirates, and then disappeared. Her ontological status may give one pause. Being on the brink is an essential condition: 'There are so many ways to buy it', Simon reflects. But the dangerous edge of things may also be the site of the miraculous: Simon talks of having sat on the edge of the Grand Canyon; Claire wonders if her discovery of a baby in the bushes was a miracle. Constant threat makes good moments seem miraculous; yet the way characters 'are there' for one another at key moments – simply cropping up, as if materialized out of nowhere – breathes a providential air: the single policeman calms the jittery girl fixated on a married man; Simon arrives as the black teenager readies his gun; Claire responds to the wailing of the abandoned baby. Kasdan's least successfully rendered character is Davis, the Hollywood exploitation director, suggesting that Kasdan cannot quite place himself in this world. (He is in a sense bifurcated between Mack and Davis, who are related in subterranean ways. Davis flirts with girls on the Hollywood lot rather as the initial roving of the camera after girls at the Lakers game has been a concealed point-of-view shot from Mack's position, both revealing and soft-pedalling his infidelity, as does the rest of the film.) If Davis's determination to move to 'life-affirming' pictures is followed by a reversion to type, does that make him a De Palma to Mack's Kasdan, or Kasdan's own dark double? Not quite, for *Grand Canyon* is not 'life-affirming' in any banal sense: it is well aware of L.A. violence, a subliminal presence tinting the smooth camera-work with back-of-the-mind dread, yet 'it isn't all bad'. And if the goodness has a source, it is perhaps in Claire, Mack's wife, who reaches out to the child's cry in the bushes, who has second thoughts about changing her jogging route to avoid an alley where the homeless sleep. (As she looks back in reality at a wino who menaced her in a dream, the clap of light that precedes the cut has a mystical edge.) She reaches into the hidden places of L.A. Presences, moments of grace, thread through the racial and other tensions, but Kasdan makes no attempt to pluck out the mystery's heart. That mystery hovers around the film's borders, cradling it and the characters, soft invisible palms one nevertheless knows are there (they have no color, the narrator's invisible palms).

PART FOUR
Lost in the stars

CHAPTER VIII
Private dancers: Valentino
and Madonna

Myth and ideology

A myth may be defined as an inconsistent story whose inconsistencies are not perceived by its receiver – either because its oral transmission prevents one from ranging freely over it, as one can over a written text, to pick out the gaps, or because gaps are deliberately engineered to yield the sense of mystery that enhances the myth's authority (as well as that of the priest or soothsayer, who is needed to interpret it). The story's version may form a cycle, but the cycle's unity will be a pseudounity. The inconsistencies may generate multiform gods or goddesses as protagonists.

The modern art-form to which the word 'myth' has most often been applied is that of cinema. Here the diverse stories are united under the double aegis of genre (the cycle) and the star system: the star's presence in a variety of films may make it seem that the system subserves the individual, but more often than not the star does not drive the vehicle but is chauffeured blindfold to an unknown destination. No one film constitutes a myth; it is the serial parade of industry production that does so. The cult film, meanwhile, will be a melting-pot of genres: as Eco describes *Casablanca*, a conference of movie archetypes.[1] What is worth noting, however, is that the cult work shuffles a plethora of incompatible stock situations so rapidly as to create by legerdemain the illusion of transcendence of the stereotypically based film system (the system of genre). Here the types are Dolby stereo-broadcast into an echo chamber; information overload prevents one from 'placing' the work. In its apparent transcendence of the genre system, the cult film is in fact its keystone, the moment at which the system seems to 'speak the truth': the moment we cynics all treasure. It justifies the genre's contemporaneity by magnetizing the random filings of its historical moment into the configuration of necessity. In becoming a series of films, this one film becomes a myth: and as Mircea Eliade has pointed out, a myth *repeats* the sacred time, the time before time (the time of the hero's origin).[2] The dominance of repetition persuades the mythical eye to either ignore difference or novelty or simply perceive it as modulation of an unchanged basic form. Hence, the domain of the mythical is that of the unchanging, where the social order can be confused with the natural one because history has been bracketed. History's absorption into nature lies, of course, at the heart of ideology, which draws paradoxical sustenance from the unpredictability of technological change: since the future's direction defies imagination (too many variables are brought into play by the multiple linkages of the world economy to permit reliable model-making), one may as well act as if it did not exist. Thus, one lives, without long-term projects, in a perpetual present – the realm of ideology.

Where once the Hollywood axis turned upon genre, however, it is now on the star's axis that its wheel revolves. Story and teleology are discarded as apparent impediments to individualism: a destination is less a destiny than an intolerable constraint upon one's shape-changing. This is now a general condition in the film industry, best exemplified by Madonna and her regal reception at Cannes 1991, but it had been adumbrated in film's silent days by the career of Valentino (whence this essay's dual focus). Each is a dancer one cannot tell from the dance, shape-changing minute by minute. In them the star embodies the fetish form of individuality: drawing on the strength of the crowd that stands behind him or her, but never admitting dependence – incarnating multiple lives to shine aloof from mortality, perhaps 'pale for weariness' at 'wandering companionless' at times, but accepting this as the price of preeminence. Baudrillard's definition of the fetish is strikingly relevant:

Fetishism is not the sanctification of a certain object, or value (in which case one might hope to see it disappear in our age, when the liberalization of values and the abundance of objects would 'normally' tend to desanctify them). It is the sanctification of the system as such, of the commodity as system.[3]

The key phrase here is the final one: the fetish is 'the commodity as system'. It is an individual object or person that stands in for the system as a whole (it has multiple tie-ins and spin-offs, like a revolving galaxy), *pars pro toto* – permitting the exhilaration and vertigo of totalization. The pathos of individuation is alien to it. The seductiveness of totalization lies in its apparent mastery of the experience of death. It is displaced by orgasm's near death. The star's existence on the screen is an out-of-body experience. De Quincey writes of the experience of 'a lady' (in fact, his mother), and the vision vouchsafed her during near drowning in childhood: 'In a moment, in the twinkling of an eye, every act – every design of her past life – arraying themselves not as a succession but as parts of a co-existence'.[4]

It is the simultaneity that is remarkable: time is spatialized into a single fetishized moment, as it is in the multiple lives of the human fetish one deems a goddess (her fundamental form – Warhol's Marilyn – endlessly recoloured, endlessly the same). The seeming self-sacrifice of identification with the star allows one both to satisfy the death instinct and outlive a death redefined as the moment of orgasm. It is thus hardly surprising that the film deity is always a love god or goddess. When the lights go down, the stage is set for love. Our step into the dark has not lost the world but permitted its total possession in condensed form, in the image of the star. His or her status as world is apparent in the magnitude of the on-screen image. We know this is not so, but...we suspend our disbelief (for a fetish is something we know to be a substitute – in this case, for the whole of humanity – but one we refuse to separate from what it represents: like onomatopoeia, as beloved of the Romantics as is the star, it creates a mutual mimesis of signified and sign to obscure the sign's arbitrariness and possible unreliability). Thus, for instance, we know Monroe is not a goddess, but we call her one. We read the sheer nervous rapidity of her flickering moods as the spiritual sign of divine flame, not the fire reflected in the panic-stricken eyes of the woman tied to the stake. We know that the Material Girl is not Marilyn, but we assent to her self-presentation as such, which draws lost time back into the fetishized moment. The world of intertextual stars – and the star is always intertextual – is one in which absence is always redefined as presence. The token respect for mutability prevents its real acknowledgement.

Valentino and the love that knows no harm

Cinematic love knows no harm: the phantom's blows always pass through one. But then, conversely, so do his or her embraces. The dark side of the utopian ideal is thus abandonment. Perhaps this is why films concerned with seduction so often show us turned backs or confront the would-be seducer with a turned back. (In the twenties it surely also stood for the partial absence present in the star's silence.)[5] To win the attention of one who turns away is to give conclusive proof of one's seductive power. And if, as Miriam Hansen has argued, the girl of Valentino's dreams is the one he looks at first, her appearance with a turned back underlines her lack of the empowered brazen gaze of the vamp.[6]

In *The Eagle*, Valentino first appears in pursuit of the runaway carriage bearing his future sweetheart (though for much of the film the love-theme will be eclipsed by that of revenge and by the lover's failure to know her own feelings as love). It is always an older woman who seeks to vamp Valentino. Her efforts may be comic (the dumpy, mannish Czarina in *The Eagle*) or menacing (Doña Sol in *Blood and Sand*). The would-be vamp is surely repudiated because she parodies – and so devalues – the image of the mother, whose first look at the male infant she repeats at an inappropriately later juncture: the look is now infantilizing. In *The Eagle,* when Valentino halts the errant carriage he finds two women inside – one modest and young and wearing the anachronistic twenties hat that shows her to be the Valentino fan wish-fulfillingly inserted into the film; and her older chaperone, who simpers that the gallant rescue reminds her of her younger days. When Valentino then follows the departing carriage with his telescope, it is comic that the older woman should lean out to wave to him; he is first disconcerted, then amused. The two women in the carriage stage the scenario of acceptable desire: woman's image has to be split. The older woman who wishes to become a lover – to turn Valentino into prey by viewing *his* retreating back – is transgressive, like the Czarina. As Valentino flees her advances, it is nicely ironic that he should be handed a note from his father asking that he appeal to her for redress in the case of the family's loss of its estates – after all, he has appealed to her already (mutely, unwillingly, as befits a silent film), for she finds him very appealing.

In *Blood and Sand,* meanwhile, Valentino repeatedly solicits the attention of women who have turned away from him. The turned backs he encounters belong both to the (paradoxically named)[7] 'good girl' Carmen, who repeatedly turns away, hurt, after seeing her toreador husband with another woman (be she his lover Doña Sol, or even his mother) and to the vamp, who seduces one by seeming to belong to another man whom one envies (usually an older one; so a subtext of the Oedipal, and of mimetic desire, is present): as Doña Sol strums her harp, one sees her naked back from Valentino's point of view, before he approaches her. The unacknowledged unity of vamp and good girl is revealed by the similarity of the positions they occupy vis-à-vis Valentino; he rules the image of woman only by dividing it. Seen from behind, the woman is anonymous, any woman, and hence *Everywoman:* to possess her is to possess all women. Her anonymity permits her male viewer to project onto her the archetype of the 'one woman' (the mother?) that the hero protests is the only person he loves. In each case it is the turned back that attracts the masochistic seducer: he has to prove himself compulsively and is not interested in women who offer themselves to him. (When a flamenco dancer offers her lips in close-up, he pushes her away, and at first he resists the embraces of Doña Sol.)

In a world in which everyone applauds Valentino (images of applauding crowds recur in the film), a turned back is a provocation. The repressed anxiety of the macho male is so chronic that a single sign of discontent suffices to shake him; his 'Casanova complex' requires its extinction through seduction. Only barriers attract him. (They express his sense that love is forbidden, a feeling reflected in the double bind that associates close-ups with transgression throughout the film – for example, the close-up of the flamenco dancer or that of the ring that seal's Valentino's union with Doña Sol, depicting a snake, and establishing him as the Mark Antony to her Cleopatra.) The flamenco dancer's rejection is followed by a cut to Carmen, being serenaded on her balcony, *behind bars.* Doña Sol, meanwhile, is alluring when she stands above the toreador (on the balcony at the bullfight, on the steps down which her dress's train flows), embodying the unattainability of both the prepossessed mother-figure and the riches for which the poor boy pays with death in the ring. (The bullring rhymes with Doña Sol's ring: it is the ring – in both senses – that slays the toreador.) Failure to persuade a woman to turn her face to him issues in death. When Doña Sol looks towards her husband, away from the toreador, she has turned her thumb down on him.

The Eagle, for its part, unfolds under the aegis of unknowing. Valentino plays Dubrovsky, whom the Czarina outlaws on his spurning of her advances: he is a Robin Hood figure seeking to avenge his father's dispossession by the brutal Kyrilla. But the Black Eagle in one incarnation is Monsieur LeBlanc in another, insinuating himself into Kyrilla's household with a double purpose – to be near Mascha, Kyrilla's daughter, with whom he is smitten, and to exact revenge. The two functions are mutually frustrating.

But Dubrovsky is not alone in his failure of self-knowledge; Mascha requires considerable time before recognizing her feelings for him as love and grasping the unity of Le Blanc with the Black Eagle. The film flirts at coy length with possibilities of recognition. When Mascha tells LeBlanc, her French tutor, that if the Black Eagle were there, 'I'd plead with him not to make vengeance his only aim in life', we may wonder whether she is being subtle, feigning ignorance, or really does not know. And there is of course irony in the fact that Valentino does indeed have other things than revenge on his mind. Definitive recognition does not occur until his defense of her from a lunging bear calls to mind her roadside encounter with the Eagle – and a shot of him in the Black Eagle mask appears where he is standing. Nevertheless, even this recognition is incomplete, as is indicated by the mask. The moment has been preceded by the most succinct scenic summation of self-unknowing. Underlining 'Vengeance is mine, saith the Lord', Mascha places a Bible on Dubrovsky's desk and retreats to the wardrobe. He responds by turning to 'an eye for an eye'. His citation of the maxim causes us, however, to suspect diminished commitment to its message, for we recall his earlier 'an eye for an eye, and a horse for a

donkey' on replacing a poor girl's confiscated donkey with the confis-
cator's horse. But we cannot be sure as yet. He opens the wardrobe's
right-hand door and pulls out a pistol; Mascha watches horrified from
her position on the left. Concealed in the wardrobe, she is Dubrovsky's
feminine side, on the left hand (where the heart is), not the right,
which acts and seeks 'the right'. Mascha becomes an American girl
trying to incline him from Latin vendetta to Christian forgiveness (to
focus on the other head of the Latin Eagle – Latin lover). Dubrovsky's
masked, shadowy figure leaning over her father is a horror film image.
Wielding a pistol herself, she disarms, but cannot shoot him. Only on
finding his pistol unloaded does she grasp that vengeance is now the
subordinate component in his constitution. His is indeed the love that
knows no harm.

And yet . . . one of the seducer's most potent weapons for luring his
prey is to play dead: as Hansen notes, Valentino is often transfixed by
the sight of the girl of his dreams.[8] The hunter dissimulates his preda-
tory purpose by adopting a vulnerable position, luring the girl to commit herself without himself being committed. Playing dead attracts the
kiss of life. In approaching, the girl is a mother whose power of seduction is denied and replaced with life-giving power: retrospectively, the
older woman's seduction of the child is rewritten as child-initiated. It
is Valentino's personal assurance concerning his masculinity, his secure inner distance from the often effeminate roles he is called on to
play, that permits him to act thus. An Italian, inevitably type-cast as
the gigolo, he seems to say, 'If they want a Latin lover, I'll give them
one with a vengeance', disdainful of the cliché he is asked to embody
and of those who view Italians through the distorting spectacles of
stereotype. The most important props in the performance of the Latin
lover are cigarettes and the whip. In the case of the cigarette, it is not
only the phallic prop that is important; equally so is the smoke whose
gradual serpentine glide envelops the girl with a slow, indirect seduction. Valentino becomes quasi-feminine, a cloud, to enwrap her gently,
harmlessly. Moreover, the apparent narcissism that takes pleasure in
itself alone – in its own cigarette – reinforces the air of harmlessness.
(It is a narcissism – a 'to-be-looked-at-ness'[9] – that may facilitate female identification with him.) To control smoke is the acme of poise.
That poise had been evident at the very start of Valentino's career, in
Four Horsemen of the Apocalypse: in an early scene, for instance, Julio, the Valentino character, on asking his mother for money, stands
quite still at emphasized moments – for example, when resting his
right hand on his knee. He presents himself as a picture for contemplation, a fetish object. In this film his primary erotic prop is a paintbrush; he is 'using painting as a pretext to surround himself with
women', the intertitle informs us. As he stands at the easel, smoking,

with paintbrush in hand, he is doubly phallicized. The ability to hold a cigarette in his mouth without touching it a sign of consummately nonchalant erotic control.

There is little suspense in Valentino's films.[10] This may be because there is no need for it when the work's most important element – the star – is ever-present. Critical evocations of the Oedipal motion of classical Hollywood narrative are fatally weakened by their omission of the often antinarrativizing effect of star presence. Valentino's ability to occupy sadistic and masochistic positions alternately testifies to the star's totalizing effect – one that situates him beyond narrative.[11] However, it can be argued that the sadistic and masochistic elements have differing aetiologies, the sadism being erotically grounded, reflecting male power over women and the masochism rooted in class and race in the Italian immigrant's inferior position in the United States. If this is so, then *Blood and Sand,* which combines the two, becomes a privileged text, permitting one to supplement Miriam Hansen's more exclusively Freudian feminist perspective with considerations of racial and class factors. If Valentino's persona does indeed activate such factors, then Hansen's contention that its 'deepest, most effective layer...is that of the whipping boy' becomes questionable.[12] Only a purely Freudian analysis could deem this the case. It can hardly be argued, for instance, that the whipping boy is typical of the fiction of adolescent girls prone to picture themselves as male whipping boys. Does not the hero of boys' fiction also suffer capture and torture, a rite of passage that precedes his victory? Is not flagellation a widespread element in Victorian male fantasy, not just in 'popular fiction devoured by adolescent girls'?[13] The foreigner's horsewhipping at the hands of the father (*Son of the Sheikh*) is the test he has to pass to be worthy of the bride. His suffering under the paternal whip corresponds to a recurrent feature of Valentino films – the generation gap underlying young lovers' (and young cinema-goers') persecution by the old. The father's whipping strips the lover of menace (unstopping the springs of the girl's maternal pity), confirming his love's status as one that knows no harm. Any threat may be met by renewed invocation of paternal protection, for the woman may well wish to take out such an insurance policy. After all, did not Julio in *Four Horsemen of the Apocalypse* promise no harm to Marguerite Laurier (glancing slyly at the camera as he did so), only to overpower her incipient resistance in his artist's studio? Valentino may redeem one from conventional love – arranged marriages such as Marguerite's, unsophisticated American males – but the uncharted seas of unconventional eros can be deep and dangerous.

Nevertheless, the whips that seem to be a Valentino film trade mark more often rest in his hands than in anybody else's. Perhaps it is less the whipping-boy than the whip that is the works' hero, for it fuses cigarette and smoke, the male and female symbols already alluded to. When the whip cracks, the smoke's drifting line hardens, masculinized. Instantaneously its flicker annuls the distance between look and touch, and so fulfils the fantasy of the female spectator: Valentino's presence in the auditorium becomes real, roping one into the action. An aside from the screen, it is a logical extension of the glance at the camera that punctuates the assurances Julio gives Marguerite in *Four Horsemen of the Apocalypse*. Violence breaches the gap between self and other, auditorium and film: the fan's wish to climb on-stage (to clutch a piece of the star) is fulfilled in the *coup de foudre* with which he lassoos her from the midst of the assembly of other watching heads.

Miniaturizing the *Gesamtkunstwerk*

If myth is achieved through the shuffling and serial alignment of inconsistent images, then its main abode now could well be the rock video. A compact, transistorized version of the *Gesamtkunstwerk*, the rock video lends credibility to a rock no longer fired and fed by the late sixties' hopes of upheaval: unable to concentrate upon either image or music, the receiver is overwhelmed by a surfeit of information. (In the terms of cybernetics, information becomes indistinguishable from the noise a group like Slade extends into a third sense by inviting us to *feel* it.) Nevertheless, only the speed with which the images are dealt deceives the eye. Removed from their original contexts, the borrowed, intertextual images of rock video lose their immanent capacity for development and so become trivial. The rapid fire of instanciations of a startling presence rapidly becomes monotonous, a flattened homogeneity. The rock video, like the *Gesamtkunstwerk*, is a merger of bankrupts.[14]

At the centre of the videos stand the rock gods and goddesses. Like the protagonists of classical mythology, they derive divine status from the multiplicity of forms they are able to adopt. Diana is tri-form and Madonna bi-form: both whore and virgin in *Like a Virgin;* both showbiz star and girl grateful for a humble bouquet in *Material Girl;* both peep-show performer and runaway big sister in *Open Your Heart.* Dual identity gives the goddess the best of both worlds, allowing her to step outside and watch (survive) herself, preserving primary narcissism into adult life: in the *Who's That Girl?* video, she views a self so well known that the cursory notation of a cartoon is sufficient to identify her. Rock videos broadcast a slew of incompatible images, and Madonna is the most proficient rock star of a new kind – the rock video star. The rock video is the appropriate art-form of a fast-track, multitrack world. At present, as Jacques Attali notes, music 'is unavoidable, as if, in a world now devoid of meaning, a background noise were increasingly necessary to give people a sense of security'.[15] One's detachment from one's own actions – be they routinized assembly line work or the sense of 'going through the motions' that afflicts one bemired in a single career – permits simultaneous prosecution of another line of action. One does homework with the radio on or – like academic Madonna-fan Camille Paglia – writes with the TV on.[16] This multiplication of channels of activity implements the internalized imperatives of consumerism, as one seeks to do as much as possible at once, to 'make the most of life' in a society lacking the compensatory hope of an afterlife. Attali deems music prophetic. Like the prophecies of most oracles, however, those of music achieve their effect by resisting disconfirmation and fulfilment: the very openness (or vagueness) of music's conceptual meaning allows one to attribute various significances to it. Music ecumenically fuses meaning with meaninglessness. (It is thus hardly surprising that most fans do not know the words of their favourite songs – Ronald Reagan's use of Springsteen's 'Born in the USA' being the classic instance.) Music becomes a form of ideology that transcends ideology ('Rock is the only true religion', the graffito tells us): anyone can subscribe to it, for it involves rhythms and patterns, not concepts. Although music is the only art-form in which the child-genius is found, the extreme simplicity of rock's rhythms ensures the participation of children who lack genius also. Music may appear to bypass ideology, and so escape the general disillusion with failed faiths, but it is one itself: one of regression. Only for the fan is the explosion in the realm of the senses a prelogical, biological revelation; the marketing agencies (and those stars who are agencies themselves, such as Madonna) are well aware of what they are doing.

Rock's message is denial of origin. This can be utopian or ideological. In its utopian mode it posits a world in which no one is limited by background: whites meet blacks on the grounds of R & B; the working class accedes to riches and fame; and white trash becomes a goddess (Madonna). But at the same time the rock video's presentation of the lip-synching, gyrating singer represses the messy moment of music's performance and creates the alarming image of the omnipotent performer. (There is something rather chilling in the mass of one-arm salutes that greet the performers in a Bon Jovi or Van Halen video, and Madonna's cropped platinum blonde hair in *Open Your Heart* awakens echoes of the Aryan ideal – the video itself becoming a miniaturized version of *Cabaret*.) The endlessly malleable self that denies origins (love 'em and leave 'em) moves mindlessly with (or a hair's breadth ahead of) the times, besotted with a progress whose cost it never ventures to consider (the cost of Madonna's move from provocation to soft porn, for instance). Where rock denies origin, rock videos go even further by virtually effacing all memory of the musical experience of the prevideo era. The clean sweep is both exhilarating and barbaric.

In *Faust*, Goethe's hero rewrites the opening sentence of the Gospel of St. John, which ascribes primacy to the Word, as 'In the Beginning was the Deed'. In the modern world, originary force is ascribed to Desire. In the realm of Desire all images are glossy, sexualized and unattainable: Desire is chronically unsatisfied, for the objects in which it seeks release are fetishes, phantoms of something forever absent. In this consumerist world of many mansions, the chief one reserved for the young is that of MTV, in which the rickety partitions separating programme from commercial in American TV collapse, causing a pansexualism that stands for the omnipresence of the advertisement; the male lead singer winks and ogles as shamelessly as the unpeople of a commercial.

The lack of linearity and teleology in MTV has been interpreted in some quarters as indicative of teen attunement to the rhythms of postmodernism. It is an argument that replays McLuhan's sixties insistence that a TV-trained youth enjoyed mystic synchronization with the electronic spirit of the age. The absence of teleology in rock videos and MTV programmes, however, is less a sign of joyful transcendence of the monotonies of plot and coherence than an imperative never to switch off (rocking around the clock with a vengeance, as Ann Kaplan notes):[17] the rhythm of continual substitution that pervades the part, the record, trains one to identify with the substitutive movement of the whole, the station. One 'buys' (swallows) everything in the substitutive train in the perhaps unconscious hope that it may include the one thing one wants. A denizen of the pre-MTV era might assume that the images lose authority through the double bind that condemns them to choose between tautologous reiteration of the lyrics or their ignoral; in actuality the image seems to have garnered authority (hardly surprising, given the inventiveness and elliptical quality of many image-tracks), displacing the lyrics to the level of noise: most fans, as already noted, do not know the words of their favourite songs. Only a few lines, or the title, remain in the mind, the detritus left from the shipwreck of the lyrics. It is possible, meanwhile, that the frequent lack of fit between image, words and music generates a sense of subconscious panic. The outpouring of disposable images can offer a dreamlike exhilaration, but it also threatens dissolution of identity. The possibility of dream becoming nightmare in the nausea of excessive consumption is dispelled by the descent of a deus ex machina, the star, who rescues one from chaos (or centres that chaos) rather as the fascist (fetishized) leader 'saves society from anarchy' through his personality cult. If videos resemble dreams, as Marsha Kinder has argued,[18] the rapid eye movement soon exhausts itself, allowing reality to return (within the text, as the singer; outside it, as the VJ). The contexts that anchor the image flow render it merely a 'minor apocalypse' (to borrow a phrase from Tadeusz Konwicki), a minor-league imitation of the postmodernism of the big brother. The reality principle is a watch-dog possessing three heads.

Most important of these is the performer: it is almost de rigueur for a rock video to return periodically to base by presenting images of the performer. In part this has a legitimizing function: it demonstrates the youth (and/or vigour – that substitute for youth among ageing rock-stars) the performer shares with the audience. If the viewer experiences the performer as an oasis of meaning in the midst of an imagistic sandstorm, the rock video is not 'decentred' at all but centred on the performer and the selling of his or her image. MTV begins each video by listing the song title and the name of the performer (from whose demiurgic presence a world issues, so no directorial credit is required), plus the record label – all the information required to achieve speedy and effective purchase. The first concentric circle surrounding the performer is the stage or recording studio. Video after video will display young people dancing in the streets: rock creates a holiday as music radiates from the performer, who is magically able to reproduce a studio sound in the streets and project his or her voice without microphones. Waves of music wash over the world. The streets are hot with desire, with the laziness of summer or winter break, but the overflow of sound-waves onto the streets also mirrors the star's ego: only a street provides a large enough auditorium to encompass the prospective audience. The expansiveness that moves from studio to a street representing the world is quite realistic from the point of view of the performer singing in the 'universal' language of English, and with the considerable forces of First World promotion agencies at his or her beck and call. The conspicuous outlay of high-tech production shows that nothing succeeds like success; after all, without a video one cannot plug into the TV promotion system. The street dancing often contravenes the protests of straw-men fuddy-duddies or the police. It is not the possibility of revolutionary protest that arouses police interest, however; a token police presence is needed to code the dancing as enticing transgression. The dance is played out in the pedestrian precinct of youth culture, and when the cops finally start dancing too (adult stiffness melted by youthful spontaneity) the sheer improbability of the imaginary reconciliation of the age gap shows just how far the videos are from reality. The protest movements and trade unions abandon the streets (there was no union parade in New York in 1986) because the performers have taken them over.

Another context anchoring the movement of the video is the sound-track. We had been prepared for the endlessness of MTV (the insatiability of a desire reared on junk food) by the endlessness of radio; synaesthesia transfers to one sense the lessons learned by another. MTV is less postmodernism for the young than colour radio – the enormous TV set the apotheosis of a boom box grown too big to carry. Unlike radio, however, MTV has little or no past. Songs from the prevideo era are marginalized, except where past songs can be dumped as a flavour of the month to undercut the products of the present. As the sphere of music consumption splits between an endlessly shifting amnesiac present on MTV and the preterition of radio (hence, the emergence of stations playing nothing but oldies), the oldie is granted a token presence on TV to hide the extent to which the market feeds on forgetting. The sheer rarity of the old shows how little of the past was worth remembering. Rock tells the truth about the past, blissfully unaware that it too will suffer the same deserved fate. Rock's translation to cable TV is yet another stage in the process that expropriated the music blacks originated: the black carries a boom box (it is *Radio* Raheem who appears in Spike Lee's *Do the Right Thing*), and the white squats before the TV. A Vanilla Ice is the exception that proves the rule of separation.

The third anchor holding the pirate lightship of MTV in place is the VJ. MTV's phone-ins and calls for audience participation (Madonna – wanting a good video on the cheap? – invites us to make one for her *True Blue* and win $25,000) are premodern, not postmodern: an antidote to the vertigo of endlessly plastic images. The lightning transformations are grounded by the safeness of the home environment mirrored on the screen: the MTV studio has been likened to a garage. The songs it purveys thus become basement tapes, and we the initiated insiders. The studio's unpretentiousness connects our world with that of the studio and the performers we can almost touch: MTV as an enormous, insanely catholic fanzine. Its minimalism corresponds to the idealism that prevents the young seeing themselves as consumers. The minimalist format reconciles celebrity glitz with the homespun and shows one can have both: are not the VJs themselves celebrities, though they appear in a homespun context? The media mediate between their own contradictions and so achieve the illusion of reconciliation. In doing so, they replicate the structure of many rock videos themselves, which alternate story and performance: Madonna's *Material Girl* has a double script, one presenting her as Monroe in *Diamonds Are a Girl's Best Friend*, the other showing her traditional wooing by a man with flowers. What makes *Material Girl* a particularly witty and subtly duplicitous video, however, is the double take it performs around the double plot. Madonna, the home-town girl, prefers unassuming men to the bigshots who rain diamonds upon her, but her virtue is rewarded with diamonds nevertheless, for the man who wins her with simple flowers is a big shot who has overheard her telephone denigration of men who give lavish gifts (and is played by Keith Carradine, already a star himself). The story-line may seem to relegate *Diamonds Are a Girl's Best Friend* to a mere dance routine, a professional necessity, but the number's sheer bravura, Madonna's final departure with the executive (albeit in disguise – but there is no hint that she might bridle later at the deception) and the title of her own framing song – 'Material Girl' – indicate that in actuality it is the portrayal of the simple girl that is the act. The dialectic of innocence and knowing is very like that of Monroe herself; and so it is clear that Madonna is seeking the mantle of Monroe, not just the colour of her hair. (The Madonna wanna-bes are themselves imitating a wanna-be.) It is this duality, of course, that permits one to become a goddess: in becoming all things to all men – and no particular thing to anyone – one becomes a female equivalent of the president, who has abandoned the realm of political programmes for that of sheer, undying symbolism: fields of wheat, flags, wide-open spaces. Like him, one is qualified to appear simultaneously on all available channels. MTV is just the start – the foot in the door.

Vox pop, vox dei: desperately seeking Marilyn

Myths, according to Mircea Eliade, are born of repetition and restage the drama of the time before time, the era when the rules of the game for all subsequent ages were laid down. The time before time is that of one's first years on earth, with their insistent, shaping, uncomprehended pressure upon one. For the baby boomers, they were the fifties; as time passed, it was hardly surprising that the horizon of awareness for nostalgia should shift to the sixties. For Madonna, the sacred figure to whose fame she seeks to accede was most refulgent on the cusp of those periods (taking her innocence from the former, her knowingness from the latter; between Doris Day and Warhol): Marilyn Monroe. Madonna's own initial and ambiguous name (of which more later) meant that even at the start of her quest, she was more than half-way to her goal. Indeed, the letter 'M' seems to mark the point of intersection of several of the key modern media myths, which might run – in a Max Headroom stutter – from the Ms of Bond and the McDonald's golden arches to those of Marilyn and Madonna herself. They are perhaps linked as code for the unity of authority, money and infantile sexuality: the 'mmm' of the child at the sight of food and mother (of mother as food); M as the logo of erect breasts; and the M of the Madonna Ron Kierkegaard terms 'Madollar', headed for heaven in what one may term the 'Concluding Unscientific Postscript' to his brilliant *Shooting Stars* cartoon book. But if Madonna began by using Monroe's image to multiply herself in a hall of mirrors to the power of a goddess – entering the emporium of abstraction and exchange, in which new lamps are best if they are also golden oldies – she later seemed to have played sorcerer's apprentice: no longer able to demythologize and remythologize the Monroe image, as she had done in *Material Girl*, she became the messageless medium of its reincarnation in *Who's That Girl?* Like Teresa Russell in Roeg's fatally named *Insignificance*, she surrendered her own selfhood to the fetishes of blondeness and cuteness. Thereafter, aware perhaps of the débâcle of *Who's That Girl?*, Madonna relinquished the effort – one that had succeeded in *Material Girl* – to emulate Monroe's staggering, quicksilver synthesis of naturalness and knowingness. She became simply knowing instead.

In the strange world of rock video, *Who's That Girl?* could be number one even as the movie bombed everywhere. Indeed, the success of the former is probably dependent on the failure of the latter, for the video thrives on the elliptical presentation of images a film would require to be fleshed out (to be given narrative detail in a plausible world); the indirections of videos are those of a partial memory, recycling fragments of old stories, or a trailer, giving snippets of the new story in which song or star features. In the *Who's That Girl?* movie, meanwhile, wildness is adopted as a tried and tested property that had shown its value shortly before in *Something Wild.* But since wildness sanitized by cuteness is simply calculating and hypocritical, the result is the same sort of self-cancelling flop as *Shanghai Surprise.* If the title of that earlier movie suggested Sternbergian delights, it was sunk by the inconsistency Madonna brings into movies from video: by the disparity between the demure words emerging from the missionary's (!) mouth and the irrepressible streetwise shrugs of her brows. The binary, flip-flop oscillations of the video aesthetic subverted the characterization, emptying the personality cult of personality. Things had been different in the *Material Girl* video.

Material Girl, of course, was a self-apotheosis. To have claimed the mantle of Monroe in an earlier video would have seemed mere absurd presumption. To do so after the success of *Like a Virgin* was simply to seem to acknowledge that one had one's foot on the stairway to heaven and could go all the way to the top. 'I feel I am becoming a goddess', one can almost hear her whispering, echoing Vespasian. The cannibalization of *Diamonds Are a Girl's Best Friend* was part of the social climbing celebrated in the song's words and the video's staircases.

The pastiche of Monroe was more than pastiche, however, for Madonna really is like Monroe in being less a person than a cloud of images. But whereas Monroe belonged in the cartoons of the fifties, in which females protruded from tight cleavage, Madonna is a creature from a fable pretending to be a human being. If Madonna is in some ways more a cartoon figure than a person, she registers the fact with empty self-congratulation in tho *Who's That Girl?* vidco. Having accn *Material Girl,* one realizes how the slithering two-dimensional vamp had been wasted in *Desperately Seeking Susan* – Susan Seidelman's wooden fable of a suburban housewife's liberation from yuppie self-dissatisfaction, laced with borrowings from Rivette, screwball comedy and *Belle de jour.* With her Bugs Bunny voice, her sucked-in cheeks and her cartoon air of detachment from everything she did, the early Madonna brought radiance to sleaze: it became the epic theatre of a sexuality reduced to quotable gestures. She became so successful because she showed how punk disorder could become elegant, all it needed being a self-disbelieving all-American smile to defuse the intensity of rage or depression and a touch of glamour to dispel the boredom. The smile identified with the mother's indulgence of her daughter dressing up in her own rags (as did the early Madonna's largely preteen audience, one of her early concerts being collective female narcissism starting small but already writ large). Punk becomes tolerable through severing its links with British working-class ennui, through reclassification as merely a passing phase. Unfortunately, it was only a phase for Madonna also.

Both virgin and whore, Madonna is a trickster goddess: Our Lady of Rock as Belladonna, the Lady of Situations. Preteens identified with her early image because it fused the sex symbol with the world of the cartoon figures with which they had grown up. The sex symbol made it clear that she was only a symbol: she (and her preteen fans) were celebrating their nonavailability, teasingly poised between feminism and mere pubescence (in a sense, the postsexual and the presexual). A Warhol paradox, the early Madonna presented herself to the public as pure image in order to preserve her privacy behind it. Madonna now, however, has the porn star's readiness for everything: one may not be able to touch the screen, but one can do what one likes with the performer in one's fantasies. *Open Your Heart* takes this step, with a tiny afterthought, as the windows come down at the peep-show allowing the rock queen censorious revenge on those she provoked to look at her in the first place. *Justify My Love* and *Truth or Dare* dispose even of the afterthought. Madonna's early success involved a coupling of feminism with traditional female display, presenting an oxymoron that could not but intrigue, a riddle demanding, and refusing, to be solved. The ambiguity that is the hallmark of the mythical figure was marvellously focused in her name. If 'Madonna', the name of one who was not merely *like* a virgin, suggested a pert pact with the devil, the fact that it was her real name offered the possibility of innocence and redemption. Madonna may subsequently have discarded the swinging crosses because she knew she was playing with fire: the disapproval of the American public. The shock effect served to gain attention, but she was neither willing nor able to elaborate it into a programme. Moreover, if, as Ernest Jones notes, it is Greek Orthodox belief that 'children born on Christmas Day are doomed to become vampires in punishment for their mother's sin of being so presumptuous as to conceive (sic) on the same Day as the Virgin Mary'[19] may not Madonna have feared that her name predestined her to be a vamp? And so even though *Material Girl* may seem to have represented a step away from the dangerous ground of *Like a Virgin,* where blasphemy confirms religion's importance by negation, and towards the pure secularism of the material, the image of the vamp may be seen to rise from the same unhallowed soil. Not that Madonna was vampirized by Monroe; the self-confidence of *Material Girl* had the salutary effect of showing women that it is possible to survive on one's own terms even as one invokes the after-image of Monroe, which has haunted popular mythology. *Material Girl* enlisted the strength of Monroe's myth rather than being crushed by it. Had Madonna played the lead in *Sid and Nancy,* as Alex Cox suggested at one point (another missed opportunity; at this rate one doubts that Madonna will ever become the movie star people have foreseen in her), doubtless Sid would have been left to stew in his own juice at the Chelsea Hotel as Nancy, dressed to kill, went on alone to fame. In the last scene she would have pressed the MTV doorbell as *Material Girl* welled up on the sound-track.

'Material Girl' was an ironic anthem for preteen consumers; paired with Dire Straits's 'Money for Nothing', it forms half of the key diptych of mid-eighties songs. But whereas at this stage of her career Madonna's lyrics and the scenarios of her videos were interacting fascinatingly with one another, in such later videos as *Who's That Girl?* and *Open Your Heart* they go separate ways. The final stock ploy of dancing with children drives the last gold-plated nail into the coffins of these two videos. Their celebration of 'fun' reminds one of the ideological aspect of that word and indicates that no apologia for rock can base itself simply on the criterion of music for pleasure. One recalls that Hitchcock termed *Psycho* a 'fun picture'. The word is employed to secure immunity for the purveyor of 'fun', consigning all objections to the realm of the unhip. The will to power behind 'fun' becomes apparent with Madonna's shift from the marvellous harlequin garb of *Dress You Up,* which had embodied the early-eighties fashion trend Rosalind Coward described as daring 'to wear the extraordinary, to look as if you don't care and still remain attractive'.[20] Instead, there is the synchronized strutting of 'Open Your Heart', whose video steamrollers any dreams the auditor may have attached to the words by imposing on them a completely incompatible scenario. The momentary hints of a congruence between words and image ('Watch out!' as a child covers alternate eyes; 'it makes me want to hang my head down and cry', as Madonna leans back and sheds her black wig) only underline the disparity by inducing expectations of something the video – a tease on this level also – refuses to deliver. At its end the peep-show manager rushes after a Madonna who has begun to prance cutely with the child on a Chaplinesque road, crying, 'Abbiamo ancora bisogno di te'. The untranslated Italian implies that if Madonna has turned her native identity into a dark wig one can discard, it is only to conquer the WASP world under cryptic coloration. But the gesture to roots is cynical. It is perhaps their loss that now causes her to change her image compulsively, blind to the fact that some images (such as those of the *Material Girl* and *Dress You Up* period) are more potent and interesting than others.

The material girl's compulsively shifting roles are now blank signs of the directionlessness that usually ends with the singer falling into the arms of the industry to collect an assured lifetime pension belting out 'That's Entertainment!' To borrow a contrast from Pauline Kael, in Madonna zeitgeist has become poltergeist. The finely ambiguous timeliness of *Material Girl* has become the hollow echoing of self-advertisement from speakers placed all around the haunted house of postmodern culture. It is not that the rebel's lack of a cause has turned her into a conformist. Rather, Madonna's right hand is truly ignorant of what the left hand is doing: such haunting songs as 'Live to Tell' and 'Like a Prayer' alternate with the meretriciousness of 'La Isla Bonita' or 'Express Yourself'. The video no longer adds significant meaning to the song, but more often than not funnels meretriciousness into it, as in *Like a Prayer*'s partial exploitation of the 'shocking' potential of liberalism in a conservative American public sphere. Paradoxically, the rebel's advocacy devalues the cause, leaving a bad aftertaste of commodification and subliminally present streetwise scepticism. (A wise lapel badge advises, 'Madonna Don't Preach!') In the end, the goddess's self-multiplication – the source of the power of media dissemination on all available channels – becomes a denial of self: the generation of alternative incarnations becomes inflationary. In Madonna, shape-changing is not utopian but protean, hysterical flight from the time that dresses up as fashion. Like the true/false Maria of the *Metropolis* she takes so strangely seriously in *Express Yourself* – quoting with reverence Von Harbou's kitschy advocacy of the heart as a lonely mediator – she is the fitting icon of a confused, contradiction-laden society.

PART FIVE

Lucid dreams

To consider the relationship between 'high' and 'low' culture is una-voidably to broach that between individual and group. Much twen-tieth-century art erects a dichotomy between the 'high', the realm of the individual, and the primeval soup of the mass out of which it has crawled. The case of cinema complicates the opposition, long before postmodernism rendered slumming fashionable: after all, its products are collectively authored. The high–low distinction can be reinstated, of course, by presenting certain films as stemming from collectivities subordinated to a single author (as Pauline Kael does, commenting on Bergman's comparison of himself to a medieval artisan: 'Bergman's team is *his* team, working to express *his* vision'),[1] while others become assembly-line products, Taylorized and instrumentalized, director less important than producer, producer subsumed under studio style and studio style itself the messenger boy of an ideology whose brazen self-camouflage is to term itself 'individualistic'. Two of the films I am about to consider – *Warning Shadows* and *The Wedding* – present col-lectivities composed of warring individuals who enter a common space of dream, from which they emerge unified: in the former case, in rec-onciliation; in the latter, under the demonic sway of a straw figure who is perhaps the dark shadow of the enlightening artist of the for-mer. In each case, the ringmaster of dreams represents both popular culture – the people – and art. The third film is more ambiguous, for in Tarkovsky's *Sacrifice,* Alexander, the actor who has seceded from the company of actors, passes through a dream that may be his own or may be shared. We never discover when he entered it, if ever. I present it second because it does indeed occupy an intermediate position in the triad. But if the hallucination of *Warning Shadows* is collective, and that of *The Sacrifice* possibly simply private, *The Wedding* com-bines the alternatives: most of the phantoms that haunt the fin-de-siècle wedding of peasant and artist are viewed in private – and yet several people witness the messianic apparition of Wernyhora. In all three works, however, the space of dream is linked both to the popular

and to madness. In all three, this realm imposes responsibilities fulfilled to a diminishing degree from film to film: completely in *Warning
Shadows,* partially in *The Sacrifice,* not at all in *The Wedding.* Even if
a dream is only one's own, it is nevertheless given to one and so in a
sense reconciles inner and outer. The artwork that mimics dream itself
seeks a similar reconciliation.

The forecast of shadows

The Cabinet of Dr. Caligari, one of the founding works of German art
cinema, may be read as an indicator of how that cinema demonizes
popular culture: the mountebank is demonic. Its most famous exegete
does likewise: for Siegfried Kracauer, 'the fair is not freedom, but anarchy entailing chaos'.[2] *Warning Shadows* offers a dialectical correc-
tive that is perhaps the road untaken by German cinema, one
recognizing − rather than repudiating − its own popular origins. Its
shadow player is not the dubious, protofascist hypnotist of *Caligari,* or
of Thomas Mann's *Mario and the Magician,* which stages its spectacle
of degradation in a cinema in the poor quarter of an Italian coastal
resort. Rather, he employs hypnosis as aversion therapy, fictionally enacting an event to forestall its actual occurrence: after all, 'they kill in
jest' (a lesson Stoppard's filmic Rosencrantz and Guildenstern are unable to learn, as the players' dumb show of the pair's hanging falls, as
it were, on deaf ears). Our shadows can become our scapegoats; and
there is no guilt in the scapegoating of shadows. After all, prophecies
can fail.

The fact that two shadows seem to meet does not necessarily mean
that their owners are touching. In other words, fantasy (the shadow)
may appear to duplicate reality, but that reality need not coincide precisely with the fantasy. It is on this basis that *Shadows* advances its
argument. The simultaneous alignment and nonalignment of fantasy
and reality furnish both one of its metaphors and its overall mechanism. One instance of the metaphor shows a jealous husband watching the conjunction of his wife's shadow with those of her admirers;
but his curtained-off position involves exclusion from his drama, an
inability to see − as *we* are allowed to − that the meeting is merely
shadowy, insubstantial. Having demonstrated this possibility, the film
will later surprise us by inverting this scene's argument: in the
shadow play-within-the-play we watch the husband revenge himself on
his faithless wife by compelling her admirers to stab her. Seeing only
shadows, we hope that no actual contact will occur. We are doubly
shocked when the rising curtain discloses her corpse.

But the simultaneous coincidence and nonalignment of fantasy and
reality also impel the narrative. The film begins with a conjurer beside

a courtyard fountain, observing two shadows embracing outlined against a curtain: his position is our own (or, at least, partly aligned with ours), that of the outsider, awaiting the curtain's ascent. Turned away from the wealthy home at first, his shadow-play with his hands persuades the husband to summon him to divert a company composed of himself, his wife, her lover and her three admirers. The shadow-player sets up his magic lantern and unfolds the story of 'a Chinese emperor whose wife was loved by a neighboring prince'; 'the Emperor overtook them one day', he adds. At this point the watching wife's hand is approaching that of her lover; the shadow-player's redirected lantern-light frustrates the encounter. The Emperor has found out – in reality, as he did in fantasy. But there is a difference to the repetition: no contact was made; the husband seems relieved and banters bluffly. (He is played by Fritz Körtner, best known for his later role as the jealous husband – clearly his stock role – in Pabst's *Pandora's Box*.) Nevertheless, as Kracauer puts it, 'the juggler senses disaster in the air, and discontinues his performance to forestall a tragedy arising out of the steady growth of conflicting passions'.[3] The shadow-player had titled his entertainment *Schatten*, the mise-en-abîme suggesting snug correspondence between inner and outer narratives (Chinese boxes). If he scents disaster, it is on the basis of knowledge of the teleology of desire delineated by his own story – the Emperor's sword will bifurcate his rival ('made two princes where only one grew before'); he seeks to prevent reality falling into its mould. The possibility of *repetition with a difference* has already been adumbrated in the husband's failure to punish the wife, despite seeing her hand spotlighted reaching out to her lover. The husband is not a Chinese emperor in reality, where he implodes into impotent self-torment.

When the shadow-player intervenes in his own performance, switching registers from the illusionism of stimulating the imagination to that of hypnosis, we experience the most virtuoso passage in the work's philosophical essay on lighting. 'Under the spell of this conjurer, they felt themselves transported – to the realm of the subconscious – enacting their parts foretold by the shadows', the intertitle informs us. The metaphorical 'transported' becomes metaphysical fact: no longer viewers safely separated from a screen that screens them, the protagonists follow their shadows, which slide from behind to before them at the behest of the illusionist's redirected light, and then themselves materialize in the shadows' new place. They have abandoned the table's left and reemerge on its right-hand side. What follows exists in the realm of possibility, an extrapolated 'alternative world' the characters finally rejoice is not their own. In this story-within-the-story, the husband commands his servants (one old, faithful, but reluctant; the other bolt-upright, leering and eager) to bind his wife: her binding is itself a shadow-play, too monstrous to be shown in actuality, and the admirers watch in shock but are also unable to intervene precisely because the scene has the unreal, overblown quality of a shadow-battle: they cannot enter its two-dimensional space. (There is nevertheless a shuttling movement between the shadow-realm of the 'two-dimensional' and the 'three-dimensional' story world: this permits the protagonists to *become* their shadows. The linkage of the two varieties of space is most striking when, for instance, the wife's shadow appears in a mirror, the husband sees *a reflection* of the shadows of wife and lover embracing, or when the husband's cuckolding is imaged in the attachment of his head's shadow to the protruding horns of a hunting trophy. In persuading the three-dimensional protagonists of the story world to enter the two-dimensional domain of shadows, the shadow-player becomes a fantastic embodiment of an extraordinarily successful *film-maker*.) Something similar occurs when the husband later commands her bound to the table that will be a sacrificial altar: he stands left of screen, holding up a candelabra and blocking the view of the wife's actual struggles, which appear only as etched in shadow on the screen's right. He then has her stabbed and then himself (having gathered flowers for her, an image of feminization and madness ever since *Hamlet*) suffers defenestration by the admirers, who have emerged from the trance of his domineering will. Like a vampire, he fades on the pavement.

At this point we return to the spectators' frozen assembly in front of the conjurer. Resetting the light (and perhaps time also), he ferries their shadows back to the position behind them, and they slowly unwind from the folds of catatonia. The wife wipes her forehead; the conjurer resumes his interrupted Chinese tale. We see the Emperor exact revenge and bifurcate his rival, but then respond to the wife's pleas and solder the two parts together. (Their reunification parallels the way in which a shadow can disappear as the light shifts and it shrinks back into its owner.) The husband applauds, the admirers and lovers slink away and the lengthy coda ends with husband and wife framed arm-in-arm in the window, gazing down at the courtyard. A servant has raised the curtain upon a spectacle of a different kind: day has broken, bringing the sight of an astonishingly detailed, bustling market, where pigs flee their peasant owners and comedy and realism displace the likelihood of a tragic outcome of fantasy. Kracauer acidly notes the meagre response the film evoked: 'Contemporaries may have felt that any acknowledgement of the healthy shock effect of reason was bound to result in an adjustment to the ways of democracy'.[4] Considering his *Theory of Film*'s prescription of realism as the right nostrum for German cinema, he might also have noted the death-blow the realistic close deals to the nocturnal effluvia of fantasy.

Upon returning from their hypnotized excursion to the other side, of reality and of the table, the protagonists are subdued, but seem not to recall what they have just undergone. It is as if the acting out of fantasy itself is insufficient to cause a change in their relationships. It has, however, sown the seed of such an alteration. The conjurer concludes his shadow-play for good measure – watering the seed. The expedition to the realm of shadows does not function like 'The Mousetrap' in *Hamlet,* holding up the mirror of conscience to a wide-awake Claudius. So what has been the point of the exercise? It is debatable, but it could be that the possible world's unfolding has rendered it impossible actually (rather like the appalling future Faust views in the mirror in René Clair's *La Beauté du Diable*): reality is never quite as foreseen. The dream enactment of possible tragedy may also have had a cathartic, draining effect. The narrative mechanism is finally mysterious: shadow and reality (*Schatten,* the film, and 'Schatten', the conjurer's performance; the Chinese play and the protagonist's excursion 'through the looking glass' of another Otherness) belong together, but they are also separate.

Of burning houses and burning bridges: *The Sacrifice*

At the time of his death in 1986, Andrei Tarkovsky was perhaps the only director in the world still working in the Grand Manner. *Fanny and Alexander* having been Bergman's deliberate valediction to the exhausting craft of film-making, Tarkovsky had assumed his mantle of expressionist prophet. Hence, it was appropriate that Bergman should have praised Tarkovsky fulsomely: 'Tarkovsky is for me the greatest, the one who invented a new language, true to the nature of film, as it captures life as a reflection, life as a dream'.[5] The appearance of consummated succession was then reinforced by *The Sacrifice,* whose multiple allusions to Bergman's work will be discussed later. Nevertheless, the two directors put their dream syntax to radically different uses. In Bergman's films, the dream mode manifests itself only in outcrops and is generally counterpoised by an (often quasi-psychoanalytic) attempt at explication. Where Bergman situates dream in a dramatic context, Tarkovsky allows its tide to ebb and flow across the entirety of the work, which it washes with chilly lyricism. His dream plays have less in common with Strindberg than with Poe, whose monologues they distend into epics.

If *The Sacrifice* gestures towards portentous statements about modern civilization (the denunciation of its incapacity for sacrifice found in *Sculpting in Time*),[6] its limpid tone suggests a director who has so distilled his themes as virtually to have lost interest in them. The core of the scenario was an old one, and this – together with the automatism of the side-on camera movements – may be a major source of this effect. Equally important, however, may have been uncertainty over the degree to which the plot is steeped in the fantasy of its main protagonist. He is Professor Alexander, who is disgusted with the wordiness of his own monologues and who may stand for the self-sickened state of a logocentric culture; it may be this malaise, or the actual imminence of nuclear disaster, that primes him to take cognizance of other, mystical orders. Midway through the celebration of Alexander's birthday amid relatives and friends, TV broadcasts reveal the imminence of nuclear war. As jets flash low overhead, the set flickers out and a darkness of world and soul supervenes. Alexander prays, promising to sacrifice all if only God will restore the vanished harmony. It seems as if his willingness could indeed stave off the threat. Otto the postman, a guest who has shown an interest in the paranormal, instructs him to cycle to the far side of the island and make love to Maria, a peasant witch. (*The Witch* had been the script's first title.) Alexander does so, and his encounter with Maria concludes in a levitation of their entwined bodies. Daylight seeps back, and Alexander consummates his sacrifice by setting fire to his house. A remarkable tour de force precedes the film's end, the camera slowly withdrawing to impassively observe the house burn as Alexander scampers among puddles and his relatives watch in consternation. An ambulance arrives – of course, he must be mad. In a final coda, Alexander's son, Little Man, waters the barren tree with which the film began and musingly asks the meaning of a phrase his father quoted to him, 'In the beginning was the Word'. This, together with other features of the film, may seem to question the word's primacy,[7] but the iconographic use of Leonardo's *Adoration of the Kings* permits a reading in which the language that was so tainted at the outset has been recovered at the end: Little Man is aligned typologically with the Logos and has indeed regained his speech. There may be a new birthday to celebrate, that of the redemptive child rather than the father; it is as if Abraham has sacrificed himself. For the film is more subtle than Tarkovsky's gloss on it: it does not conclude by setting a revelatory image against a speech that has 'become mere chatter',[8] but rather seeks a Logos whose mediation includes a linkage of image (both Leonardo and film) and language. It is as if Alexander's sacrifice has translated the kings' gift into reality, enabling the redemptive child to step out of the picture also: *The Adoration of the Kings* is no longer blocked, rendered sinister, by the father's reflection in the glass that overlays it.

The Sacrifice is neoexpressionistic. In expressionist works the seen world is an emanation of the disordered mind of a central figure or a mind unseen. Insofar as *The Sacrifice* is expressionistic, however, its interpretation becomes problematic. Tarkovsky himself noted the problem, though without grasping its possibly devastating effect on his work's reception. Having asserted the possibility of various readings, he concludes that 'there will doubtless be others for whom all the events of the film are merely the fruits of a sick imagination, since no nuclear war is actually happening'.[9] The sick imagination, one presumes, belongs to Alexander. But if the night's redemptive events are merely oneiric phantasms, the film becomes a close-up portrait of a diseased mind and forfeits its religious pretensions. The possibility of a definitive change in register three-quarters of the way through the narrative, recategorizing preceding events as delusion, may cause one to feel cheated, for all the occasional earlier hints of such a possibility. The serious tone precludes Buñuelian playfulness. It is as if Tarkovsky has awakened suddenly to his own lugubriousness, effectively annihilating a nearly completed work. If Tarkovsky did not abandon his film at this point, it was perhaps because on another interpretive level the retrospective rewriting can be deemed indicative of the efficacy of Alexander's prayer: it is not just the nuclear night, but the entire world that issued naturally in it, that has undergone decreation – in other words, Tarkovsky's own, albeit in a different context, 'We could be said to be turning time back through conscience', a remark that sits ambiguously with the one that precedes it in *Sculpting in Time* ('But, having made its effect, the cause is not then discarded like the used stage of a rocket'),[10] for 'revolution' may betoken reversion to, or overturning of, the past. *The Sacrifice* equivocates – one is tempted to say, fatally – between these two senses. The equivocation refuses resolution in terms of the narrative itself. Only if one argues that the egotism of the actor who has renounced roles belongs also to the director obsessed with his own exile – that 'Alexander' represents Tarkovsky – does the work's progression become justifiable and genuine. The closing section of *The Sacrifice* can then be read as an immolation of the darkness of *Nostalgia*, its perverse eclipse of the Italian light. Indeed, the film's closing dedication – to Tarkovsky's son – virtually compels an autobiographical reading. And this dedication too *comes at the end.*

If 'cinema lives by its capacity to resurrect the same event on the screen time after time'[11] – a remark deeply reminiscent of *Solaris* – the resurrected body is always new nevertheless, as St. Paul notes: 'And that which thou sowest, thou sowest not that body that shall be, but bare grain'.[12] The first three-quarters of *The Sacrifice* are the 'bare grain' that finally arises with another body. It may well be the body of Japanese culture. Japanese elements (the kimono, the music, the parched tree) have pervaded the work and cluster densely in its coda – unsurprisingly, for Tarkovsky associates self-effacement with the East: 'In the Eastern tradition they never utter a word about themselves'.[13] At the film's close, the Japanese tree is no longer juxtaposed with, and dependent on, the tree in Leonardo's painting; it is no longer simply an interface, a turning hinge, between Japanese and Christian culture, but stands separate, transcendent. Whereas the constant shifting between the two cultural registers had suggested confusion in the first three-quarters of the film, finally there is a fusion, perhaps an absorption: Little Man speaks of the Logos beside the Japanese tree. Its association with the son, however, consigns it to utopian futurity.

Iconographically the film is pleasingly dense. Its opening credits are superimposed on a portion of Leonardo's *Adoration of the Kings* depicting one king kneeling before the crib to present his gift; the camera climbs the picture's tree, which then becomes the barren stump Alexander is planting near the sea-shore. The painting will recur, its glass-covered reproduction deemed 'sinister' (perhaps because it encompasses the characters' reflections and enacts self-alienation, uncannily forecasting the movement towards expressionism in one of the narrative strands). Alexander repeats the king's gesture as he kneels at one point before relatives and friends in the closing sequence, his – and their – house ablaze in the background. On presenting Alexander with a sixteenth-century map of Europe, Otto had justified his munificence by stating that all true giving entails sacrifice. He thus voices the film's theme: Alexander's sacrifice of his house is his gift to Little Man, as if Little Man's model house has rendered the larger one superfluous and will grow to its size given time. As Alexander's birthday echoes that of the Christ child, it becomes the appropriate time (the *kairos*) both for his own second birth and for the world's.

One of the film's key motifs is that of the self-moving object. Before and after the crisis, the doors of display cabinets and wardrobes creak open of their own accord, presenting reflecting surfaces that uncannily double events. During the crisis itself, the sonic boom of low-flying jets sends glasses shuddering across surfaces and over their edges. (One may recall the opening of *Stalker.*) Alexander himself enters this mysterious realm of self-propulsion when sleeping with Maria. The levitation of their linked bodies seems to humanize the motif and banish the crisis.

But for all the satisfaction one garners from analysis of the film's iconographic correspondences, watching its first three-quarters is far less rewarding an experience. The Chekovian echoes merely underline Tarkovsky's lack of Chekov's musical instinct for groups' interaction: and Sven Nykvist's panning camera circles the crepuscular tableaux so inexorably as to seem mechanical, tranced in numbness. The presentation of the women is particularly inadequate, even chauvinistic: no longer does the strange ontological status of a Harey provide an alibi for failure to comprehend female reality. Where the male figures are merely sketched, Alexander's wife Adelaide is a caricature of the hysterical virago. It is hard not to see the return of the light, the mystical renewal of world and soul, as a wish-fulfilment. One may welcome the relief from the visual monotony of the semidark crisis period, while wondering that so much should hang on the idiosyncratic actions of so attenuated a believer as Alexander. The mystical schema is compromised by the sheer lugubriousness of its unfolding. Otto may declare that there are other worlds, but adds, 'We are blind, we see nothing', and collapses. The Lord may uplift all those who fall, and the fall may be merely the epileptic consequence of the visionary moment that precedes it, but the vision is presented too cryptically and enjoys too ambiguous a status to be uplifting. It may be that Tarkovsky's mysticism is so morose because of its marginal, threatened position in the desacralized modern world. The lack of a religious framework to support the spirituality further debilitates it, rendering it fatally dependent on the shifts of personal mood: a mood inevitably darkened during the film's gestation by cancer and the solitude of exile. *Nostalgia*'s theme of homelessness recurs here: the final incineration of the house may seek to make a virtue out of necessity. The barren tree taking root is surely Tarkovsky's dream of his own successful transplantation. The tree becomes the transformed image of the father, his son at his feet. As the last image appears (sun blazing beyond bare branches, an epiphanic hieroglyph that recalls Celan's 'Thread Suns,' with its 'treehigh thought' tuning into the light's tone), so does a title dedicating the film to Tarkovsky's son. Words are reborn, superimposed on the image, but they are *written* words: it is now the father who is mute (the film has come full circle), who soon in fact will be dead. The torching of the house is the director's sublime valediction to life itself.

Much of *The Sacrifice* may be said to anticipate this final immolation through its submergence of Tarkovsky's preoccupations in those of Bergman. The island and apocalyptic war of *Shame*, Alexander's rejection of acting (cf. Elisabet's withdrawal in *Persona*), the disgust with words: one recognizes them all. When Little Man precipitates himself at Alexander's neck, he is for a moment the demon-child of *Hour of the Wolf*. One need hardly add that the casting of Erland Josephson and the use of Swedish cement the air of the Bergmanesque. The closing scenes, however, seem to redefine this self-abnegation as a false version of sacrifice – even as signifiers of falsity per se. For the last section, whose central image is the blazing house, is paradoxically instinct with a sense of homecoming, braiding together a concatenation of echoes of Tarkovsky's earlier films, like an orchestral finale. In front of the burning house stand large pools of water, the juxtaposition recalling the co-presence of water and fire in one of the key images of *Mirror,* a shot from behind of several figures watching a barn blaze as water dripped from the eaves of the porch on which they stood. (A pun in the collective linguistic unconscious may link 'barn', 'burn' and 'bairn' here: it is in the burning barn, as it were, that one witnesses the adored Christ child, the burning babe, the light-source.) The drawback from the water-surrounded house replays the vertiginous final shot of *Solaris.* The model of Alexander's house that Little Man has fashioned as his birthday present is reminiscent of the the house Solaris re-creates from the astronaut's thought-waves. Little Man's speechlessness, due to a throat operation – and its final transcendence – recall the stuttering of the boy in *Mirror.* The preoccupation with justified madness renews a theme of *Nostalgia.* And the Leonardo painting, which has preceded the film, closes it in the same manner as Rembrandt's *Return of the Prodigal Son* concludes *Solaris:* by entry into *reality.*

The *Sacrifice* seeks to fuse a dream and a sermon. One is thus compelled to ask how effectively Tarkovsky adapts his dream syntax to what is clearly the presentation of a 'message'. The film's trajectory happily replaces the morose despair of *Nostalgia* with the sublimely transplanted tree rooted in exile. Yet the pattern of rebirth is confused, perhaps undermined, by the problems of interpretation already considered. Alexander's final actions eclipse the image of redemption they also represent – rather as, earlier on, his face had darkened the glass above Leonardo's painting. For it is arguable that an artwork's openness to various interpretations should involve homology, an interlocking of its levels, rather than mutual contradiction. Where they contradict each other, and with equal justification, the result is either (a) incoherence or (b) intentional conundrum. Given the seriousness of Tarkovsky's intent, (b) has to be ruled out; one has to opt for (a). The *Sacrifice* resembles an anthology of starting-points for films, none of them entirely carried through; the accumulation of pointers to the unattainable may be the inscription of imminent death. Disparate scenarios even colour trivial details of costuming, the female characters seeming to issue from different eras (Adelaide, from the turn of the century, and hence from Chekov or Strindberg; Marta, from the present). It would indeed have been some recompense for the cruelty of his early death had Tarkovsky's last film been a work of the order of *Mirror.* Nevertheless, its first three-quarters breathe a malaise that seems to afflict so many Russian artists in exile. Their decline is so precipitous because, unlike a Lang or a Skolimowski, they see no virtue in their new abode. The closed Soviet society has shown them so little of the world outside that they cannot function beyond its borders. Transplanted to the West, they become parochial and/or mystical. And this, of course, suits the Soviet regime very well, demonstrating the barrenness of a West they often join it in denouncing, albeit in very different terms. (Lack of spirituality would not have been one of the official Soviet criticisms, though it was one of Tarkovsky's.) The inhumanity of the politics of exile is borne out appallingly in the decline in the work of a Tarkovsky or a Solzhenitsyn. For each, the world outside Russia was an airless, alien planet. Is leaving Russia the ultimate sacrifice?

Revolutionary spirits: the wedding of Wajda and Wyspiański

Wesele (The wedding), a fin-de-siècle play by Stanisław Wyspiański, is known outside Poland largely through the influence it has exerted on the films of Andrzej Wajda. The hypnotic circular polonaise at the end of *Ashes and Diamonds* is borrowed from Wyspiański's work; an urge to distil a universal import from the bickerings of a closely circumscribed artistic milieu is common to both *Wesele* and Wajda's *Everything for Sale*, each of which transports real events and personalities into the space of fiction; Wajda stands in the Polish Romantic tradition of the 'seer' who speaks for the nation, the indirections of art pointing directions out when more explicit utterance is censored – and it was to this tradition that the first audience of *Wesele* immediately ascribed Wyspiański. Where Wyspiański was a visual artist, among other things, Wajda began as an art student. And so it was almost inevitable that in the end Wajda would seek to film Wyspiański's great play.

As one emerges from Wajda's screen version, stunned by the whirling, zooming, multicoloured agitation of the work, and sobered by the plasmic hues of its disillusioned close, one is hardly surprised to hear that the original contains levels of allusion obscure to non-Poles. Yet although this symbolist play is grounded in a local Polish anecdote, it echoes beyond the Polish context as part of the stubborn study of Hamletism and the obstacles to action conducted by the Romantics. To the eye alone, Wajda's film is hypnotic, and the pungent imagism is appropriate: it has been remarked that Wyspiański not only saw with the eye but thought with it too. But when one realizes that the characters are the stolen shadows of Wyspiański's own contemporaries, one begins to grasp why the first audiences, who knew this, emerged in a state of shock (and why Wajda's *Everything for Sale* is finally closer in method to *The Wedding* than his film of the play). Wyspiański was declared a seer, the spokesman of the nation, and presented with bouquets wrought with the number 44 – according to Adam Mickiewicz, whose early-nineteenth-century *Forefathers' Eve* inaugurates the tradition of political supernaturalism continued by Wyspiański, the mystical number of the Polish messiah. Clearly, the play had tapped the numerological hopes attached to the date of its appearance – 1900 – in a partitioned Poland.

The play's underlying anecdote was as follows. Lucjan Rydel, a poet in the throes of the 'peasant mania' prevalent among Cracow intellectuals of the time, chose to act upon the aesthete's idealization of redemptive peasant strength and proposed marriage to a village girl, who accepted him. The wedding reception took place in a village just below Cracow, draped with folk decorations and steeped in alcoholic mist. All Rydel's Cracovian acquaintances, among them Wyspiański, attended the celebrations. Wyspiański is the absent centre of the play, as he had been of the original event, when he stood by a door, a spectator, protesting that vodka gave him a headache. The play's characters are walking shadows of the whirling guests. The bridegroom is modelled on Rydel, who is drawn with the friendly irony with which Wyspiański viewed him in everyday life; the poet Tetmajer is the host; 'Nose' is based on the perennially intoxicated metaphysician of sex ('In the beginning was lust...'), Stanisław Przybyszewski, known to the Berlin Bohème as 'der geniale Pole'; and so on. Only in the case of Rachel, the play's flamboyant aesthete Jewess, is there a possible divergence between character and prototype – though the widespread contention that Pepa Singer was pallid, passive and modelled herself subsequently on her distorted mirror image has been disputed by her friends and acquaintances.

During the middle section of the three-act play, appropriate visions afflict several of the characters. The dovetailing of their visions with the known preoccupations of their beholders enables Wyspiański to adopt a rationalist and a romantic standpoint simultaneously. The Tetmajer figure, for instance, sees a vision of a black knight who appears in one of his poems: this may be a private projection, Wyspiański's way of identifying Tetmajer, or a companionable shape assumed by the Other. Another guest, based on a conservative journalist for whom Wyspiański had considerable respect, is confronted by the figure of Stańczyk, a court jester who sits dejectedly apart from a feast in a painting by Matejko, stunned by the Polish defeat at the Battle of Smolensk: the figure had become emblematic of the Cracow conservatives, who were critical of the Polish uprisings of 1830 and 1863, mindful of how the ravages of repression had succeeded romantic revolt. The chief characters sit paralysed by these projections, rather as Wyspiański himself faces the splintered, clouded mirror of his own play.

The Wedding is rigorously composed in three parts, advancing from realism to the fantastic and concluding in the exhaustion that supervenes after a night's drunken grappling with the traumas of a subjugated country. At the end the characters dance in a circle to a tune played by the Straw Man. The first section introduces the guests, cutting prismatically and protocinematically among them, allowing each only a couple of short, clipped lines whose subordination to rhyme already suggests dependence on some external force. They spin on and off stage, or in and out of the spotlight, like dolls in a *szopka,* the Polish traditional Christmas puppet play often seen as the source of this stylization. Their hopes and fears emerge from their gossip. Underlying it are dark memories of the appalling events of 1846, when Jakub Szela, a peasant manipulated by an Austrian government intent on smothering any germs of an alliance between the local Polish gentry and the peasantry, led a revolt against masters who were rumoured to be planning a peasant massacre. During Szela's revolt many a master was edged in a hollow tree-trunk and sawn in two. (Wajda's graphic accentuation of Szela's importance was to be a controversial point in the film.) Szela's shadow indicates the frailty of the artist–peasant union. Indeed, it is as if only the pressure of closely packed bodies in a single room generates a sense of oneness: the moment a person leaves it he or she splits into near schizophrenia.

The second section records the state of mind of those who have reeled away temporarily from the alcoholic carousel. Towards the first act's close, Rachel, the Jewish aesthete, had invited the Straw Man, who stands outside shielding a heart of roses against the winter chill, to enter the hut. Her invitation to the chthonic forces goes far beyond a jeu d'esprit. (I will return to the figure of Rachel and her particular significance in Wajda's film towards the end of this essay.) The Straw Man enters through the children's room, to then disappear and reappear in fearsome guise at the play's close. Like a demonic parody of Christ, he comes twice. Once, benignly, to children who have no memory of the past and bear no responsibility to liberate their country; the second time, as ringmaster to the guests whose god has failed and who have failed themselves because their gods – and here the play echoes Feuerbach – are born of the self-alienation of human power. After the Straw Man's appearance, the various guests step outside the room and see the visions mentioned earlier. One notes that there is no religious vision among them. Although the characters expect the Virgin Mary, Queen of Poland, to direct the uprising from Wawel Hill, the old Cracow seat of the Polish monarchy, her absence – the absence of any religious figure – problematizes the visions, rather as the ghost in *Hamlet* is problematic. The vacillation between a world of earth spirits, one of projections and one ordered by Christianity, creates a real similarity between Wyspiański's play and Shakespeare's; it is hardly surprising that one of his most intriguing works should have been a commentary on *Hamlet* that proposes saving the play's spirit by banning its ghost.[14] In each case, uncertainty regarding the status of the other world's injunctions prompts hesitancy in their execution. There is thus a sense in which Wyspiański himself is the Ghost in his contemporaries' *Hamlet*. The degree of his frustration by their inaction is apparent in his remark that there was no need to stage his play in Warsaw: the more radicalized Russian partition had no need of its violent spur to uprising.

At the end of the second act the final vision appears, bearing directives for collective action. The only vision to be witnessed by more than one person is that of Wernyhora: a profoundly ambiguous figure, he is known to Poles as the Ukrainian peasant of a Słowacki play who participates in an eighteenth-century revolt against the Polish gentry. Nevertheless, at the sound of his lyre the corpse of Polish nationhood will be resurrected. The ambiguity of Wernyhora's apparition – an ambiguity both of meaning and of form (he is both Polish and Ukrainian; he appears to the host and yet is seen by others) – sums up in a single figure the various modes whereby the phantoms manifest themselves in Wajda's film. Its staging of their appearances runs from one end of the spectrum of possible explanation to the other, so that in the end everything hangs in doubt. The first two visions – the child's of the Straw Man, a peasant woman's of her dead lover – end with awakenings, as if the images had been merely dreams. A sequence follows in which the characters see visions in isolation (the poet, the groom, the beggar, the journalist). The brief and subliminal quality of the apparitions, who have none of the relative loquacity of Wyspiański's phantoms, combined with this isolation, generates an air of febrile hallucination. Finally Wernyhora appears. His image in the window illusively meshes with, and separates itself from, that of the host: the Other is virtually a double – the materialization, as it were, of the host's identification with the Matejko *Wernyhora* that hangs on the wall of his house. Wernyhora hands the host a golden horn, to be blown at sunrise to summon all Poles to rebel.

The final act begins in the somnolent weariness of the small hours. Slowly the host's words concerning his visitation circulate among the guests, who begin to anticipate some tremendous event. Kneeling as if to pray, they prick up their ears for the return of Jasiek, the servant boy the host has dispatched to rouse the surrounding peasants and instruct them to whet their scythes. He returns as the scythes approach: blades as ultimately feeble, for all their serried mass, as the blades of grey grass they suggest in Wajda's version. Jasiek, it seems, has lost the horn by the wayside; and the film concludes with the low mocking tones of the Straw Man's song, as the guests move in a hypnotized circle and the camera – at the edge of the maelstrom perhaps, but caught up in its movement nevertheless – does likewise, describing a 360-degree pan.

Originally, Wyspiański wanted the actual wedding guests to play themselves. (This was achieved by Wajda in *Everything for Sale*.) But Rydel was offended by what appeared to be satire, and real actors had to be employed instead. (Here again the parallel with *Everything for Sale* is striking: Bogumił Kobiela, a close friend of Cybulski, the film's dead and absent subject, was to walk off the set of Wajda's film, deeming it an act of imaginative cannibalism.) Thus, the total, dizzying interpenetration of art and life was to prove unattainable. Wyspiański baffled the actors by refusing to issue directions on how to play the characters. Perhaps he agreed with the Straw Man that the characters essentially lacked personality; and he may well have been reaching out for the form of acting shortly to be made possible by film, in which the actor always in a sense 'plays himself'. (He cannot be separated from his role.) This would further justify the act of filming the play. The decision is validated even more by Wyspiański's interest in the *Gesamtkunstwerk* – the total artwork whose mantle, arguably, was to fall on the shoulders of film. This is perhaps why Krzysztof Teodor Toeplitz could remark that 'never in my experience as a theatregoer has it been my lot to see a "complete" "Wedding", that is, one in which all the threads, all the possibilities, all the consequences, are developed on the stage'.[15] Yet Wajda's film is deeply flawed, for all its virtuoso evocation of what might have been a participant's experience of the festivities, dancers fleeting by like tracers streaking past a cockpit. The camera of Witold Sobociński may move with great brio, figures pouring semitransparently across the middle distance, but its desire to dance with the dancers dispels the unremitting objectivity forced upon the theatre audience by Wyspiański, who dematerializes himself from the wedding to draw the viewer into the spectatorial detachment of his own position at the festivities. The quest to bring together all the threads can even issue in the lack of an organizing idea of which Krzysztof Mętrak complains.[16] The Aesopian possibility of reference to seventies Poland borders on academicism and ironically exemplifies the very inability to criticize the system pilloried by Wyspiański himself. It may well be as compensation for this that Wajda fetishizes technique, setting the camera zooming compulsively to engender the sense of instability that heralds, and then accompanies, the manifestations of the other-worldly. (Thus, the journalist, whose nervousness is strikingly incarnated by Wojciech Pszoniak, sees his own double very early on in the film, well before his confrontation with himself in the form of the jester Stańczyk.) The semisubliminal editorial dislocations that accompany the spirit projections prevent one from dwelling on their visual impressiveness and frustrate attention to the actual words they use. Wajda's film has some good ideas for staging – the peasants Czepiec has armed march out past an enormous copy of the *Panorama of Racławice,* depicting Kosciuszko's famed defeat of the Russians; and the beggar's traumatic hallucination of peasants handing their masters' severed heads to Austrian soldiers graphically underlines the uncertainty of the marriage of the classes – but it lacks the incendiary force of the original. Indeed, the film may even undercut Wyspiański's work by suggesting that the supernatural hovers spectrally around the edge of everyday life, rather than remaining locked in a feared political unconscious, entered only when one's awareness has been safely dulled by alcohol. For the blue lighting of the face of Rachel's father – a Jew – the presentation of the poet on the far side of a fire's hazy exhalations and the enigmatic shots of the misty orange-lit fields suggest a conflation of the supernatural with anything that is unexpected and other: the otherness of the past holds the otherness of the supernatural in suspension and in check. Consequently, the dialectic Wyspiański concentrates in the middle section of his play is dissipated into the totality of the film's body. But if at the time of the film's release it seemed to countermand Wyspiański's incendiarism through academicism, indirection and even fetishistic evocation of the past – if the dispersal of the supernatural throughout the work implied the absence of the very reality the phantoms exhorted their beholders to transform – in retrospect the fact that for Wajda it is only a step from the natural to the supernatural may be read as symptomatic of rebellion's increased proximity to the surface of everyday Polish life. In this respect, the film may dimly anticipate the Solidarity revolt. And yet the film's possibly prophetic aspect is barely compatible with its grimly vulgar Marxist version of the class struggle. Hence, Wajda's decision to show the peasants with their scythes at their masters' throats – an interpretive move lambasted by Słonimski – lends substance to Mętrak's charge that the film's interpretation of Wyspiański is frozen in the mould of 1954.[17] Wajda's version may simply be incoherent – perhaps because the poetic rhythms that create order amid the chaos are lost in the dance, rather than diverting the dance's movement into the form of its own imitation.

Wyspiański's play works simultaneously on a series of levels, examining the irascible disparity between the peasants and the intellectuals at play, the relationship between imagination and religion, the conflicts within individuals in a frustrated society and the way collective symbols can both instigate and compensate for the absence of rebellion. Rising through various locks, it begins as a satire, proceeds through a quasi-psychoanalysis of a series of individuals and finally (like the oeuvre of Freud himself) unfolds a visionary diagnosis of an entire repressed society. Beginning with the word, it ends with the enigmatic - image; which is why Wajda's version deals more effectively with the conclusion (the peasants' scythes like spectral grass, the tremendous tracking of the hand-held camera scanning the wedding guests frozen in catatonic expectation) than with the beginning. If the first act is realist, the third is symbolist. The phantoms of liberty that haunt the work's midsection are cruel personifications of the rebellion one cannot express in everyday life: that life unfolding under the watchful eye of the Austrian soldiers Wajda adds. (His own society is more thoroughly controlled, more deeply held in place by the watching totalitarian eye, than Wyspiański's had been.) Freud might have described the revellers as cowed by their superegos, for the latter are animated by the energy the ego suppresses, which can achieve expression only through disavowal and projection. The aggression the ego surrenders is appropriated by the superego to augment its own assault on the ego. As the phantoms are to the revellers, so the play itself is to Wyspiański (a point Stanisław Brzozowski was to stress):[18] a vision of such personal torment – earth's molestation by the suffering spirits the guests invite in from their own unconscious – that it resists appropriation by any other man. Perhaps that is why Wajda's version, for all its inventiveness, leaves us dissatisfied. Wajda's own *Wedding* is in fact dispersed over two films, *Everything for Sale* and *Man of Marble;* he cannot reproduce Wyspiański's astonishing *fusion* of political and artistic self-interrogation. (In *Man of Marble,* the use of two director figures, both Agnieszka and Burski, allows the image of Wajda himself to make its getaway.) It is as if his film is touched by Wyspiański's spirit as the wedding guests are by their phantoms.

Nevertheless, one aspect of the film is haunting, and this by virtue of its foregrounding of a theme Wyspiański places in the background: the Jewish question. Rachel's father, blue-lit, becomes akin already to a phantom, and like phantoms he admonishes the conscience. Though real, he has already been assimilated to the Other: as such, he is already marked by a fate that still lay in the future of Wyspiański's Jews and reflects the phantom nature of the Jewish presence in contemporary Poland. The broaching of the theme is all the more welcome a mere few years after the government-instigated anti-Semitic campaign of 1968. For Wajda, however, the Other is as much Woman as the Jew. When Rachel drifts in across the fields, she is in a sense the first ghost to arrive. The power of the female exacts Jewish revenge on the excluding Catholic culture of Poland. Her flapping sleeves may be spectral, but as Maja Komorowska incarnates her, she has a stronger, more human presence than almost any other woman in Wajda's films. The casting of Komorowska in the role clearly strengthens its importance. Since the Straw Man's advent follows Rachel's departure and she herself has issued the invitation for his entry, the phantoms' visitations may be read as metaphorical embodiments of her revenge. Indeed, she has likened herself to the Straw Man: 'No need to worry about me; / the worst frost will not freeze the one / who has the fragrance of roses; / just bind her up in dead straw, / unwrap her in the spring, / and she will bloom'.[19] The twanging rhythm of the music that accompanies the outdoor scenes suggests the lilt of the Jew's harp, implying a link between Jewishness and the fields from which the phantoms come. One may recall how she has been mocked by the poet and may seek supernatural redress; how she has appeared staring through the barred window, as if she were an imprisoned spirit; and how the appearance of her reflection as she enters the hut establishes her divided status. It is as if Rachel exists on two planes: the individual may indeed be pretentious, draped in ecstasies of pseudorhapsody, but what is false poeticism at the individual level becomes true poetry by virtue of her Jewishness, which lends her the witchlike power society confers upon the Other. The split may be interpreted as corresponding to the dual sense of 'speculation': her father's financial speculations fuel her poetic speculations. They bestow a form on airy nothing: that of the phantoms. Rejected, Rachel in essence reappears as the Straw Man; and as such, she has the last word.

European cinema (and in particular Fritz Lang) goes to Hollywood

The introduction to this book invokes the hope of an injection of 'the European' into the genre-based cinema of the United States, one of potential mutual benefit. The odds against such an enterprise succeeding can be gauged from the collapse of the careers of such 'Europeanized' directors as Altman, Coppola and De Palma, as well as from the Hollywood vicissitudes of the European – particularly German – exiles of the thirties. The trip the Germans took has been billed 'Expressionism Goes to Hollywood'. Yet it can be argued that expressionism never went to Hollywood but died in the mid-twenties before it could pack its bags. The widespread use of sets in both Hollywood and Neubabelsberg hardly necessitates resemblance in other domains, while the mere Hollywood presence of numerous Germans after Hitler's ascent is far from tantamount to an invasion by expressionism. It is arguable that only the least 'expressionist' German directors produced Hollywood films of comparable weight to their German work. (One thinks of *Sunrise* and David Thomson's remarks on Murnau's extraterritoriality to expressionism.)[1] If Pabst, seemingly the best candidate for the trip, a metteur-en-scène in the American mould, succeeded nevertheless in avoiding departure, it was not simply because his talent was inferior to that of Lang or Murnau, but also because for him the traffic went the other way: his realist style, and use of Louise Brooks, brought Hollywood to Europe. Meanwhile, although expressionism clearly influenced the style of film noir, similar stylistic elements had already surfaced in American film in passages of Stroheim. The sense of horror in expressionism being linked to silent fascination by an image, wordy post-thirties Hollywood was unreceptive to it. And the Madonna–whore opposition still extant in expressionism dissolves in film noir, whose actresses' shoulder pads place inverted commas around the one-dimensional stereotypes they stand behind, manipulating them languidly and knowingly, whistling all the while. In film noir the realm of sexuality is defined very differently than in expressionism.

In Weimar cinema the realm of sexuality represents chaos: Nosferatu's love brings the plague; the false Maria incites apocalypse (her falsity the plot device whereby Freder disavows the sexuality secreted in the love-object he pursues); Becker in 'M.' is the victim of his urges; and Lola Lola and Lulu shed destruction upon males. Here it is not Woman that means trouble, as in Hollywood, but sexuality itself. Film noir, by way of contrast, is always already sexualized, and the hero's weary worldliness (or hidden hurt) stems from past experience; the protagonist of Weimar cinema is the adolescent entering a sexual realm fraught with threats to his identity. (There is much in Kracauer concerning the pubescent nature of Weimar film fantasies.) This is the source of the obstacles to attaining love in Weimar plots, in the mise-en-scène that freezes motion into tableaux and in the editing practices that – as Elsaesser notes apropos the films of Lang[2] – interpose shots of mute objects to frustrate glance meeting glance. Fearful of sexuality, the son is the son of his father, who persists in isolation. The contrast between Hollywood's version of sexuality and the Weimar one becomes apparent when expressionism and film noir are juxtaposed. Although it might seem as if film noir is preoccupied with sexuality and expressionism with power, in actuality they link the two elements in opposite ways. Matriarchal in film noir ('Put the Blame on Mame'), power is patriarchal in expressionism, which reflects the relatively disadvantaged position of German women.

Where the noir protagonist seeks power indirectly, through possession of a woman (and plotting with her to kill her husband), the expressionist does so directly, through confrontation with the father. Even the most powerful expressionist women act on behalf of men: the false Maria or Kriemhild's revenging of the absent Siegfried. There is also, of course, a pacifist strain in expressionism, opposed to the seizure of power, combating the father for the right to love, for freedom from the regimes of sublimation and repression that subtend patriarchal power. The father has no wife – no compunction or 'feminine side' – but is awesomely unified. Joh Frederson's sole mate is all hardness, not feminine softness, a robot. In *Caligari, Waxworks* and *Metropolis,* the father stands alone, as a youth seeks to break his daughter's Electra complex.[3] Particularly interesting in this context, however, is *Metropolis,* whose opposition to power has a dark subtext. Maria's indistinguishability from Hel, Freder's dead mother, turns her appearance in his father's arms into a temporally free-floating primal scene; and so the desire for a younger woman, apparently expressive of a wish to shed power, becomes a roundabout way to achieve it, by securing the image of the mother. Consciously, Freder may be an Oedipus who fails to kill the father through fear of marriage with Jocasta, but unconsciously he is a true Oedipus: he gets the girl whose double is his mother. Elsewhere in expressionist film, the son's will to power manifests itself in disavowed doubles, such as Nosferatu, Cesare and Jack the Ripper (*Waxworks* and *Pandora's Box*). The two identities — ostensible libertine pacifism, hidden identification with power — succeed one another in the split career of that key figure of interwar German cinema, Frederick the Great: the youthful, maternally swayed rebel and devotee of French fripperies is harshly pressed into the service of his father's Spartan ideals. Kracauer's ground-breaking dissection of Weimar film might best have been titled *From Frederick to Hitler*.[4]

Onetime German expressionists may have gone to Hollywood, but only after passing through the deexpressionizing antechamber of the New Objectivity. The expressionist utopias and dystopias of the machine faded in tandem as machines became banal normality. On entering Hollywood, expressionist themes and style break up and disperse, percolating in part into film noir and partly into horror film. Poe may have argued in the preface to his *Tales of Grotesque and Arabesque* that a terror of the self 'is not of Germany, but of the soul', but the widespread association of the horrific and the Germanic is partly justified by the Weimar cinema's preoccupation with scapegoating, cruelty, humiliation and pain. The horror motif of the unstable self acquires its most political meaning in the uncertainty of German self-definition: both 'inside' itself and 'outside', in the penumbra of other German-speaking lands. But horror film's generic channelling of the expressionist unease before the world serves only to contain it — just as elsewhere the dream sequence becomes the limiting locus of stylistic excess. (The momentariness of such excess, and its comfortable linkage to inebriation in *The Last Laugh*, is surely the cause of American admiration of that film.[5]) The expressionist images that bridge discontinuities through the violence of their reverberation occur only here and there in Hollywood film. Dreams are merely interludes. One does not wake up without waking up, as in *Caligari*, whose framing device melts into the picture it frames, displaying the same mise-en-scène. It is thus hardly surprising that an American Lang film like *Scarlet Street* — for instance — should be 'Langian' only at its edges, the beginning and end: the opening's male group round a circular table in a smoke-filled room recalling *M.*, as does the play with sound near the outset and the close, be it during the initial sighting of the femme fatale (Joan Bennett) (beaten up as an insistent drone drowns all natural sound and renders this a hallucinatory regression to silent cinema) or when 'she' is last seen in the supposed self-portrait carried across an art dealer's window. Other elements of *M.* are the window reflection as image of baffled desire (cf. *Woman at the Window*); the auditory hallucinations of unquenchable jealousy in the expressionistic, neon-flashlit coda, reminiscent of the voices impelling Becker (Peter Lorre); and the

Kafkaesque finality and inscrutability of the execution chamber door's closure on the man the painter framed for his own murder of the girl. Edward G. Robinson as the cashier who steps regressively into a youthful dream of love is just such a Little Big Man, diminutive in appearance yet grandiose in desire, as is Becker, though for most of the film he bears the mask of ordinariness. The masking amounts virtually to a repression, for *Scarlet Street* is far inferior to *M.*, with none of its tonic, fiercely and jubilantly ironic counterpoint. Since almost all of Lang's American films may be read as footnotes to *M.*, his first sound film, the auteurist case for these works is destroyed by *M.*'s demonstration of his ability to achieve austere thematic seriousness even when working in Germany and with Von Harbou. It is where the co-operation with Von Harbou is concerned that *Scarlet Street* is most piquant, for on learning that Kitty has affixed her name to his pictures, the cashier-painter remarks: 'What difference does it make whose name is on those pictures, your name or mine? Why, it's like we're married – only I take your name'. An art critic says of the putative painter, 'Sometimes it seems as if she were two people'; it is surely Lang's joke about a past phase of his career. It is as if Lang is implying that his own work was more powerful when its authorship was double, both his own and his wife's, and conceding the superiority of his own German work, in which the duality of films was rendered explicit by their pairing, rather than left implicit, as in his American work (e.g., *Scarlet Street* and *Woman at the Window*).

Elements of *M.* also crop up in the margins of *Fury*, Lang's first American film – particularly near the end, when the protagonist, seeking revenge for a southern town's efforts to lynch him, stands before shop windows and suffers auditory hallucinations of his girl-friend's objections to his design. Enno Patalas has described this film as '*The Nibelungen* and *M.* rolled into one and corrected by Hollywood'.[6] Those two German films are not the only ones *Fury* rolls into its mix: the barber's definition of sanity as the ability to resist murderous impulses and the question of lynch law do indeed recall *M.*, and Joe Wilson is indeed an American Kriemhild, corrected by the conscience embodied in his fiancée, but the woman hurling a firebrand towards the jailhouse repeats the incendiary agitation of the false Maria, while Joe beside the radio, listening to the trial of his would-be lynchers, is Mabuse redivivus, the hidden *eminence grise*. Hollywood's correction of the German Lang is primarily aesthetic denaturing, however, for all Pauline Kael's pinpointing of its stylistics as Germanic.[7] The disquieting slides of the camera between groups of menacing men, a visual quicksand, are among the work's few interesting formal features. Suggestions of a critique of American self-satisfaction may surface – the immigrant barber who has read the Constitution has a firmer grasp of the rule of law than do the natives, while Wilson concludes that his experiences have destroyed his belief in his country's difference from others – but they are only incidental. Seeds of a critique of film itself are also stifled before germination: Joe may lambast the blood-lust of the audience that delights in newsreel lynchings, thereby placing it on the same plane of culpability as the lynch mob itself, but film is exonerated when newsreel footage of the riot unmasks the back-scratching perjury of the townspeople. Closer to *M.* in time than is *Scarlet Street, Fury* is in fact further removed from expressionism; its first half is almost as demagogic as the lynch mob itself. Thus, expressionist elements come and go in Lang's American work, their intensity fluctuating rather than fading step by ordered step.

It is worth remembering, however, that even *M.* had been positioned at some remove from expressionism – despite its use of the doppelgänger motif. In it – as in the near-contemporary *Threepenny Opera* – we see a waning of the shadow that was the substance of expressionism. Formally motivated by the expressionist commitment to artifice, to emphasizing the degree to which the apparently real characters traced patterns in a *Lichtspiel* ('play of light' – that now-defunct German word for film); thematically grounded in the preoccupation with the shadow side of the self, its inauthenticity, and by the shadow's propensity to wax much larger than its owner, its growth indicating an individual's engulfment by overwhelming desire – in the late twenties the shadow departs German cinema. Reflections, particularly ones in shop windows, take its place, signs of the triumph of the New Objectivity: reflections are almost always the same size as the persons who cast them and do not tower over them. (One exception is the mirror maze, as in *Lady from Shanghai.*) The shadow that persists has been cast across the Atlantic: Orson Welles is the Shadow who knows the evil lurking in men's hearts. For insofar as expressionism enters Hollywood in earnest, it does so less through exiled Germans locked into a client relation to the studio system than through the ample frame of that American maverick, Welles, who combines expressionism's lighting and preoccupation with themes of tyranny and self-division with such motifs as the mirror and the demonic fun-fair. And Welles, of course, was to be only problematically a 'Hollywood' director, his post-*Kane* vicissitudes a powerful testimony to Tinseltown's inhospitability to expressionism.

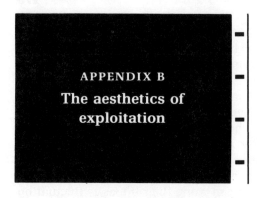

APPENDIX B

The aesthetics of exploitation

The success of *The Fly, Aliens* and many other films of SF horror indicates the degree to which mainstream film-making has been penetrated by imagery that once defined the area of address of the low-budget exploitation picture. The industry seems to have realized that the horror film can be fully exploited only if it shifts from low budget to high tech. The transition has been facilitated by the two-edged nature of the interest in the aesthetics of the exploitation picture displayed by the disciples and pupils of Roger Corman, and by Scorsese and Schrader in particular, for whom self-mortification becomes a road to salvation. Traditional exploitation pictures generally include ostensible disclaimers of a moral or sociological nature, allowing their makers to contend (in a court of law if necessary) that to present images of prostitution, drug addiction or putative 'white slavery' is to expose a social evil rather than cash in on prurient public interest in it. The dubious material is presented together with a mechanism for its disavowal: it has built-in 'credible deniability'. This split within the consciousness of the films permits them to address a divided self, a divided community. It is the separation of ego and id that is constitutive of the expressionist world of *Mean Streets* (in *Goodfellas* the id prevails). Scorsese, Schrader and others are further interested in exploitation flicks because the films' position outside Hollywood tradition and mainstream distribution makes it possible to discern in them an alternative tradition. The marginality of the exploitation movie (which, as it tries to appeal to and appease everybody, is paradoxically *representative* of the contradictoriness of society as a whole) corresponds to these film-makers' own sense of being out on a limb, on the dangerous, existential edge of things. And so, during the seventies, Scorsese, Schrader, De Palma and others – following in the footsteps of the French auteurs' apologias for the B picture – were to inject an 'exploitation ideology' into a mainstream that no longer knew what it wanted (genres having collapsed) and so was prepared to fall back on the reliably bankable staple cinematic experience of *shock.*

An audience of film buffs alone could never, however, have brought exploitation aesthetics into the mainstream. That could be achieved only with the aid of an audience that is now central to the Hollywood mainstream: the adolescent one. Many critics have described the modern schlock horror audience as composed of adolescents who find in such films an opportunity to distance, and laugh at, the possible and impossible effects of the strange bodily changes they themselves are undergoing. James Twitchell and Walker Evans have even likened the experience of such films to tribal rites of initiation. Thus, Evans declares, 'Monster movies clearly reproduce ritual patterns to focus on those social and personal needs which were satisfied in premodern cultures by rites of initiation into adulthood.'[1] The analogy is shaky: whereas tribal initiations are socially imposed as a way of marking officially the transition from puberty to adulthood and occur once and for all, teen attendance at horror flicks is more like a way of entering a gang within whose confines time and the maturation process are arrested. If you can look at this, the dare goes, then you are one of us. So if teenagers can be said to identify with adult society when attending such movies, it is in the sense of absorbing hegemony, accepting what adults think they want, not that of submitting to a ritual. Twitchell can note that teenagers approve of material that shocks their parents[2] without grasping how this audience feature undermines the initiation rite analogy.

Adolescents may think they are transgressing, but the boundaries of permissible wrongdoing are clearly marked. Cinema becomes the marginal space that is the only one teenagers can call their own (a magnified version of the alternative, the living room when parents are away, TV set digesting a gory video). The sense of a lack of space is linked to another characteristic of the schlock horror movie: what Gareth Sansom has termed its preoccupation with territoriality. In one of the scenarios of territoriality, the Other invades, possesses or mutilates the body (sometimes all three), while in another – as Sansom puts it – 'the viewing subject is positioned as a mobile locus on a disturbing trajectory through territorialized diegetic space'.[3] Sansom's remarks on territoriality provide a useful starting-point for sketching the psychology of the implicit viewer of these films, since it is the teenager – about to enter society – who experiences space thus. The recent prevalence of the horror movie surely also reflects a suspicion entertained by all the inhabitants of a global economy: that no space is truly 'their own' any longer. If it is the adolescent who experiences this lack of personal space most intensely, the current phase of capitalism can be said to render us all adolescent. Ominous breathing or music combines with the jittery hand-held camera to evoke a fear of the return of the space's owner from the absence that has tempted one to enter it. On occasions, that which returns may be the nature that has mutated under the shocks administered to it, or the child repressed by the pressures to speedy maturation. Necessity then compels delivery of the final shock. In other cases it may be a demonized image of the parent or the working class. (Each provides the labour that furnishes one's leisure to watch.) The ghostly owner of the house is defined as diabolic; the parent ought already to be a ghost and leave the home to the teenager. The existing owner is demonized so as to legitimate his destruction and replacement by the adolescent spearheading the next generation: and that adolescent's identification with the machine and its artificial intelligence has reached the point of self-reification – as the use of 'generation' with reference to computers indicates. Frustration over one's inability to enter into the riches wasteful ancestors enjoyed boils over into forcible, murderous evacuation of all others from the home one cannot have. Thus, the modern American horror film is not simply, as Twitchell argues, an initiation into sexual knowledge (though the vacuum that requires to be filled, the space to be invaded, may of course also represent the vagina); it is a rehearsal for the invasion of the territory of the Other in general, be it the older generation, woman, nature, outer space or enemy soil.

Such films offer an imaginary training ground for colonialism, a translation of colonialism into a purely imaginary space that may then leave one entrapped in a virtual reality of fantasy. Colonialism is internalized because the possible consequences of its externalization in a world bristling with nuclear weapons might be so horrendous. The anxiety the protagonist feels on entering this prepossessed space is that of the individualist without allies; the monstrosity of one's individualism has alienated all possible confrères. The Other the film destroys is among other things the denied sign of the adolescent's exile in pimply monstrosity. The horror film's concern with isolation and its transcendence is profoundly pubescent. The creature's isolation mirrors your own and so renders you its most likely victim. Safety lies in the crowd that shouts at the screen monster – the monstrous screen – like the audience during the three-minute hate of *Nineteen Eighty-Four*. If, nevertheless, the horror film contains a utopian element, its dreamed removal of defiling forces from the earth we inhabit is checkmated by its inability to locate the true culprit, its willingness to vent rage on scapegoats instead. The horror film's images may be cast by light, but it fails to perceive the darkness behind the mask of the light-bringing angel.

Horror films dramatize frustrated identifications between an individual and a community. The monster is an outsider, and hero and heroine are caught between it and society. If, for most of the film, they are unable to reach the safety of the group, it is because of their unconscious unwillingness to pay the price of conformity. In the end they are driven into the community's arms by the realization that isolation could cause them also to be classified as monsters. (In *Night of the Living Dead* the black who survives – who remains outside – is then shot by the mopping-up soldiers.) Paradoxically, the ultimate bugaboo in the American horror film is the one it is least able consciously to acknowledge, American individualism itself: to stand out from the crowd is to be a target (presidents are assassinated); it is to have destruction's mark of Cain inscribed on one's brow, one's look so distorted that murder claims justification as a euthanizing coup-de-grâce. As democracy proscribes the outstanding individual (who does he think he is?), his powers become malevolent and monstrous. Democracy projects its fascist underside onto an Other that is its own mobile mirror.

APPENDIX C
A note on ideology

The notion that society was melting into a classless homogeneity, widely propagated in the sixties, was accompanied by the proposition that we were witnessing the end of ideology. As always, however, the apparent end was really a transmutation. Whereas previously 'ideology' had designated the consciously held beliefs of a single class, group or society, in the sixties the word began to be used to denote an unconscious mental structure. The old usage had presupposed a rationalist faith in the possibility of dispelling false consciousness by unmasking social relations, carrying the torch of enlightenment to the slaves in the cavern. The past thirty years, however, have seen a growing suspicion that a false consciousness of one's position can outlive its unmasking: fearing the loss of relative material gains rather than believing in the possibility of losing its chains, the working class was seen to have suffered *embourgeoisement.* More leg-room within the chains seemed to be the primary aim, and the structure of ideology seemed to be a deep one. Remarking on the paradoxical inability of the bourgeoisie to name itself within bourgeois society, Roland Barthes was to conclude that this caused it to disappear as an ideological fact. But if the bourgeoisie is unnameable, it is not simply because it is unspeakable, but because it is simultaneously hemmed in to the point of nonexistence (between capital and labour) and limitless. (The extremes for which it is the excluded middle can themselves be absorbed into it – the capitalist using it for camouflage, the worker unable to grasp that to enjoy greater material wealth than one's forebears is not to escape oppression.) To seek to oppose 'the bourgeoisie' thus becomes a task as endless, romantic and harmless as that of Don Quixote. To conflate a system with one of its parts and term it 'bourgeois' is to fail to recognize the true falsity that pervades the polarized whole. It is to be caught up in the repetitive compulsion of fighting yesterday's battles. Althusser's notion that ideology had no history was merely the most blatant example of Marxism's blindness to current change. With nothing existing outside ideology and ideology itself anchored in inaccessibly deep mental structures, change became no more than a utopian mirage. Left-wing fatalism was augmented by the conviction that all that words of protest could alter was a superstructure no longer attached to ('relatively autonomous of', in the Althusserian formulation) the base. If false consciousness survives the recognition of its own falsity, it is because the lack of real alternatives (real socialism was never really socialistic) causes the exploited to resign themselves to exploitation and pursue instead the tiny areas of breathing space micropolitics aims to secure. After all, would not an end of exploitation mean a partial evaporation of the privilege of the Western and Northern societies themselves? Meanwhile, the multinational system of capital so diversifies itself that any merely local attack misses the target, which can be secreted in another part of the system. Only in a society with a strong centre, whose securing can credibly stand for a taking of the whole, is revolution possible. And the system persists by generating the spectre of a world of short resources we can no longer afford to share. 'We' are threatened – by Third World demographics, fanaticism, debt and environmental devastation. 'We' must hold what we have against all comers, since to give 'them' an inch is ruefully to discover them annexing the miles of *Lebensraum* their pullulating masses require. And it is surely this 'us'–'them' distinction that is the fundamental form of ideology.

Notes

Preface

1 Pauline Kael, 'Trash, Art and the Movies', in *Going Steady* (London: Temple Smith, 1970), p. 129.
2 T. W. Adorno, 'Der Essay als Form', in *Noten zur Literatur I* (Frankfurt am Main: Suhrkamp, 1975), p. 29.
3 Walter Benjamin, 'Theses on the Philosophy of History', in *Illuminations,* trans. Harry Zohn (London: Collins/Fontana 1973), p. 265.
4 Kael, 'Trash', p. 106.
5 Ibid., p. 129.

Introduction

1 See Hermann Broch, 'Zum Problem des Kitsches', in *Die Idee ist ewig: Essays und Briefe* (Munich: Deutscher Taschenbuch Verlag, 1968), pp. 117–32.
2 See Eco's useful definition: 'One could define Kitsch in structural terms as *a stylistic device torn from its proper context and inserted in another context, the general structure of which lacks the homogeneous and necessary qualities of the original structure, whilst – by means of this unlawful insertion – the message is presented as an original work*' ('The Structure of Bad Taste', in *Italian Writing Today* [Harmondsworth: Penguin, 1967], p. 119). One may note here the recurrence of the part–whole relationship considered in my preface.
3 For more on *Clarissa*, see '*Clarissa*, Dialectic and Unreadability', in my *The Realist Fantasy: Fiction and Reality since 'Clarissa'* (London: Macmillan; New York: St. Martin's, 1983), pp. 23–49.
4 Hans-Jürgen Syberberg, Introduction to *Hitler: A Film from Germany* (New York: Farrar, Straus & Giroux, 1982), p. 9: 'In kitsch, in banality, in triviality and their popularity lie the remaining rudiments and germ cells of the vanished traditions of our myths, deteriorated but latently effective'.
5 T. W. Adorno, *Minima Moralia,* trans. Rodney Livingston (London: New Left Books, 1974), pp. 146–8.
6 A subtle examination of this question may be found in Peter Stallybrass and Allon White, *The Politics and Poetics of Transgression* (Ithaca, N.Y.: Cornell University Press, 1986).
7 Walter Benjamin, 'The Work of Art in the Age of Mechanical Reproduction',

182

in *Illuminations,* trans. Harry Zohn (London: Collins/Fontana, 1973), p. 252n19.

8 I describe this process at greater length in the chapter entitled 'Auteurs' in my *The Story of the Lost Reflection* (London: Verso, 1985).

9 T. W. Adorno, 'On Popular Music', in *Zeitschrift für Sozialforschung,* vol. 9 (New York: Institute of Social Research, 1941; photomechanical reprint, Munich: Deutscher Taschenbuch Verlag, 1980), p. 43.

10 Fredric Jameson, *The Political Unconscious: Narrative as a Socially Symbolic Act* (Ithaca, N.Y.: Cornell University Press, 1981), pp. 281–99.

11 David Bordwell and Kristin Thompson, *Film Art* (New York: Knopf, 1986), pp. 325–30.

12 See Adorno's reading of Stravinsky in *Philosophie der neuen Musik* (Frankfurt am Main: Ullstein, 1974), pp. 121–89.

I. Getting in on the act

1 Nathanael West, *The Day of the Locust,* in *Miss Lonelyhearts and The Day of the Locust* (New York: New Directions, 1962), p. 144.

2 Pauline Kael, 'Charmer', in *State of the Art* (New York: Dutton, 1985), pp. 335–40.

II. We see in part

1 For more on *Vertigo,* see ' "Vertigo", Visual Pleasure and the End of *Film Noir*', in my *The Gorgon's Gaze* (Cambridge University Press, 1991), pp. 177–86.

2 See René Girard, *Violence and the Sacred* (Baltimore: Johns Hopkins University Press, 1984), pp. 143–68.

3 Kael, 'Charmer', p. 263.

4 Gabriel Josipovici, *The Book of God* (New Haven, Conn.: Yale University Press, 1988), p. 193.

III. Limits of our language, limits of our world

1 Ryszard Kapuściński, *Lapidarium* (Warsaw: Czytelnik, 1990), p. 132.

2 Robert Scholes, *Structural Fabulation: An Essay on Fiction of the Future* (Notre Dame, Ind.: University of Notre Dame Press, 1975), p. 17.

3 Ibid., p. 18.

4 Roland Barthes, *Mythologies* (Paris: Seuil, 1957), pp. 144–6.

5 Ursula Le Guin, Introduction to *The Left Hand of Darkness* (New York: New Ace Science Fiction Books, 1976). The introduction is unnumbered, but the penultimate page contains the following piquant declaration: 'I write science fiction, and science fiction isn't about the future'.

6 It is surely significant that the English translation of Stanisław Lem's mammoth *Fantastyka i futurologia* should be *Science Fiction and the Fantastic.* The confusion of science fiction with futurology is clearly a widespread one. Here again, Le Guin is salutary: 'I am not predicting or prescribing. I am describing. I am describing certain aspects of psychological reality in the novelist's way, which is by inventing elaborately circumstantial lies' (Introduction to *Left Hand of Darkness*).

7 Robert M. Philmus, *Into the Unknown: The Evolution of Science Fiction from Francis Godwin to H. G. Wells* (Berkeley and Los Angeles: University of California Press, 1970), p. vii.

8 Brian W. Aldiss, *Billion Year Spree: The True History of SF* (Garden City, N.Y.: Doubleday, 1973), p. 245.

9 Scholes, *Structural Fabulation*, p. 40.

10 A waning of the imagination of the other may be a concomitant of postmodernism, which stages the past as spectacle, depthless fashion. (Similarly, the second-generation 'Saturday Night Live' is comprehensible only to a person steeped in the trivial pursuit of American TV – the counterculturalist's degeneration into tube addict sadly manifest in Pynchon's *Vineland* also.)

11 One may thus be sceptical of Robin Wood's efforts to discern a 'progressive' strain in the genre, based on the auteurist's chronic identification of low budget and subversive value. See his 'An Introduction to the American Horror Film,' in *Movies and Methods*, vol. 2., ed. Bill Nichols (Berkeley and Los Angeles: University of California Press, 1985), pp. 210–20 in particular. The distinction between SF and horror is fundamental, since its absence can cause far too cavalier a dismissal of one of the most illuminating hermeneutics of the horror genre, the psychoanalytic one. Thus, although Noël Carroll, in *The Philosophy of Horror, or Paradoxes of the Heart* (New York: Routledge, 1990), pp. 173–6, rightly notes that the unthought is not the same as the repressed, his failure to separate horror from SF leads him to ignore the different status of monsters in each genre. Their purely theoretical status in SF does indeed mean that in that genre the unthought is not necessarily the repressed. But in horror the monsters are secretly familiar, and to unthink them is to repress them (so psychoanalytic language is appropriate to their discussion). Carroll confuses the intellectual and combinatory procedures of SF with the more emotionally laden ones of horror, and this vitiates his otherwise lively and stimulating book.

12 One may recall the anecdotes according to which the audiences of early cinema read a close-up as a mutilation of the actor.

13 Stuart Cornfeld, *Dialogue on Film,* Interview in *American Film* 12, no. 6 (April 1987), p. 11.

14 T. S. Eliot, 'Tradition and the Individual Talent', in *Selected Prose,* ed. John Hayward (Harmondsworth: Penguin, 1965), p. 23: 'The existing order is complete before the new work arrives; for order to persist after the supervention of novelty, the *whole* existing order must be, if ever so slightly, altered'.

15 Karol Irzykowski, *X Muza* (Warsaw: Wydawnictwo artystyczne i filmowe, 1977 [1924]).

16 For further comment on this phenomenon, and in particular its connection with the emergence of cinema, see my *The Double and the Other: Identity as Ideology in Post-Romantic Fiction* (London: Macmillan; New York: St. Martin's, 1988), p. 54.

17 This is what happens in the work of D. H. Lawrence, who seeks to do away with our culture's emphasis on sight, which grounds relationships in the maintenance of safe *distances,* replacing it with touch: the touch relied on by Birkin and Gerald as they wrestle in *Women in Love,* as Birkin says he's tired of people he can see: tired of distance. Lawrence's protagonists are often associated with animals, whose forms they enter, like Zeus, to prosecute human designs more effectively by rendering them invisible. One may be reminded of the amorality of Wells's invisible man, whose invisibility allows him to attack others with impunity. The dream of escape into invisibility, like so many other utopian images, can be traced back to the Garden of Eden – first, because to become invisible is to be as God, to become a spirit within one's own lifetime, i.e., to die without dying. The serpent, the subtlest of all beasts, had said that to partake of the fruit of the forbidden tree would render the eater divine. It is the idea of invisibility that procures the forbidden fruit (first, one thinks one is unseen) and is itself that fruit. Ironically, in hiding from God after their offence, Adam and Eve are seeking to be like him. Their concealment is the helpless parody of the true invisibility that would render humans shameless, no longer possessed of naked private parts of which to be ashamed. Wells's invisible man walks the streets naked (he has to, for if he wore anything he would become visible): his nakedness becomes apparent only in the moment of death. Similarly, Sophocles' Oedipus blinds himself in a magical effort to achieve the shamelessness of invisibility. If there are no eyes in my world, why should there be any in yours? At least no one can look him in the eye and cause him to flinch with shame at his deeds. Oedipus is shameless both before and after his blinding. He does indeed resemble Wells's invisible man: each is irritable and splenetic. Each, in becoming invisible, has separated himself from society and thereby become – confounding the binarism of Aristotle's distinction – *both* a beast and a god.

18 Stanisław Lem, *Solaris,* trans. from the French (*sic*) by Joanna Kilmartin and Steve Cox (New York: Walker, 1970), p. 60.

19 John Donne, 'The Dreame', in *Poetical Works,* ed. Sir Herbert Grierson (London: Oxford University Press, 1966), p. 33.

20 Lem, *Solaris,* p. 62.

21 Andrew Marvell, *The Complete Poems,* ed. Elizabeth Story Donno (Harmondsworth: Penguin, 1978), p. 49.

22 Lem, *Solaris,* p. 61.

23 Andrey Tarkovsky, *Sculpting in Time* (New York: Knopf, 1987), p. 72.

24 Simonetta Salvestroni, 'The Science-Fiction Films of Andrei Tarkovsky', *Science-Fiction Studies,* 14, pt. 3 (November 1987), p. 305.

25 Tarkovsky, *Sculpting in Time,* p. 138.

26 The camera's movement past a litter of objects corresponds to Tarkovsky's conviction that 'the artistic image is always a metonym, where one thing is substituted for another, the smaller for the greater' (*Sculpting in Time,* p. 38). The frame's impotence to encompass everything becomes patent. The part directs one to the whole of which it is a fragment. But because the image is only ever a fragment, capable only of suggesting wholeness, it is unable finally to convince us such wholeness exists. Perhaps this is why Tarkovsky then uses some tell-tale words: 'To tell of what is living, the artist uses something dead' (ibid.). He uses the corpse of Harey.

IV. Crying in the dark

1 René Girard, *Violence and the Sacred* (Baltimore: Johns Hopkins University Press, 1984 [1977]), pp. 68–72.

2 Peter Brooks, *The Melodramatic Imagination: Balzac, Henry James, Melodrama, and the Mode of Excess* (New York: Columbia University Press, 1985), p. 2.

3 Ibid., p. 11.

4 Mary Ann Doane, *The Desire to Desire: The Women's Film of the 1940's* (Bloomington: Indiana University Press, 1987), p. 95.

5 Julian Jaynes, *The Origin of Consciousness in the Breakdown of the Bicameral Mind* (Boston: Houghton Mifflin, 1976), p. 98. If many theorists of cinematic experience define it as involving a sense of entry into 'a world', this may well be because the enveloping qualities of sound make us feel we are 'inside'. Unfortunately, in line with the widespread tendency to speak of film as exclusively (rather than primarily) a visual medium, they tend to attribute the sense of being 'inside' to identification with the camera. (This tendency has been criticized incisively by Gregory Currie, who terms it 'the participation thesis'; nevertheless, he also ascribes too little importance to sound and concentrates on cinema's visual aspect.)

6 For further remarks on melodrama and tragedy, see Appendix I to my *The Gorgon's Gaze: German Cinema, Expressionism and the Image of Horror* (Cambridge University Press, 1991), pp. 232–6.

7 Although there has been much play with the notion of hysteria in recent theorization of melodrama, its linkage to bisexuality in Freud's theories has passed unmentioned, perhaps because such a linkage would complicate, and compromise, attempts to valorize melodrama as 'a woman's form'. See Freud, 'Hysterical Phantasies and their Relation to Bisexuality', *Collected Papers*, vol. 2 (London: Hogarth Press and the Institute of Psychoanalysis, 1950), p. 57 ('An hysterical symptom is the expression of both a masculine and a feminine unconscious sexual phantasy') and p. 58 (which speaks of 'certain hysterical attacks in which the patient acts at one and the same time both parts of the underlying sexual phantasy – for instance, in one case I observed the patient pressed her dress to her body with one hand [as the woman] while trying to tear it off with the other [as the man]').

8 Garry Wills, *Reagan's America: Innocents at Home* (Garden City, N.Y.: York, 1987), p. 380: 'The lone bomber...is imposing his or her will, and winning, against the joint wills of all those who lifted several hundred people into the air inside their large tubular capsule. That is why the terrorist is the true individualist of our time, the lone defier (and defeater) of the common will'.

9 Thomas Elsaesser reaches a similar conclusion in his fine 'Tales of Sound and Fury: Observations on the Family Melodrama', in *Movies and Methods*, vol. 2, ed. Bill Nichols (Berkeley and Los Angeles: University of California Press, 1985), p. 185: 'One of the characteristic features of melodramas in general is that they concentrate on the point of view of the victim: what makes the films mentioned above exceptional is the way they manage to present *all* the characters convincingly as victims'.

10 Here, Sun Yu's *Daybreak* (1931) becomes of particular interest as a zoologi-

cal garden in which three of the genre's subspecies are assembled. Its progression is one from early-twenties melodrama to that of the mid-twenties, concluding in that of the late twenties. Griffith, Stroheim, Pabst and Sternberg succeed one another; in other words, one has Victorian melodrama, followed by political melodrama, followed by revolutionary kitsch. The closing pastiche of Sternberg is particularly glaring, an amalgam of *The Blue Angel* and *Dishonored* that plays havoc with the film's earlier characterization. Where the midsection deems prostitution the stigma of a country girl's city degradation, an ignominy that calls out for revolution, in the final third her fishnet-stockinged leg unfolds in confident self-display: victim becomes Material Girl. Any spectator inclined to laugh when a relative asks if she's going to see her friends again (one assumes she has left that sphere behind) finds laughter choked when she does indeed do so. Once the signifier of degradation, prostitution is now a Brechtian/Sternbergian (!) way of redistributing wealth. There is an unacknowledged shift from a feminist to a Marxist position. Sun Yu's lead actress, Lili Li, can hardly have been bothered by the incoherence, for it permits her to play every big part in the book.

11 Jack Zipes, 'Political Dimensions of *The Lost Honor of Katharina Blum*', *New German Critique*, no. 12 (Fall 1977), p. 83.

12 'Tales of Sound and Fury', Elsaesser, p. 185; quoted in Zipes, 'Political Dimensions', p. 82.

13 Zipes, 'Political Dimensions', p. 82.

14 An even more confusing use of melodrama is found in the previous Von Trotta–Schlöndorff collaboration, *Strohfeuer*, which is usually located in the filmography of the latter. On the one hand, Elisabeth, whose unfeeling husband is well able to mobilize public preconceptions to deprive her of custody of her child, is a victim, Virtue in distress. On another, however, the victim is *blamed:* her female lawyer describes her efforts at emancipation as 'a flash in the pan' (to dream of singing in American musicals is hardly to want to change the world), and the film endorses this perspective. *Strohfeuer*, its title, denotes a fleeting enthusiasm. The close shows Elisabeth remarrying to the sound-track's first-person song about a woman who did as she was told, avoided violence – and ended up with nothing. More ambiguous condemnation is provided when an art gallery owner capable of quoting Reich when it suits his aims of seduction likens her to a drawing of Nana, a woman in revolt with big heart and minuscule head. His remark is odious yet true. The name 'Nana' is particularly interesting, since Schlöndorff's use of his wife resembles Godard's simultaneously adoring and objectifying use of Karina in *Vivre sa vie* and *Une Femme est une femme:* indeed, Schlöndorff fuses elements of those two films (woman as victim – but also victim of the director, who gets her to do cute, excruciating things, such as sing and dance despite a minimal talent). A picture of Schlöndorff himself appears at one point. Is it a casual detail or an indication of his awareness that he too is the repressive husband, keeping his wife in place (*before* the camera)? The film leaves one queasy, as if Von Trotta's consent to participate in this scenario had indeed rendered *her* like Elisabeth or Nana, not quite conscious of what is going on. Schlöndorff himself seems to share this partial awareness: does he realize that his camera's fixation on his wife's legs recalls the thinly disguised lust of the Cranach

Lucretia he has the art historian condemn (the slightly obtuse use of 'an authority' another Godardian feature)?

15 See Michael Rutschky, 'Realität träumen', *Merkur*, no. 363 (July 1978), pp. 773–85, quoted in translation in Elsaesser, *New German Cinema: A History* (New Brunswick, N.J.: Rutgers University Press, 1989), pp. 56–60.

16 Elias Canetti, *Crowds and Power* (London: Gollancz, 1962), p. 173.

17 Raymond Durgnat, *Franju* (London: Studio Vista, 1967).

18 Mary Ann Doane, 'The Abstraction of a Lady: *La Signora di tutti*', *Cinema Journal* 28, no. 1 (Fall 1988), pp. 65–84.

V. Doubles and male fantasies

1 George M. Wilson, *Narration in Light: Studies in Cinematic Point of View* (Baltimore: Johns Hopkins University Press, 1986), p. 49.

2 Brian Henderson, '*The Searchers*: An American Dilemma', in *Movies and Methods*, vol. 2, ed. Bill Nichols (Berkeley and Los Angeles: University of California Press, 1985), pp. 444–9 in particular.

3 See Joseph McBride and Michael Wilmington, *John Ford* (New York: Da Capo, 1975), p. 179.

4 Henderson, '*The Searchers*', p. 437.

5 Kaja Silverman, 'Dis-Embodying the Female Voice', in *Re-Vision: Essays in Feminist Film Criticism*, ed. Mary Ann Doane, Patricia Mellenkamp and Linda Williams (Frederick, Md.: University Publications of America, 1984), p. 134.

6 See my *The Gorgon's Gaze: German Cinema, Expressionism and the Image of Horror* (Cambridge University Press, 1991), pp. 246–8.

7 Ibid., p. 170.

VI. How near are the far-away places

1 Alexander Solzhenitsyn, *The Nobel Lectures* (quoted in Michael Scammell, *Solzhenitsyn: A Biography* [London: Norton, 1984], p. 771).

2 The widespread theoretical suspicion that production values necessarily entail commodification becomes harder to sustain when Third World cinema, having begun in the monochrome that signified virtuous impoverishment in the sixties, later moved into colour. Perhaps the most interesting attempt to incorporate this shift into a revised theory of third cinema is found in Fredric Jameson's 'On Magic Realism in Film', *Critical Inquiry*, 12, no. 2 (Winter 1985), pp. 301–25, which, in contradistinction to most critiques of the 'dominant cinema', values the 'intensely visual pleasure' (p. 303) these films afford and argues that there is a 'necessary and constitutive relationship between intensities of colors and bodies in these works and their process of de-narrativization which has ultimately been shown to be a process of ideological analysis and deconstruction' (p. 323). The intensity Jameson notes may nevertheless have monochrome as background in a double sense: the memory of monochrome as a *recent* form of film and the relatively limited colour palette of environments devoid of (and often polemically opposed to) the constant stimuli of billboards.

3 If film can be likened to a dream, then voice-over may perhaps be the speech of the subconscious (*not* the unconscious): a level of speech that manifests itself in insomnia, as it says things and keeps one awake, without logical progression or transitions. (This voice of insomnia, the self telling itself the garbled story of its own identity, may be the purest form of the inner speech of which Eikhenbaum writes.) Whence the leaps in progression in the films of a Godard, a Kidlat Tahimik, a Harun Farocki? One of the most powerful examples of the use of sound-track to speak the subconscious is surely David Lynch's *Eraserhead*. Its sound-track swarms with strange rumbling, hissing and humming noises, the squeals of a baby, the sibilants of piping and elevator doors, wind blowing and water bubbling. Lynch's concern with piping, like that of Terry Gilliam in *Brazil*, indicates a willingness to go below surfaces and examine the body as the chugging source of the rumbling Americans know from the world of TV laxative commercials. If, in the United States, plumbing represents the repressed – as I have argued in my 'Unfinished Business: Thomas Pynchon and the Quest for Revolution', *New Left Review* (November–December 1986), p. 160 – Lynch's sound-track can be described punningly as a plumbing of the unconscious, transmitting it up to the level of the subconscious. The imperfect nature of world and body betrayed by the irregular growling is the fundamental theme of Lynch's work, expressed most poignantly in *The Elephant Man*.

4 See Chapter III, the section entitled 'Visions and Revisions of *Solaris*'.

5 Raymond Williams, *The Country and the City* (St. Alban's: Paladin, 1975), p. 334.

6 Ryszard Kapuściński, *Lapidarium* (Warsaw: Czytelnik, 1990), pp. 209–10.

7 Ibid., p. 98.

8 Alexis de Tocqueville, *Democracy in America*, vol. 2 (New York: Vintage, 1945), p. 18. It is generalization that effects the transition from thinking in terms of behaviours to thinking in terms of innate propensity – a transition central to the emergence of modernity. Ivan Illich discusses the change in connection with 'the historical discovery of the homosexual as a special kind of human' (in *Gender* [New York: Pantheon, 1982), p. 148n), noting the first appearance of the word 'homosexual' in 1890 (*OED*). In the historical moment of naturalism, all classes of humans are special kinds, not only homosexual ones. In the same way as single action is generalized into mind-set, the individual becomes a replication of family, class, race. Sartre's account of how Genet became a thief after being called one demonstrates the devastating power of such typing. It is a loss of the particular within the totality that contributes to the archaeology of fascism and makes the fascist affinity for various thinkers of the 1890s no surprise.

9 See my 'Unfinished Business', p. 125.

10 It may thus be contrasted with *Sammy and Rosie Get Laid*, the second Frears–Kureishi co-operation, which is far more problematic and strangely evasive. It begins with London street fighting between blacks and police; standing to one side is a refined, melancholy black, Victoria, who would like to fight but is appalled by the violence. His dilemma mirrors that of Frears and Kureishi. While demonstrating that the impossibility of democratic systemic change sows the seeds of violence, they stand back from it. They wish only to scandalize and safely displace outrage from political to sexual

transgression. The agonizing dilemmas of British political life in the eighties – the paralysis of the Left in the face of Thatcherism – are repressed and replaced with a pseudoproblem, the question of how the liberal Sammy and Rosie are to cope with the torturer's role Sammy's father played in Pakistan. Rafi, the father, is a convenient diversion, allowing the film to sacrifice radicalism to etiolated radical chic, rendering it decorative and brittle.

VII. White noise

1 Richard Dyer, *Heavenly Bodies* (London: Macmillan/British Film Institute, 1987), p. 45.

2 Ibid., p. 46.

3 See Maureen Turim, 'Gentlemen Consume Blondes', in *Movies and Methods,* vol. 2, ed. Bill Nichols (Berkeley and Los Angeles: University of California Press, 1985), p. 371. For David Thomson ('Baby Go Boom!' *Film Comment* [September–October 1982], pp. 34–41), Marilyn is most impressive in her photographs. Here one must distinguish between the shots for which she posed and the stills from her films. The photographs are controlled, even manipulated by Marilyn herself, with an often hard unpleasant edge of successful self-reification. They are all too self-consciously 'quotable'. The stills, by way of contrast, are far more ambiguous and touch the imagination. Marilyn's nervousness means she exists only as a series of moments, flickering anxiety matching the flicker of film itself. Notoriously unable to remember lines from one moment to the next (in the photographs the absence of the need to say anything generates the air of control), she may indeed change twenty-four times per second.

4 For more on *King Kong,* see my *Gorgon's Gaze: German Cinema, Expressionism and the Image of Horror* (Cambridge University Press, 1991), pp. 77–81; and for Dietrich, see ibid., pp. 54–72.

5 Norman Mailer, 'King of the Hill', in *Existential Errands* (Scarborough: Signet, 1972), p. 27.

6 Ibid., p. 28.

7 Garry Wills, 'Muhamad Ali', in *Lead Time: A Journalist's Education* (Garden City, N.Y.: Doubleday, 1983), p. 338.

8 Mailer 'King of the Hill', p. 31.

9 T. W. Adorno, *Minima Moralia,* trans. Rodney Livingston (London: New Left Books, 1974), p. 28. It might be more accurate, however, to state that such glorification of the system is implicit, a result of the work's vaunting of its own ability to restore fairy-tale justice and hence of the system that permits that work's existence.

10 See the transmutation of noir into tragedy effected by Jacques Tourneur in *Out of the Past,* analysed in Chapter V in the section entitled 'The Voice-over and the Mute'.

VIII. Private dancers

1 Umberto Eco, '*Casablanca:* Cult Movies and Intertextual Collage', in *Travels in Hyperreality* (New York: Harcourt, Brace, Jovanovich, 1986), p. 208 in

particular: '*Casablanca* became a cult movie because it is not *one* movie. It is "movies" ' – whence the title of his subsection: 'The Archetypes Hold a Reunion' (ibid.).

2 Mircea Eliade, *Myths, Dreams and Mysteries,* trans. Philip Mairet (London: Collins, 1968), pp. 36–7: 'The re-living of that which the Gods and Heroes had lived *in illo tempore* imparted a sacramental aspect to human existence'. Cult works or stars may thus be read as seeking to counter the 'fall into time' of secularization.

3 Jean Baudrillard, *For a Critique of the Political Economy of the Sign* (St. Louis, Mo.: Telos Press, 1981), p. 92.

4 Thomas De Quincey, 'Suspiria de Profundis', in *Confessions of an Opium Eater and Other Writings,* ed. Grevel Lindop (Oxford: Oxford University Press, 1985), p. 145. My Baudrillard and De Quincey quotations parallel Ernest Becker's more strictly psychoanalytic terminology: 'The transference object always looms larger than life size because it represents all of life and hence all one's fate' (*The Denial of Death* [New York: Free Press, 1973], p. 147). Love and hate transference creates overblown objects (so Nosferatu's defeat is imminent when the enormous shadow accompanying him up the stairs is scaled down to a reflection in his female adversary's room). Although the twentieth century drained the authority of the parents, the primal objects of transference, by rendering their skills of scant use to their offspring, the will to transference simply sought other havens: arguably, ones more harmful to the individual, more prone to fracture his or her identity, because more distantly related. (The leader needs *charisma* to elevate his or her authority, and fear and envy of the parents dictate the subversion of the family under fascism and communism.) The emergence of cinema can provide towering new figures for identification and yet further diminish the authority of such figures. (They are merely fictions.) Could it be that the overwhelming impact of Hollywood stars on American life provided a set of foci for transference that helped prevent the emergence of fascism in the United States? (This conclusion is underwritten by Nathanael West's confusion of the star-struck groupie and the fascist, which intuits a real connection but misreads its meaning.) Becker remarks that 'the human face is really an awesome primary miracle; it naturally paralyzes you by its splendor if you give in to it as the fantastic thing it is', adding that 'we mostly repress this miraculousness' (ibid.). In the cinema, however, we become aware of it once more, though we forget that the god one can bear to look at must be false.

5 For further reflections on the turned back in modernism, see my *The Gorgon's Gaze: German Cinema, Expressionism and the Image of Horror* (Cambridge University Press, 1991), pp. 55–60.

6 Miriam Hansen, 'Pleasure, Ambivalence, Identification: Valentino and Female Spectatorship', *Cinema Journal* 25, no. 4 (Summer 1986), p. 11.

7 Although the attribution to the good girl of the name of Bizet's femme fatale might prompt a psychoanalytic reader to speak of her fundamental ambivalence, in actuality in this case it functions in terms of the code of exoticism and signifies no more than 'recognizably Spanish'.

8 Hansen, 'Pleasure, Ambivalence, Identification', p. 15.

9 Ibid., p. 12: 'Valentino's appeal depends, to a large degree, on the manner in

which he combines masculine control of the look with the feminine quality of "to-be-looked-at-ness," to use Mulvey's rather awkward term'.

10 Ibid., p. 17.

11 Ibid., p. 19.

12 Ibid., p. 20.

13 Ibid.

14 For more on the merging of the arts in the late nineteenth century as a joint venture by bankrupts, see my *The Realist Fantasy: Fiction and Reality since 'Clarissa'* (London: Macmillan; New York: St. Martin's, 1983), pp. 69–70. For more on the *Gesamtkunstwerk* in general, see my 'Cinema, Symbolism and the *Gesamtkunstwerk*', in *Comparative Criticism Yearbook,* vol. 4 (Cambridge University Press, 1982), pp. 213–29.

15 Jacques Attali, *Noise: The Political Economy of Music* (Minneapolis: University of Minnesota Press, 1985), p. 3.

16 See her intriguing dialogue with Neil Postman (*Harper's* [March 1991], pp. 44–55), particularly pp. 46–7.

17 E. Ann Kaplan, *Rocking Around the Clock: Music Television, Postmodernism and Consumer Culture* (New York: Methuen, 1987).

18 Marsha Kinder, 'Music Video and the Spectator: Television, Ideology and Dream', in *Film Quarterly,* vol. XX (Fall 1984), pp. 2–15.

19 Ernest Jones, *On the Nightmare of Bloodsucking,* in *On the Nightmare* (New York: Liveright, 1971), quoted in *Focus on the Horror Film,* ed. Roy Huss and T. J. Ross (Englewood Cliffs, N.J.: Prentice Hall, 1972), p. 58n2.

20 Rosalind Coward, *Female Desires: How They Are Sought, Bought and Packaged* (New York: Grove, 1985), p. 35.

IX. Dreams and responsibilities

1 Pauline Kael, 'A Sign of Life', in *Going Steady* (London: Temple Smith, 1970), p. 214.

2 Siegfried Kracauer, *From Caligari to Hitler: A Psychological History of the German Film* (Princeton, N.J.: Princeton University Press, 1974), p. 73.

3 Ibid., p. 113.

4 Ibid., p. 114.

5 Press notes to New York opening of *The Sacrifice* (1986).

6 Andrey Tarkovsky, *Sculpting in Time* (New York: Knopf, 1987), pp. 232–6.

7 This is Peter Schwenger's argument in an essay he kindly let me see, 'Word and Image in Tarkovsky's *Sacrifice*'. Such a subversion of language may indeed have been Tarkovsky's intention (see Ian Christie, 'Against Interpretation: An Interview with Andrei Tarkovsky', *Framework,* 14 [1981], p. 49); whether it is the final effect of his films remains debatable.

8 Tarkovsky, *Sculpting,* p. 228.

9 Ibid., p. 224. The problem surrounding the film's transitions from 'dream' to 'reality' has been noted by Jim Leach also (' "Hideousness and Beauty": A Reading of Tarkovsky's *The Sacrifice*', in *Before the Wall Came Down: Soviet and East European Filmmakers Working in the West,* ed. Graham Petrie and Ruth Dwyer [Lanham, Md.: University Press of America, 1990], pp. 211–12). He reads the resultant crisis of representation as drawing us 'into the world of the "fantastic" where natural explanations seem insufficient but cannot be ruled out' (ibid., p. 212). To speak of 'the fantastic', however, runs the risk of losing sight of the dilemmas raised by the film's straddling of the supernatural and the real, of replacing it safely on one side of the divide.

10 Tarkovsky, *Sculpting*, p. 59.

11 Ibid., p. 140; I am grateful to Schwenger's piece for bringing this quotation to my attention.

12 I Corinthians 15: 37.

13 Tarkovsky, *Sculpting*, p. 240.

14 Wyspiański locates the core of Shakespeare's play in its elevation of theatre to the court before which sinners blench. *Hamlet* is thus cast in the image of *The Wedding*, his own verdict on his contemporaries. Wyspiański terms the ghost 'incomprehensible' and suggests that in act 3, scene 4, it is rendered unnecessary by the adjacent portraits of Hamlet père and Claudius. The portrait 'removed the necessity of the ghost's appearance in this scene, and thereby in other scenes also' (*Hamlet* [Wrocław – Warszawa – Kraków – Gdańsk: Zakład narodowy imienia Ossolińskich, 1976], p. 48). Just as Shakespeare corrects the legend, so Wyspiański corrects Shakespeare: the ghost is an inessential residue of legendary material, for a ghost 'appears only to criminals as an outgrowth of their crime and terror' (ibid.; as in *Macbeth*). If the same generalization applies to *The Wedding*, the implication is that only Szela is truly a ghost, other figures being projections.

15 Krzysztof Teodor Toeplitz, ' "Wesele": Jak najdalej od kolorowej bajki', in *Próba sensu, czyli notatnik leniwego kinomana* (Warsaw: Wydawnictwo artystyczne i filmowe, 1974), p. 297.

16 Krzysztof Mętrak, 'W czyichze rękach byłem manekinem . . .', in *Autografy na ekranie* (Warsaw: Wydawnictwo artystyczne i filmowe, 1974), pp. 22–9.

17 Ibid., p. 24.

18 See, e.g., Brzozowski's *Legenda Młodej Polski* (Lwów: Nakładem księgarnii Polskiej Bernarda Połonieckiego, 1910; photomechanical reprint Kraków: Wydawnictwo literackie, 1983), p. 529: 'In fact from beginning to end only Wyspiański himself is present on the stage'. Similarly, 'When Wyspiański thought, *he in fact viewed his own tragic double thinking*' (ibid., p. 565).

19 Stanisław Wyspiański, *The Wedding*, trans. with notes and introduction by Gerard T. Kapolka (Ann Arbor, Mich.: Ardis, 1990), p. 79.

Appendix A

1 David Thomson, *A Biographical Dictionary of the Cinema* (London: Secker & Warburg, 1980), pp. 426–7.

2 Thomas Elsaesser, 'Innocence Restored', *Monthly Film Bulletin* 51, no. 611 (1984), pp. 363–6.

3 These films desexualize the father (and thus emphasize his status as embodiment of power) by pairing him with a daughter. Father–daughter relations are of enormous importance in expressionism, and perhaps even in German life in general. (Think of the father–daughter relationship in Von Trotta's *Marianne and Juliane*). Perhaps the degree of submissiveness the German father requires is something only a daughter could be comfortable with; perhaps the

daughter is the image of the disenfranchised wife. The young man seeking to prise her away from the father is reenacting the fairy-tale conquest of obstacles placed before the princess. So if Maria in *Metropolis* seems at first hardly designable as Fredersen's daughter, her physical identity with his dead wife must give one pause. *Metropolis* may even be read anthropologically, as an essay on how endogamy is camouflaged as exogamy in order to preserve the incest taboo apparently intact (while its actual, unacknowledged violation is the source of the air of chaos). The stratagem is characteristic of dynasties wishing to concentrate power or threatened with extinction.

4 Cf. Siegfried Kracauer, *From Caligari to Hitler: A Psychological History of the German Film* (Princeton, N.J.: Princeton University Press, 1974), pp. 115–19 and 265–9. Kracauer does indeed devote ample space to the Fridericus films, but nevertheless underestimates their centrality and generative force. They are far better candidates for ideological indictment than the expressionist works whose warning shadows were coded prophecies.

5 Lotte Eisner, *Murnau* (London: Secker & Warburg, 1973), pp. 167–8.

6 Enno Patalas, in *Fritz Lang*, ed. Friede Grafe, Enno Patalas, Hans Helmut Prinzler and Peter Syr (Munich: Carl Hanser, 1976), p. 105.

7 Pauline Kael, *5001 Nights at the Movies* (New York: Henry Holt, 1991), p. 273.

Appendix B

1 Walker Evans, 'Monster Movies and Rites of Initiation', *Journal of Popular Film* 4, no. 2 (1975), p. 138.

2 James Twitchell, *Dreadful Pleasures: An Anatomy of Modern Horror* (New York: Oxford University Press, 1985), p. 89.

3 Gareth Sansom, 'Fangoric Horrality: The Subject and Ontological Horror in a Contemporary Cinematic Sub-genre', *Discours social* 2, nos. 1–2 (Spring–Summer 1989), p. 166.

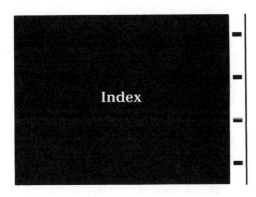

Index

195

DATE DUE
